LECTIONARY FOR WORSHIP

REVISED COMMON LECTIONARY

Cycle B

Augsburg Fortress
Minneapolis

LECTIONARY FOR WORSHIP, CYCLE B
Study Edition

Design: Lecy Design
Typesetting: Peregrine Graphics Services

The paper used in this publication meets the minimum requirements of American National Standard for Information Sciences—Permanence of Paper for Printed Library Materials, ANSI Z329.48-1984. ∞

Manufactured in U.S.A.   ISBN 0-8066-0195-7   AF 3-382

| 05 | 04 | 03 | 02 | 01 | 00 | 99 | 98 | 97 | 96 | 1 | 2 | 3 | 4 | 5 | 6 | 7 | 8 | 9 | 10 |

CONTENTS

INTRODUCTION

The word of God

The Scriptures speak of the word of God as light and lamp, imperishable seed, spiritual food and drink, healing balm, cleansing fire. The word sustains life, produces faith, strengthens hope, and inflames love. As the Bible attests, the word of God created the world and all living things. The word of the Lord liberated the Hebrew people from slavery and sustained them on their journey to the promised land. Throughout the history of Israel, this word inspired the judges and spoke to the prophets. In time, the great acts of God's mercy were written down and then proclaimed in the daily and weekly gatherings of the Jewish people. Through an annual cycle of lessons, the Hebrew Scriptures were read, sung, and interpreted in communal worship.

The word among us

"Long ago God spoke to our ancestors in many and various ways by the prophets, but in these last days he has spoken to us by a Son" (Hebrews 1:1-2). In the worship of his people, Jesus read the ancient scriptures and interpreted them anew: "Today this scripture has been fulfilled in your hearing" (Luke 4:21). In his own life, he proclaimed the good news of salvation in word and deed. To his disciples on the road, the risen Lord interpreted in all the scriptures the things concerning himself. In breaking open the word, he gave himself as the bread of life. Indeed, for the early Christian community, Jesus himself was the living Word to be proclaimed and interpreted in new places among new people. "We declare to you what was from the beginning, what we have heard, what we have seen with our eyes, what we have looked at and touched with our hands, concerning the word of life" (1 John 1:1).

The word proclaimed in worship

When the Scriptures are proclaimed in the worshiping assembly today, the living Word continues to speak to his disciples. Through the power of the Holy Spirit, the risen Christ is truly present when the Scriptures are read. Through the ministry of readers, the written word becomes a lively, spoken word addressed to all who listen with faith.

Gathered around the table of God's word, the church follows Christ's pattern of reading and interpreting the Scriptures, so that when the holy book is opened and read, Christ speaks anew this living and active word. In the hearing of this word the church is sustained in faith, drawn to the font and holy supper, and strengthened for witness in the world.

The proclamation of the word

In various ways the word of God is proclaimed in the liturgy by the worshiping assembly and its ministers. In particular, the word is proclaimed in the biblical readings (the Hebrew Scriptures, the New Testament letters, and the Gospels); in the singing of the psalms, hymns, and acclamations surrounding the readings; and in preaching.

The proclamation of the Gospel in reading and preaching is the high point of the word service. The other readings illuminate this central reading while the psalms, hymns, and acclamations offer musical responses to the readings. Because of the centrality of the Gospel reading, the assembly stands to welcome the Lord who speaks anew in this place and time.

In these varied actions, the dialogue between God and the worshiping assembly takes place. In order to take the word of God to heart and ponder its meaning, intervals of silence are often kept by the assembly and its readers. Just as haste hinders reflection on the word, so a tendency to wordiness on the part of worship leaders can detract from the clear and simple voice of the word proclaimed.

In most instances, baptized members of the worshiping assembly who have been trained in this ministry read the first and second readings. After brief silences, a cantor or choir leads the people in singing the psalm as well as the song or acclamation that greets the Gospel reading. Normally, the preacher reads the Gospel and then preaches the good news for the community and the world. A hymn responds to this word with thanksgiving. A proclamation of faith often continues the assembly's response, leading the community to pray for the church, the world, and those in need.

The medieval custom of two places for the word (lectern and pulpit) has yielded, in many congregations, to a single place (lectern or ambo) from which the readings are proclaimed and the sermon is preached. Here the book of life is opened; here the banquet of scripture is set forth; here the people of God are nourished on the word.

"He interpreted to them the things about himself in all the scriptures. He took bread, blessed and broke it, and gave it to them. Then their eyes were opened, and they recognized him" (Luke 24:27, 30-31). From the table of God's word, the worshiping assembly gathers at the table of the holy supper to receive the bread of life and the cup of blessing. In word and meal, the living Word welcomes, enlightens, and nourishes the people of God for service in the world.

The lectionary

The lectionary sets forth many of the stories, images, and actions through which the living Word sustains the Christian community gathered in public worship during the seasons of the year. It is ordered around the first reading, psalm, second reading, and Gospel reading. Appropriate introductions and conclusions to the readings are provided in this lectionary book. After announcing the reading with the introduction, the reader/minister pauses and then begins the proclamation. At the end of each of the first two readings, the reader pauses and then says, "The word of the Lord." The people respond, "Thanks be to God." At the conclusion of the Gospel reading, the minister says, "The Gospel of the Lord." The people respond with the words, "Praise to you, O Christ" or another appropriate acclamation.

In this lectionary book, the readings and psalms appointed for Lesser Festivals are printed after the Sunday and principal festival readings.

In places where the New Revised Standard Version versification for the psalms differs from that of the translation used in *Lutheran Book of Worship* and *Book of Common Prayer,* LBW/BCP alternate versification is noted in italics.

During the Sundays after Pentecost, an alternate set of semi-continuous first readings and psalms are provided in an appendix. Where it is the practice to read the semi-continuous first reading and psalm response, the lectionary should be opened first to the appropriate page in the appendix. The page in the body of the lectionary where the readings continue will need to be marked clearly.

In a few instances, the Revised Common Lectionary appoints readings and responses from selected books of the Apocrypha. These readings and responses are printed in a second appendix.

May this lectionary assist the worshiping assembly in the proclamation of the word and the preaching of the holy gospel.

SEASON OF ADVENT

FIRST SUNDAY IN ADVENT

DECEMBER 1, 1996   NOVEMBER 28, 1999   DECEMBER 1, 2002

FIRST READING: ISAIAH 64:1–9

A reading from Isaiah:

¹O that you would tear open the heavens and come down,
    so that the mountains would quake at your presence—
²as when fire kindles brushwood
    and the fire causes water to boil—
to make your name known to your adversaries,
    so that the nations might tremble at your presence!

³When you did awesome deeds that we did not expect,
    you came down, the mountains quaked at your presence.
⁴From ages past no one has heard,
    no ear has perceived,
no eye has seen any God besides you,
    who works for those who wait for him.
⁵You meet those who gladly do right,
    those who remember you in your ways.

But you were angry, and we sinned;
    because you hid yourself we transgressed.
⁶We have all become like one who is unclean,
    and all our righteous deeds are like a filthy cloth.
We all fade like a leaf,
    and our iniquities, like the wind, take us away.
⁷There is no one who calls on your name,
    or attempts to take hold of you;
for you have hidden your face from us,
    and have delivered us into the hand of our iniquity.

⁸Yet, O LORD, you are our Father;
    we are the clay, and you are our potter;
    we are all the work of your hand.
⁹Do not be exceedingly angry, O LORD,
    and do not remember iniquity forever.
    Now consider, we are all your people.

The word of the Lord.

PSALMODY: PSALM 80:1–7, 17–19   *Psalm 80:1–7, 16–18* LBW/BCP

SECOND READING: 1 Corinthians 1:3–9

A reading from First Corinthians:

³Grace to you and peace from God our Father and the Lord Jesus Christ.

⁴I give thanks to my God always for you
because of the grace of God that has been given you in Christ Jesus,
⁵for in every way you have been enriched in him,
in speech and knowledge of every kind—
⁶just as the testimony of Christ has been strengthened among you—
⁷so that you are not lacking in any spiritual gift
as you wait for the revealing of our Lord Jesus Christ.

⁸He will also strengthen you to the end,
so that you may be blameless on the day of our Lord Jesus Christ.
⁹God is faithful;
by him you were called into the fellowship of his Son,
Jesus Christ our Lord.

The word of the Lord.

GOSPEL: MARK 13:24–37

The Holy Gospel according to Mark, the 13th chapter.

Jesus said:
24"In those days, after that suffering,
    the sun will be darkened,
        and the moon will not give its light,
      25and the stars will be falling from heaven,
        and the powers in the heavens will be shaken.
26Then they will see 'the Son of Man coming in clouds' with great power
        and glory.
27Then he will send out the angels,
and gather his elect from the four winds,
from the ends of the earth to the ends of heaven.

28"From the fig tree learn its lesson:
as soon as its branch becomes tender and puts forth its leaves,
you know that summer is near.
29So also, when you see these things taking place,
you know that he is near, at the very gates.
30Truly I tell you,
this generation will not pass away until all these things have taken place.
31Heaven and earth will pass away,
but my words will not pass away.

32"But about that day or hour no one knows,
neither the angels in heaven, nor the Son,
but only the Father.
33Beware, keep alert; for you do not know when the time will come.
34It is like a man going on a journey,
when he leaves home and puts his slaves in charge, each with his work,
and commands the doorkeeper to be on the watch.
35Therefore, keep awake—
for you do not know when the master of the house will come,
in the evening, or at midnight,
or at cockcrow, or at dawn,
36or else he may find you asleep when he comes suddenly.
37And what I say to you I say to all:
Keep awake."

The Gospel of the Lord.

Second Sunday in Advent

DECEMBER 8, 1996   *DECEMBER 5, 1999*   *DECEMBER 8, 2002*

FIRST READING: Isaiah 40:1–11

A reading from Isaiah:

¹Comfort, O comfort my people,
    says your God.
²Speak tenderly to Jerusalem,
    and cry to her
that she has served her term,
    that her penalty is paid,
that she has received from the Lord's hand
    double for all her sins.

³A voice cries out:
"In the wilderness prepare the way of the Lord,
    make straight in the desert a highway for our God.
⁴Every valley shall be lifted up,
    and every mountain and hill be made low;
the uneven ground shall become level,
    and the rough places a plain.
⁵Then the glory of the Lord shall be revealed,
    and all people shall see it together,
    for the mouth of the Lord has spoken."

⁶A voice says, "Cry out!"
    And I said, "What shall I cry?"
All people are grass,
    their constancy is like the flower of the field.
⁷The grass withers, the flower fades,
    when the breath of the Lord blows upon it;
    surely the people are grass.
⁸The grass withers, the flower fades;
    but the word of our God will stand forever.

⁹Get you up to a high mountain,
    O Zion, herald of good tidings;
lift up your voice with strength,
    O Jerusalem, herald of good tidings,

lift it up, do not fear;
say to the cities of Judah,
    "Here is your God!"
¹⁰See, the Lord GOD comes with might,
    and his arm rules for him;
his reward is with him,
    and his recompense before him.
¹¹He will feed his flock like a shepherd;
    he will gather the lambs in his arms,
and carry them in his bosom,
    and gently lead the mother sheep.

The word of the Lord.

PSALMODY: PSALM 85:1–2, 8–13

SECOND READING: 2 PETER 3:8–15a

A reading from Second Peter:

⁸Do not ignore this one fact, beloved,
that with the Lord one day is like a thousand years,
and a thousand years are like one day.
⁹The Lord is not slow about his promise, as some think of slowness,
but is patient with you,
not wanting any to perish,
but all to come to repentance.

¹⁰But the day of the Lord will come like a thief,
and then the heavens will pass away with a loud noise,
and the elements will be dissolved with fire,
and the earth and everything that is done on it will be disclosed.
¹¹Since all these things are to be dissolved in this way,
what sort of persons ought you to be in leading lives of holiness and godliness,
¹²waiting for and hastening the coming of the day of God,
because of which the heavens will be set ablaze and dissolved,
and the elements will melt with fire?

¹³But, in accordance with his promise,
we wait for new heavens and a new earth,
where righteousness is at home.
¹⁴Therefore, beloved, while you are waiting for these things,
strive to be found by him at peace, without spot or blemish;
¹⁵and regard the patience of our Lord as salvation.

The word of the Lord.

GOSPEL: MARK 1:1–8

The Holy Gospel according to Mark, the first chapter.

[1]The beginning of the good news of Jesus Christ, the Son of God.

[2]As it is written in the prophet Isaiah,
    "See, I am sending my messenger ahead of you,
        who will prepare your way;
    [3]the voice of one crying out in the wilderness:
        'Prepare the way of the Lord,
        make his paths straight,' "
[4]John the baptizer appeared in the wilderness,
proclaiming a baptism of repentance for the forgiveness of sins.
[5]And people from the whole Judean countryside
and all the people of Jerusalem were going out to him,
and were baptized by him in the river Jordan, confessing their sins.
[6]Now John was clothed with camel's hair,
with a leather belt around his waist,
and he ate locusts and wild honey.
[7]He proclaimed,
"The one who is more powerful than I is coming after me;
I am not worthy to stoop down and untie the thong of his sandals.
[8]I have baptized you with water;
but he will baptize you with the Holy Spirit."

The Gospel of the Lord.

THIRD SUNDAY IN ADVENT

DECEMBER 15, 1996   DECEMBER 12, 1999   DECEMBER 15, 2002

FIRST READING: ISAIAH 61:1–4, 8–11

A reading from Isaiah:

¹The spirit of the Lord GOD is upon me,
    because the LORD has anointed me;
he has sent me to bring good news to the oppressed,
    to bind up the brokenhearted,
to proclaim liberty to the captives,
    and release to the prisoners;
²to proclaim the year of the LORD's favor,
    and the day of vengeance of our God;
    to comfort all who mourn;
³to provide for those who mourn in Zion—
    to give them a garland instead of ashes,
the oil of gladness instead of mourning,
    the mantle of praise instead of a faint spirit.
They will be called oaks of righteousness,
    the planting of the LORD, to display his glory.
⁴They shall build up the ancient ruins,
    they shall raise up the former devastations;
they shall repair the ruined cities,
    the devastations of many generations.

⁸For I the LORD love justice,
    I hate robbery and wrongdoing;
I will faithfully give them their recompense,
    and I will make an everlasting covenant with them.
⁹Their descendants shall be known among the nations,
    and their offspring among the peoples;
all who see them shall acknowledge
    that they are a people whom the LORD has blessed.

¹⁰I will greatly rejoice in the LORD,
    my whole being shall exult in my God;
for he has clothed me with the garments of salvation,
    he has covered me with the robe of righteousness,

as a bridegroom decks himself with a garland,
   and as a bride adorns herself with her jewels.
[11]For as the earth brings forth its shoots,
   and as a garden causes what is sown in it to spring up,
so the Lord God will cause righteousness and praise
   to spring up before all the nations.

The word of the Lord.

PSALMODY: PSALM 126 or LUKE 1:47–55

SECOND READING: 1 THESSALONIANS 5:16–24

A reading from First Thessalonians:

[16]Rejoice always,
[17]pray without ceasing,
[18]give thanks in all circumstances;
for this is the will of God in Christ Jesus for you.
[19]Do not quench the Spirit.
[20]Do not despise the words of prophets, [21]but test everything;
hold fast to what is good;
[22]abstain from every form of evil.

[23]May the God of peace himself sanctify you entirely;
and may your spirit and soul and body be kept sound and blameless
at the coming of our Lord Jesus Christ.
[24]The one who calls you is faithful, and he will do this.

The word of the Lord.

GOSPEL: JOHN 1:6–8, 19–28

The Holy Gospel according to John, the first chapter.

[6]There was a man sent from God, whose name was John.
[7]He came as a witness to testify to the light,
so that all might believe through him.
[8]He himself was not the light,
but he came to testify to the light.

[19]This is the testimony given by John
when the Jews sent priests and Levites from Jerusalem to ask him,
"Who are you?"
[20]He confessed and did not deny it, but confessed, "I am not the Messiah."
[21]And they asked him, "What then? Are you Elijah?"
He said, "I am not."
"Are you the prophet?"
He answered, "No."
[22]Then they said to him, "Who are you?
Let us have an answer for those who sent us.
What do you say about yourself?"
[23]He said,
    "I am the voice of one crying out in the wilderness,
    'Make straight the way of the Lord,' "
as the prophet Isaiah said.

[24]Now they had been sent from the Pharisees.
[25]They asked him,
"Why then are you baptizing if you are neither the Messiah, nor Elijah,
        nor the prophet?"
[26]John answered them, "I baptize with water.
Among you stands one whom you do not know,
[27]the one who is coming after me;
I am not worthy to untie the thong of his sandal."
[28]This took place in Bethany across the Jordan where John was baptizing.

The Gospel of the Lord.

Fourth Sunday in Advent

DECEMBER 22, 1996 *DECEMBER 19, 1999* *DECEMBER 22, 2002*

FIRST READING: 2 SAMUEL 7:1–11, 16

A reading from Second Samuel:

¹Now when David the king was settled in his house,
and the LORD had given him rest from all his enemies around him,
²the king said to the prophet Nathan,
"See now, I am living in a house of cedar,
but the ark of God stays in a tent."
³Nathan said to the king,
"Go, do all that you have in mind; for the LORD is with you."

⁴But that same night the word of the LORD came to Nathan:
⁵Go and tell my servant David:
Thus says the LORD: Are you the one to build me a house to live in?
⁶I have not lived in a house
since the day I brought up the people of Israel from Egypt to this day,
but I have been moving about in a tent and a tabernacle.
⁷Wherever I have moved about among all the people of Israel,
did I ever speak a word with any of the tribal leaders of Israel,
whom I commanded to shepherd my people Israel, saying,
"Why have you not built me a house of cedar?"

⁸Now therefore thus you shall say to my servant David:
Thus says the LORD of hosts: I took you from the pasture,
from following the sheep to be prince over my people Israel;
⁹and I have been with you wherever you went,
and have cut off all your enemies from before you;
and I will make for you a great name,
like the name of the great ones of the earth.
¹⁰And I will appoint a place for my people Israel and will plant them,
so that they may live in their own place, and be disturbed no more;
and evildoers shall afflict them no more, as formerly,
¹¹from the time that I appointed judges over my people Israel;
and I will give you rest from all your enemies.
Moreover the LORD declares to you that the LORD will make you a house.

^{16}Your house and your kingdom shall be made sure forever before me;
your throne shall be established forever.

The word of the Lord.

PSALMODY: Luke 1:47–55 or Psalm 89:1–4, 19–26

SECOND READING: Romans 16:25–27

A reading from Romans:

^{25}Now to God who is able to strengthen you
according to my gospel and the proclamation of Jesus Christ,
according to the revelation of the mystery
that was kept secret for long ages ^{26}but is now disclosed,
and through the prophetic writings is made known to all the Gentiles,
according to the command of the eternal God,
to bring about the obedience of faith—
^{27}to the only wise God, through Jesus Christ,
to whom be the glory forever! Amen.

The word of the Lord.

The Holy Gospel according to Luke, the first chapter.

[26]In the sixth month the angel Gabriel was sent by God
to a town in Galilee called Nazareth,
[27]to a virgin engaged to a man whose name was Joseph,
of the house of David.
The virgin's name was Mary.
[28]And he came to her and said,
"Greetings, favored one!
The Lord is with you."
[29]But she was much perplexed by his words
and pondered what sort of greeting this might be.
[30]The angel said to her,
"Do not be afraid, Mary,
for you have found favor with God.
[31]And now, you will conceive in your womb and bear a son,
and you will name him Jesus.
[32]He will be great, and will be called the Son of the Most High,
and the Lord God will give to him the throne of his ancestor David.
[33]He will reign over the house of Jacob forever,
and of his kingdom there will be no end."

[34]Mary said to the angel,
"How can this be, since I am a virgin?"
[35]The angel said to her,
"The Holy Spirit will come upon you,
and the power of the Most High will overshadow you;
therefore the child to be born will be holy;
he will be called Son of God.
[36]And now, your relative Elizabeth in her old age has also conceived a son;
and this is the sixth month for her who was said to be barren.
[37]For nothing will be impossible with God."
[38]Then Mary said, "Here am I, the servant of the Lord;
let it be with me according to your word."
Then the angel departed from her.

The Gospel of the Lord.

SEASON OF CHRISTMAS

The Nativity of Our Lord
Christmas Eve (I)

DECEMBER 24

FIRST READING: Isaiah 9:2–7

A reading from Isaiah:

²The people who walked in darkness
    have seen a great light;
those who lived in a land of deep darkness—
    on them light has shined.
³You have multiplied the nation,
    you have increased its joy;
they rejoice before you
    as with joy at the harvest,
    as people exult when dividing plunder.
⁴For the yoke of their burden,
    and the bar across their shoulders,
    the rod of their oppressor,
    you have broken as on the day of Midian.
⁵For all the boots of the tramping warriors
    and all the garments rolled in blood
    shall be burned as fuel for the fire.

⁶For a child has been born for us,
    a son given to us;
authority rests upon his shoulders;
    and he is named
Wonderful Counselor, Mighty God,
    Everlasting Father, Prince of Peace.
⁷His authority shall grow continually,
    and there shall be endless peace
for the throne of David and his kingdom.
    He will establish and uphold it
with justice and with righteousness
    from this time onward and forevermore.

The zeal of the LORD of hosts will do this.

The word of the Lord.

PSALMODY: Psalm 96

SECOND READING: Titus 2:11–14

A reading from Titus:

[11]The grace of God has appeared,
bringing salvation to all,
[12]training us to renounce impiety and worldly passions,
and in the present age
to live lives that are self-controlled, upright, and godly,
[13]while we wait for the blessed hope
and the manifestation of the glory
of our great God and Savior, Jesus Christ.

[14]He it is who gave himself for us
that he might redeem us from all iniquity
and purify for himself a people of his own
who are zealous for good deeds.

The word of the Lord.

GOSPEL: Luke 2:1–14 [15–20]

The Holy Gospel according to Luke, the second chapter.

[1]In those days a decree went out from Emperor Augustus
that all the world should be registered.
[2]This was the first registration
and was taken while Quirinius was governor of Syria.
[3]All went to their own towns to be registered.
[4]Joseph also went from the town of Nazareth in Galilee to Judea,
to the city of David called Bethlehem,
because he was descended from the house and family of David.
[5]He went to be registered with Mary,
to whom he was engaged and who was expecting a child.
[6]While they were there, the time came for her to deliver her child.
[7]And she gave birth to her firstborn son
and wrapped him in bands of cloth,
and laid him in a manger,
because there was no place for them in the inn.

[8]In that region there were shepherds living in the fields,
keeping watch over their flock by night.
[9]Then an angel of the Lord stood before them,
and the glory of the Lord shone around them,
and they were terrified.
[10]But the angel said to them,
"Do not be afraid;
for see—
I am bringing you good news of great joy for all the people:
[11]to you is born this day in the city of David
a Savior, who is the Messiah, the Lord.
[12]This will be a sign for you:
you will find a child wrapped in bands of cloth
and lying in a manger."
[13]And suddenly there was with the angel
a multitude of the heavenly host, praising God and saying,
   [14]"Glory to God in the highest heaven,
     and on earth peace among those whom he favors!"

[[15]When the angels had left them and gone into heaven,
the shepherds said to one another,
"Let us go now to Bethlehem
and see this thing that has taken place,
which the Lord has made known to us."
[16]So they went with haste
and found Mary and Joseph, and the child lying in the manger.
[17]When they saw this,
they made known what had been told them about this child;
[18]and all who heard it were amazed at what the shepherds told them.
[19]But Mary treasured all these words and pondered them in her heart.

[20]The shepherds returned,
glorifying and praising God for all they had heard and seen,
as it had been told them.]

The Gospel of the Lord.

The Nativity of Our Lord
Christmas Dawn (II)

DECEMBER 25

FIRST READING: ISAIAH 62:6–12

A reading from Isaiah:

⁶Upon your walls, O Jerusalem,
    I have posted sentinels;
all day and all night
    they shall never be silent.
You who remind the LORD,
    take no rest,
⁷and give him no rest
    until he establishes Jerusalem
    and makes it renowned throughout the earth.

⁸The LORD has sworn by his right hand
    and by his mighty arm:
I will not again give your grain
    to be food for your enemies,
and foreigners shall not drink the wine
    for which you have labored;
⁹but those who garner it shall eat it
    and praise the LORD,
and those who gather it shall drink it
    in my holy courts.

¹⁰Go through, go through the gates,
    prepare the way for the people;
build up, build up the highway,
    clear it of stones,
    lift up an ensign over the peoples.
¹¹The LORD has proclaimed
    to the end of the earth:
Say to daughter Zion,
    "See, your salvation comes;
his reward is with him,
    and his recompense before him."

12They shall be called, "The Holy People,
    The Redeemed of the LORD";
and you shall be called, "Sought Out,
    A City Not Forsaken."

The word of the Lord.

PSALMODY: PSALM 97

SECOND READING: TITUS 3:4–7

A reading from Titus:

4When the goodness and loving kindness of God our Savior appeared,
5he saved us,
not because of any works of righteousness that we had done,
but according to his mercy,
through the water of rebirth
and renewal by the Holy Spirit.
6This Spirit he poured out on us richly
through Jesus Christ our Savior,
7so that, having been justified by his grace,
we might become heirs
according to the hope of eternal life.

The word of the Lord.

GOSPEL: LUKE 2:[1–7] 8–20

The Holy Gospel according to Luke, the second chapter.

[1In those days a decree went out from Emperor Augustus
that all the world should be registered.
2This was the first registration
and was taken while Quirinius was governor of Syria.
3All went to their own towns to be registered.
4Joseph also went from the town of Nazareth in Galilee to Judea,
to the city of David called Bethlehem,
because he was descended from the house and family of David.
5He went to be registered with Mary,
to whom he was engaged and who was expecting a child.
6While they were there, the time came for her to deliver her child.
7And she gave birth to her firstborn son
and wrapped him in bands of cloth,
and laid him in a manger,
because there was no place for them in the inn.]

⁸In that region there were shepherds living in the fields,
keeping watch over their flock by night.
⁹Then an angel of the Lord stood before them,
and the glory of the Lord shone around them,
and they were terrified.
¹⁰But the angel said to them,
"Do not be afraid;
for see—
I am bringing you good news of great joy for all the people:
¹¹to you is born this day in the city of David
a Savior, who is the Messiah, the Lord.
¹²This will be a sign for you:
you will find a child wrapped in bands of cloth
and lying in a manger."
¹³And suddenly there was with the angel
a multitude of the heavenly host, praising God and saying,
    ¹⁴"Glory to God in the highest heaven,
        and on earth peace among those whom he favors!"

¹⁵When the angels had left them and gone into heaven,
the shepherds said to one another,
"Let us go now to Bethlehem
and see this thing that has taken place,
which the Lord has made known to us."
¹⁶So they went with haste
and found Mary and Joseph, and the child lying in the manger.
¹⁷When they saw this,
they made known what had been told them about this child;
¹⁸and all who heard it were amazed at what the shepherds told them.
¹⁹But Mary treasured all these words and pondered them in her heart.

²⁰The shepherds returned,
glorifying and praising God for all they had heard and seen,
as it had been told them.

The Gospel of the Lord.

THE NATIVITY OF OUR LORD
CHRISTMAS DAY (III)
DECEMBER 25

FIRST READING: ISAIAH 52:7–10

A reading from Isaiah:

[7]How beautiful upon the mountains
    are the feet of the messenger who announces peace,
who brings good news,
    who announces salvation,
    who says to Zion, "Your God reigns."

[8]Listen! Your sentinels lift up their voices,
    together they sing for joy;
for in plain sight they see
    the return of the LORD to Zion.

[9]Break forth together into singing,
    you ruins of Jerusalem;
for the LORD has comforted his people,
    he has redeemed Jerusalem.
[10]The LORD has bared his holy arm
    before the eyes of all the nations;
and all the ends of the earth shall see
    the salvation of our God.

The word of the Lord.

PSALMODY: PSALM 98

SECOND READING: HEBREWS 1:1–4 [5–12]

A reading from Hebrews:

¹Long ago God spoke to our ancestors
in many and various ways by the prophets,
²but in these last days
he has spoken to us by a Son,
whom he appointed heir of all things,
through whom he also created the worlds.
³He is the reflection of God's glory
and the exact imprint of God's very being,
and he sustains all things by his powerful word.
When he had made purification for sins,
he sat down at the right hand of the Majesty on high,
⁴having become as much superior to angels
as the name he has inherited is more excellent than theirs.

[⁵For to which of the angels did God ever say,
    "You are my Son;
        today I have begotten you"?
Or again,
    "I will be his Father,
        and he will be my Son"?
⁶And again, when he brings the firstborn into the world, he says,
    "Let all God's angels worship him."
⁷Of the angels he says,
    "He makes his angels winds,
        and his servants flames of fire."

⁸But of the Son he says,
    "Your throne, O God, is forever and ever,
        and the righteous scepter is the scepter of your kingdom.
    ⁹You have loved righteousness and hated wickedness;
    therefore God, your God, has anointed you
        with the oil of gladness beyond your companions."
¹⁰And,
    "In the beginning, Lord, you founded the earth,
        and the heavens are the work of your hands;
    ¹¹they will perish, but you remain;
        they will all wear out like clothing;
    ¹²like a cloak you will roll them up,
        and like clothing they will be changed.
    But you are the same,
        and your years will never end."]

The word of the Lord.

GOSPEL: JOHN 1:1–14

The Holy Gospel according to John, the first chapter.

[1]In the beginning was the Word,
and the Word was with God,
and the Word was God.
[2]He was in the beginning with God.
[3]All things came into being through him,
and without him not one thing came into being.
What has come into being [4]in him was life,
and the life was the light of all people.
[5]The light shines in the darkness,
and the darkness did not overcome it.

[6]There was a man sent from God, whose name was John.
[7]He came as a witness to testify to the light,
so that all might believe through him.
[8]He himself was not the light,
but he came to testify to the light.
[9]The true light, which enlightens everyone,
was coming into the world.

[10]He was in the world,
and the world came into being through him;
yet the world did not know him.
[11]He came to what was his own,
and his own people did not accept him.
[12]But to all who received him,
who believed in his name,
he gave power to become children of God,
[13]who were born,
not of blood or of the will of the flesh or of the will of man,
but of God.

[14]And the Word became flesh and lived among us,
and we have seen his glory,
the glory as of a father's only son,
full of grace and truth.

The Gospel of the Lord.

FIRST SUNDAY AFTER CHRISTMAS

DECEMBER 29, 1996   DECEMBER 26, 1999   DECEMBER 29, 2002

FIRST READING: Isaiah 61:10—62:3

A reading from Isaiah:

10I will greatly rejoice in the LORD,
　　my whole being shall exult in my God;
for he has clothed me with the garments of salvation,
　　he has covered me with the robe of righteousness,
as a bridegroom decks himself with a garland,
　　and as a bride adorns herself with her jewels.
11For as the earth brings forth its shoots,
　　and as a garden causes what is sown in it to spring up,
so the Lord GOD will cause righteousness and praise
　　to spring up before all the nations.

62:1For Zion's sake I will not keep silent,
　　and for Jerusalem's sake I will not rest,
until her vindication shines out like the dawn,
　　and her salvation like a burning torch.

2The nations shall see your vindication,
　　and all the kings your glory;
and you shall be called by a new name
　　that the mouth of the LORD will give.
3You shall be a crown of beauty in the hand of the LORD,
　　and a royal diadem in the hand of your God.

The word of the Lord.

PSALMODY: Psalm 148

SECOND READING: GALATIANS 4:4–7

A reading from Galatians:

⁴When the fullness of time had come,
God sent his Son,
born of a woman, born under the law,
⁵in order to redeem those who were under the law,
so that we might receive adoption as children.
⁶And because you are children,
God has sent the Spirit of his Son into our hearts, crying,
"Abba! Father!"
⁷So you are no longer a slave but a child,
and if a child then also an heir, through God.

The word of the Lord.

GOSPEL: LUKE 2:22–40

The Holy Gospel according to Luke, the second chapter.

²²When the time came for their purification according to the law of Moses,
Joseph and Mary brought Jesus up to Jerusalem to present him to the Lord
²³(as it is written in the law of the Lord,
"Every firstborn male shall be designated as holy to the Lord"),
²⁴and they offered a sacrifice according to what is stated in the law of the Lord,
"a pair of turtledoves or two young pigeons."

²⁵Now there was a man in Jerusalem whose name was Simeon;
this man was righteous and devout,
looking forward to the consolation of Israel,
and the Holy Spirit rested on him.
²⁶It had been revealed to him by the Holy Spirit
that he would not see death before he had seen the Lord's Messiah.
²⁷Guided by the Spirit, Simeon came into the temple;
and when the parents brought in the child Jesus,
to do for him what was customary under the law,
²⁸Simeon took him in his arms and praised God, saying,
²⁹"Master, now you are dismissing your servant in peace,
according to your word;
³⁰for my eyes have seen your salvation,
³¹which you have prepared in the presence of all peoples,
³²a light for revelation to the Gentiles
and for glory to your people Israel."
³³And the child's father and mother were amazed at what was being said
about him.

[34]Then Simeon blessed them and said to his mother Mary,
"This child is destined for the falling and the rising of many in Israel,
and to be a sign that will be opposed [35]so that the inner thoughts of many
         will be revealed—
and a sword will pierce your own soul too."

[36]There was also a prophet,
Anna the daughter of Phanuel, of the tribe of Asher.
She was of a great age,
having lived with her husband seven years after her marriage,
[37]then as a widow to the age of eighty-four.
She never left the temple
but worshiped there with fasting and prayer night and day.
[38]At that moment she came, and began to praise God
and to speak about the child to all who were looking for the redemption of
         Jerusalem.

[39]When they had finished everything required by the law of the Lord,
they returned to Galilee, to their own town of Nazareth.
[40]The child grew and became strong, filled with wisdom;
and the favor of God was upon him.

The Gospel of the Lord.

SECOND SUNDAY AFTER CHRISTMAS

JANUARY 5, 1997   JANUARY 2, 2000   JANUARY 5, 2003

FIRST READING: JEREMIAH 31:7–14   *Alternate Reading: Sirach 24:1–12 (p. 403)*

A reading from Jeremiah:

⁷Thus says the LORD:
Sing aloud with gladness for Jacob,
    and raise shouts for the chief of the nations;
proclaim, give praise, and say,
    "Save, O Lord, your people,
    the remnant of Israel."

⁸See, I am going to bring them from the land of the north,
    and gather them from the farthest parts of the earth,
among them the blind and the lame,
    those with child and those in labor, together;
    a great company, they shall return here.
⁹With weeping they shall come,
    and with consolations I will lead them back,
I will let them walk by brooks of water,
    in a straight path in which they shall not stumble;
for I have become a father to Israel,
    and Ephraim is my firstborn.

¹⁰Hear the word of the LORD, O nations,
    and declare it in the coastlands far away;
say, "He who scattered Israel will gather him,
    and will keep him as a shepherd a flock."
¹¹For the LORD has ransomed Jacob,
    and has redeemed him from hands too strong for him.

¹²They shall come and sing aloud on the height of Zion,
    and they shall be radiant over the goodness of the Lord,
over the grain, the wine, and the oil,
    and over the young of the flock and the herd;
their life shall become like a watered garden,
    and they shall never languish again.

¹³Then shall the young women rejoice in the dance,
    and the young men and the old shall be merry.
I will turn their mourning into joy,
    I will comfort them, and give them gladness for sorrow.
¹⁴I will give the priests their fill of fatness,
    and my people shall be satisfied with my bounty,
                                                    says the LORD.

The word of the Lord.

PSALMODY: PSALM 147:12–20   *Psalm 147:13–21 LBW/BCP*
                                          Alternate Psalmody: Wisdom of Solomon 10:15–21

SECOND READING: EPHESIANS 1:3–14

A reading from Ephesians:

³Blessed be the God and Father of our Lord Jesus Christ,
who has blessed us in Christ
with every spiritual blessing in the heavenly places,
⁴just as he chose us in Christ before the foundation of the world
to be holy and blameless before him in love.
⁵He destined us for adoption as his children through Jesus Christ,
according to the good pleasure of his will,
⁶to the praise of his glorious grace
that he freely bestowed on us in the Beloved.

⁷In him we have redemption through his blood,
the forgiveness of our trespasses,
according to the riches of his grace ⁸that he lavished on us.

With all wisdom and insight
⁹he has made known to us the mystery of his will,
according to his good pleasure that he set forth in Christ,
¹⁰as a plan for the fullness of time,
to gather up all things in him,
things in heaven and things on earth.

¹¹In Christ we have also obtained an inheritance,
having been destined according to the purpose of him
who accomplishes all things according to his counsel and will,
¹²so that we, who were the first to set our hope on Christ,
might live for the praise of his glory.
¹³In him you also, when you had heard the word of truth,
the gospel of your salvation, and had believed in him,
were marked with the seal of the promised Holy Spirit;

¹⁴this is the pledge of our inheritance
toward redemption as God's own people,
to the praise of his glory.

The word of the Lord.

GOSPEL: JOHN 1:[1–9] 10–18

The Holy Gospel according to John, the first chapter.

[¹In the beginning was the Word,
and the Word was with God,
and the Word was God.
²He was in the beginning with God.
³All things came into being through him,
and without him not one thing came into being.
What has come into being ⁴in him was life,
and the life was the light of all people.
⁵The light shines in the darkness,
and the darkness did not overcome it.

⁶There was a man sent from God, whose name was John.
⁷He came as a witness to testify to the light,
so that all might believe through him.
⁸He himself was not the light,
but he came to testify to the light.
⁹The true light, which enlightens everyone,
was coming into the world.]

¹⁰He was in the world,
and the world came into being through him;
yet the world did not know him.
¹¹He came to what was his own,
and his own people did not accept him.
¹²But to all who received him,
who believed in his name,
he gave power to become children of God,
¹³who were born, not of blood or of the will of the flesh
or of the will of man,
but of God.

¹⁴And the Word became flesh and lived among us,
and we have seen his glory,
the glory as of a father's only son,
full of grace and truth.

¹⁵(John testified to him and cried out,
"This was he of whom I said,
'He who comes after me ranks ahead of me because he was before me.' ")
¹⁶From his fullness we have all received,
grace upon grace.
¹⁷The law indeed was given through Moses;
grace and truth came through Jesus Christ.

¹⁸No one has ever seen God.
It is God the only Son,
who is close to the Father's heart,
who has made him known.

The Gospel of the Lord.

SEASON OF EPIPHANY

THE EPIPHANY OF OUR LORD

JANUARY 6

FIRST READING: ISAIAH 60:1–6

A reading from Isaiah:

¹Arise, shine; for your light has come,
     and the glory of the LORD has risen upon you.
²For darkness shall cover the earth,
     and thick darkness the peoples;
but the LORD will arise upon you,
     and his glory will appear over you.
³Nations shall come to your light,
     and kings to the brightness of your dawn.

⁴Lift up your eyes and look around;
     they all gather together, they come to you;
your sons shall come from far away,
     and your daughters shall be carried on their nurses' arms.

⁵Then you shall see and be radiant;
     your heart shall thrill and rejoice,
because the abundance of the sea shall be brought to you,
     the wealth of the nations shall come to you.
⁶A multitude of camels shall cover you,
     the young camels of Midian and Ephah;
     all those from Sheba shall come.
They shall bring gold and frankincense,
     and shall proclaim the praise of the LORD.

The word of the Lord.

PSALMODY: PSALM 72:1–7, 10–14

SECOND READING: EPHESIANS 3:1–12

A reading from Ephesians:

[1]This is the reason that I Paul am a prisoner for Christ Jesus
for the sake of you Gentiles—
[2]for surely you have already heard of the commission of God's grace
that was given me for you,
[3]and how the mystery was made known to me by revelation,
as I wrote above in a few words,
[4]a reading of which will enable you
to perceive my understanding of the mystery of Christ.

[5]In former generations this mystery was not made known to humankind,
as it has now been revealed to his holy apostles and prophets by the Spirit:
[6]that is, the Gentiles have become fellow heirs,
members of the same body,
and sharers in the promise in Christ Jesus through the gospel.

[7]Of this gospel I have become a servant
according to the gift of God's grace
that was given me by the working of his power.
[8]Although I am the very least of all the saints,
this grace was given to me
to bring to the Gentiles the news of the boundless riches of Christ,
[9]and to make everyone see
what is the plan of the mystery hidden for ages in God
who created all things;
[10]so that through the church
the wisdom of God in its rich variety
might now be made known to the rulers and authorities
in the heavenly places.
[11]This was in accordance with the eternal purpose
that he has carried out in Christ Jesus our Lord,
[12]in whom we have access to God
in boldness and confidence through faith in him.

The word of the Lord.

The Holy Gospel according to Matthew, the second chapter.

[1]In the time of King Herod,
after Jesus was born in Bethlehem of Judea,
wise men from the East came to Jerusalem, [2]asking,
"Where is the child who has been born king of the Jews?
For we observed his star at its rising,
and have come to pay him homage."

[3]When King Herod heard this, he was frightened,
and all Jerusalem with him;
[4]and calling together all the chief priests and scribes of the people,
he inquired of them where the Messiah was to be born.
[5]They told him,
"In Bethlehem of Judea;
for so it has been written by the prophet:
    [6]'And you, Bethlehem, in the land of Judah,
        are by no means least among the rulers of Judah;
      for from you shall come a ruler
        who is to shepherd my people Israel.' "

[7]Then Herod secretly called for the wise men
and learned from them the exact time when the star had appeared.
[8]Then he sent them to Bethlehem, saying,
"Go and search diligently for the child;
and when you have found him,
bring me word so that I may also go and pay him homage."

[9]When they had heard the king, they set out;
and there, ahead of them,
went the star that they had seen at its rising,
until it stopped over the place where the child was.
[10]When they saw that the star had stopped,
they were overwhelmed with joy.
[11]On entering the house, they saw the child with Mary his mother;
and they knelt down and paid him homage.
Then, opening their treasure chests,
they offered him gifts of gold, frankincense, and myrrh.

[12]And having been warned in a dream not to return to Herod,
they left for their own country by another road.

The Gospel of the Lord.

The Baptism of Our Lord
First Sunday after the Epiphany

FIRST READING: Genesis 1:1–5

A reading from Genesis:

^{1}In the beginning when God created the heavens and the earth,
^{2}the earth was a formless void and darkness covered the face of the deep,
while a wind from God swept over the face of the waters.
^{3}Then God said, "Let there be light"; and there was light.
^{4}And God saw that the light was good;
and God separated the light from the darkness.
^{5}God called the light Day, and the darkness he called Night.
And there was evening and there was morning, the first day.

The word of the Lord.

PSALMODY: Psalm 29

SECOND READING: Acts 19:1–7

A reading from Acts:

^{1}While Apollos was in Corinth,
Paul passed through the interior regions and came to Ephesus,
where he found some disciples.
^{2}He said to them,
"Did you receive the Holy Spirit when you became believers?"
They replied, "No, we have not even heard that there is a Holy Spirit."
^{3}Then he said, "Into what then were you baptized?"
They answered, "Into John's baptism."
^{4}Paul said, "John baptized with the baptism of repentance,
telling the people to believe in the one who was to come after him, that is, in Jesus."
^{5}On hearing this, they were baptized in the name of the Lord Jesus.
^{6}When Paul had laid his hands on them, the Holy Spirit came upon them,
and they spoke in tongues and prophesied—
^{7}altogether there were about twelve of them.

The word of the Lord.

The Holy Gospel according to Mark, the first chapter.

[4]John the baptizer appeared in the wilderness,
proclaiming a baptism of repentance for the forgiveness of sins.
[5]And people from the whole Judean countryside
and all the people of Jerusalem were going out to him,
and were baptized by him in the river Jordan, confessing their sins.
[6]Now John was clothed with camel's hair,
with a leather belt around his waist,
and he ate locusts and wild honey.
[7]He proclaimed,
"The one who is more powerful than I is coming after me;
I am not worthy to stoop down and untie the thong of his sandals.
[8]I have baptized you with water;
but he will baptize you with the Holy Spirit."

[9]In those days Jesus came from Nazareth of Galilee
and was baptized by John in the Jordan.
[10]And just as he was coming up out of the water,
he saw the heavens torn apart and the Spirit descending like a dove on him.
[11]And a voice came from heaven,
"You are my Son, the Beloved;
with you I am well pleased."

The Gospel of the Lord.

Second Sunday after the Epiphany

JANUARY 19, 1997   JANUARY 16, 2000   JANUARY 19, 2003

Jan 15, 2006

FIRST READING: 1 SAMUEL 3:1–10 [11–20]

A reading from First Samuel:

¹Now the boy Samuel was ministering to the LORD under Eli.
The word of the LORD was rare in those days; visions were not widespread.
²At that time Eli,
whose eyesight had begun to grow dim so that he could not see,
was lying down in his room;
³the lamp of God had not yet gone out,
and Samuel was lying down in the temple of the LORD,
where the ark of God was.
⁴Then the LORD called, "Samuel! Samuel!"
and he said, "Here I am!"
⁵and ran to Eli, and said, "Here I am, for you called me."
But he said, "I did not call; lie down again."
So he went and lay down.

⁶The LORD called again, "Samuel!"
Samuel got up and went to Eli, and said,
"Here I am, for you called me."
But he said, "I did not call, my son; lie down again."
⁷Now Samuel did not yet know the LORD,
and the word of the LORD had not yet been revealed to him.

⁸The LORD called Samuel again, a third time.
And he got up and went to Eli, and said, "Here I am, for you called me."
Then Eli perceived that the LORD was calling the boy.
⁹Therefore Eli said to Samuel,
"Go, lie down; and if he calls you, you shall say,
'Speak, LORD, for your servant is listening.'"
So Samuel went and lay down in his place.

¹⁰Now the LORD came and stood there,
calling as before, "Samuel! Samuel!"
And Samuel said, "Speak, for your servant is listening."

[[11]Then the Lord said to Samuel,
"See, I am about to do something in Israel
that will make both ears of anyone who hears of it tingle.
[12]On that day I will fulfill against Eli all that I have spoken concerning his
        house,
from beginning to end.
[13]For I have told him that I am about to punish his house forever,
for the iniquity that he knew,
because his sons were blaspheming God, and he did not restrain them.
[14]Therefore I swear to the house of Eli
that the iniquity of Eli's house shall not be expiated by sacrifice or offering
        forever."

[15]Samuel lay there until morning;
then he opened the doors of the house of the Lord.
Samuel was afraid to tell the vision to Eli.
[16]But Eli called Samuel and said, "Samuel, my son."
He said, "Here I am."
[17]Eli said, "What was it that he told you? Do not hide it from me.
May God do so to you and more also,
if you hide anything from me of all that he told you."
[18]So Samuel told him everything and hid nothing from him.
Then he said, "It is the Lord; let him do what seems good to him."

[19]As Samuel grew up,
the Lord was with him and let none of his words fall to the ground.
[20]And all Israel from Dan to Beer-sheba
knew that Samuel was a trustworthy prophet of the Lord.]

The word of the Lord.

PSALMODY: PSALM 139:1–6, 13–18   *Psalm 139:1–5, 12–17* LBW/BCP

SECOND READING: 1 CORINTHIANS 6:12–20

A reading from First Corinthians:

[12]"All things are lawful for me," but not all things are beneficial.
"All things are lawful for me," but I will not be dominated by anything.
[13]"Food is meant for the stomach and the stomach for food,"
and God will destroy both one and the other.
The body is meant not for fornication but for the Lord,
and the Lord for the body.
[14]And God raised the Lord and will also raise us by his power.

[15]Do you not know that your bodies are members of Christ?
Should I therefore take the members of Christ and make them members
        of a prostitute?

Never!

16Do you not know that whoever is united to a prostitute becomes one body with her?

For it is said, "The two shall be one flesh."

17But anyone united to the Lord becomes one spirit with him.

18Shun fornication!

Every sin that a person commits is outside the body;

but the fornicator sins against the body itself.

19Or do you not know that your body is a temple of the Holy Spirit within you, which you have from God, and that you are not your own?

20For you were bought with a price;

therefore glorify God in your body.

The word of the Lord.

GOSPEL: JOHN 1:43–51

The Holy Gospel according to John, the first chapter.

43The next day Jesus decided to go to Galilee.

He found Philip and said to him, "Follow me."

44Now Philip was from Bethsaida, the city of Andrew and Peter.

45Philip found Nathanael and said to him,

"We have found him about whom Moses in the law and also the prophets wrote,

Jesus son of Joseph from Nazareth."

46Nathanael said to him, "Can anything good come out of Nazareth?"

Philip said to him, "Come and see."

47When Jesus saw Nathanael coming toward him, he said of him,

"Here is truly an Israelite in whom there is no deceit!"

48Nathanael asked him, "Where did you get to know me?"

Jesus answered,

"I saw you under the fig tree before Philip called you."

49Nathanael replied,

"Rabbi, you are the Son of God! You are the King of Israel!"

50Jesus answered,

"Do you believe because I told you that I saw you under the fig tree?

You will see greater things than these."

51And he said to him, "Very truly, I tell you,

you will see heaven opened

and the angels of God ascending and descending upon the Son of Man."

The Gospel of the Lord.

THIRD SUNDAY AFTER THE EPIPHANY

JANUARY 26, 1997   JANUARY 23, 2000   JANUARY 26, 2003

Jan 27, 2006

FIRST READING: JONAH 3:1–5, 10

A reading from Jonah:

¹The word of the LORD came to Jonah a second time, saying,
²"Get up, go to Nineveh, that great city,
and proclaim to it the message that I tell you."
³So Jonah set out and went to Nineveh, according to the word of the LORD.
Now Nineveh was an exceedingly large city, a three days' walk across.
⁴Jonah began to go into the city, going a day's walk.
And he cried out, "Forty days more, and Nineveh shall be overthrown!"
⁵And the people of Nineveh believed God;
they proclaimed a fast, and everyone, great and small, put on sackcloth.

¹⁰When God saw what they did, how they turned from their evil ways,
God changed his mind about the calamity that he had said he would bring
        upon them;
and he did not do it.

The word of the Lord.

PSALMODY: PSALM 62:5–12   *Psalm 62:6–14* LBW/BCP

SECOND READING: 1 CORINTHIANS 7:29–31

A reading from First Corinthians:

²⁹Brothers and sisters, the appointed time has grown short;
from now on, let even those who have wives be as though they had none,
³⁰and those who mourn as though they were not mourning,
and those who rejoice as though they were not rejoicing,
and those who buy as though they had no possessions,
³¹and those who deal with the world as though they had no dealings with it.
For the present form of this world is passing away.

The word of the Lord.

GOSPEL: MARK 1:14–20

The Holy Gospel according to Mark, the first chapter.

[14]Now after John was arrested,
Jesus came to Galilee, proclaiming the good news of God, [15]and saying,
"The time is fulfilled, and the kingdom of God has come near;
repent, and believe in the good news."

[16]As Jesus passed along the Sea of Galilee,
he saw Simon and his brother Andrew casting a net into the sea—
for they were fishermen.
[17]And Jesus said to them, "Follow me and I will make you fish for people."
[18]And immediately they left their nets and followed him.
[19]As he went a little farther,
he saw James son of Zebedee and his brother John,
who were in their boat mending the nets.
[20]Immediately he called them;
and they left their father Zebedee in the boat with the hired men,
and followed him.

The Gospel of the Lord.

FOURTH SUNDAY AFTER THE EPIPHANY

FEBRUARY 2, 1997   JANUARY 30, 2000   FEBRUARY 2, 2003

FIRST READING: DEUTERONOMY 18:15–20

A reading from Deuteronomy:

¹⁵The LORD your God will raise up for you a prophet like me
from among your own people;
you shall heed such a prophet.
¹⁶This is what you requested of the LORD your God at Horeb
on the day of the assembly when you said:
"If I hear the voice of the LORD my God any more,
or ever again see this great fire, I will die."
¹⁷Then the LORD replied to me:
"They are right in what they have said.
¹⁸I will raise up for them a prophet like you from among their own people;
I will put my words in the mouth of the prophet,
who shall speak to them everything that I command.
¹⁹Anyone who does not heed the words that the prophet shall speak in my
         name,
I myself will hold accountable.
²⁰But any prophet who speaks in the name of other gods,
or who presumes to speak in my name
a word that I have not commanded the prophet to speak—
that prophet shall die."

The word of the Lord.

PSALMODY: PSALM 111

SECOND READING: 1 Corinthians 8:1–13

A reading from First Corinthians:

[1]Now concerning food sacrificed to idols:
we know that "all of us possess knowledge."
Knowledge puffs up, but love builds up.
[2]Anyone who claims to know something does not yet have the necessary
     knowledge;
[3]but anyone who loves God is known by him.

[4]Hence, as to the eating of food offered to idols,
we know that "no idol in the world really exists,"
and that "there is no God but one."
[5]Indeed, even though there may be so-called gods in heaven or on earth—
as in fact there are many gods and many lords—
[6]yet for us there is one God, the Father,
from whom are all things and for whom we exist,
and one Lord, Jesus Christ,
through whom are all things and through whom we exist.

[7]It is not everyone, however, who has this knowledge.
Since some have become so accustomed to idols until now,
they still think of the food they eat as food offered to an idol;
and their conscience, being weak, is defiled.
[8]"Food will not bring us close to God."
We are no worse off if we do not eat, and no better off if we do.
[9]But take care that this liberty of yours
does not somehow become a stumbling block to the weak.
[10]For if others see you, who possess knowledge,
eating in the temple of an idol,
might they not, since their conscience is weak,
be encouraged to the point of eating food sacrificed to idols?
[11]So by your knowledge those weak believers for whom Christ died
     are destroyed.
[12]But when you thus sin against members of your family,
and wound their conscience when it is weak,
you sin against Christ.
[13]Therefore, if food is a cause of their falling, I will never eat meat,
so that I may not cause one of them to fall.

The word of the Lord.

GOSPEL: MARK 1:21–28

The Holy Gospel according to Mark, the first chapter.

²¹Jesus and his disciples went to Capernaum;
and when the sabbath came, he entered the synagogue and taught.
²²They were astounded at his teaching,
for he taught them as one having authority, and not as the scribes.

²³Just then there was in their synagogue a man with an unclean spirit,
²⁴and he cried out, "What have you to do with us, Jesus of Nazareth?
Have you come to destroy us?
I know who you are, the Holy One of God."
²⁵But Jesus rebuked him, saying, "Be silent, and come out of him!"
²⁶And the unclean spirit, convulsing him and crying with a loud voice,
came out of him.
²⁷They were all amazed, and they kept on asking one another,
"What is this? A new teaching—with authority!
He commands even the unclean spirits, and they obey him."

²⁸At once his fame began to spread throughout the surrounding region
of Galilee.

The Gospel of the Lord.

FIFTH SUNDAY AFTER THE EPIPHANY

FEBRUARY 6, 2000   FEBRUARY 9, 2003

FIRST READING: Isaiah 40:21–31

A reading from Isaiah:

²¹Have you not known? Have you not heard?
    Has it not been told you from the beginning?
    Have you not understood from the foundations of the earth?
²²It is he who sits above the circle of the earth,
    and its inhabitants are like grasshoppers;
who stretches out the heavens like a curtain,
    and spreads them like a tent to live in;
²³who brings princes to naught,
    and makes the rulers of the earth as nothing.

²⁴Scarcely are they planted, scarcely sown,
    scarcely has their stem taken root in the earth,
when he blows upon them, and they wither,
    and the tempest carries them off like stubble.

²⁵To whom then will you compare me,
    or who is my equal? says the Holy One.
²⁶Lift up your eyes on high and see:
    Who created these?
He who brings out their host and numbers them,
    calling them all by name;
because he is great in strength,
    mighty in power,
    not one is missing.

²⁷Why do you say, O Jacob,
    and speak, O Israel,
"My way is hidden from the Lord,
    and my right is disregarded by my God"?
²⁸Have you not known? Have you not heard?
The Lord is the everlasting God,
    the Creator of the ends of the earth.

He does not faint or grow weary;
    his understanding is unsearchable.
²⁹He gives power to the faint,
    and strengthens the powerless.
³⁰Even youths will faint and be weary,
    and the young will fall exhausted;
³¹but those who wait for the Lord shall renew their strength,
    they shall mount up with wings like eagles,
they shall run and not be weary,
    they shall walk and not faint.

The word of the Lord.

PSALMODY: PSALM 147:1–11, 20c　　　　　　　　　　*Psalm 147:1–12, 21c* LBW/BCP

SECOND READING: 1 CORINTHIANS 9:16–23

A reading from First Corinthians:

¹⁶If I proclaim the gospel, this gives me no ground for boasting,
for an obligation is laid on me, and woe to me if I do not proclaim the gospel!
¹⁷For if I do this of my own will, I have a reward;
but if not of my own will, I am entrusted with a commission.
¹⁸What then is my reward?
Just this:
that in my proclamation I may make the gospel free of charge,
so as not to make full use of my rights in the gospel.

¹⁹For though I am free with respect to all,
I have made myself a slave to all,
so that I might win more of them.
²⁰To the Jews I became as a Jew, in order to win Jews.
To those under the law I became as one under the law
(though I myself am not under the law)
so that I might win those under the law.
²¹To those outside the law I became as one outside the law
(though I am not free from God's law but am under Christ's law)
so that I might win those outside the law.
²²To the weak I became weak, so that I might win the weak.
I have become all things to all people, that I might by all means save some.
²³I do it all for the sake of the gospel,
so that I may share in its blessings.

The word of the Lord.

GOSPEL: MARK 1:29–39

The Holy Gospel according to Mark, the first chapter.

^{29}As soon as Jesus and the disciples left the synagogue,
they entered the house of Simon and Andrew, with James and John.
^{30}Now Simon's mother-in-law was in bed with a fever,
and they told him about her at once.
^{31}He came and took her by the hand and lifted her up.
Then the fever left her, and she began to serve them.

^{32}That evening, at sundown,
they brought to him all who were sick or possessed with demons.
^{33}And the whole city was gathered around the door.
^{34}And he cured many who were sick with various diseases,
and cast out many demons;
and he would not permit the demons to speak, because they knew him.

^{35}In the morning, while it was still very dark,
he got up and went out to a deserted place,
and there he prayed.
^{36}And Simon and his companions hunted for him.
^{37}When they found him, they said to him,
"Everyone is searching for you."
^{38}He answered, "Let us go on to the neighboring towns,
so that I may proclaim the message there also;
for that is what I came out to do."
^{39}And he went throughout Galilee,
proclaiming the message in their synagogues and casting out demons.

The Gospel of the Lord.

Sixth Sunday after the Epiphany

PROPER 1

FEBRUARY 13, 2000   FEBRUARY 16, 2003

FIRST READING: 2 KINGS 5:1–14

A reading from Second Kings:

¹Naaman, commander of the army of the king of Aram,
was a great man and in high favor with his master,
because by him the LORD had given victory to Aram.
The man, though a mighty warrior, suffered from leprosy.
²Now the Arameans on one of their raids
had taken a young girl captive from the land of Israel,
and she served Naaman's wife.
³She said to her mistress,
"If only my lord were with the prophet who is in Samaria!
He would cure him of his leprosy."
⁴So Naaman went in and told his lord
just what the girl from the land of Israel had said.
⁵And the king of Aram said,
"Go then, and I will send along a letter to the king of Israel."

He went, taking with him ten talents of silver,
six thousand shekels of gold, and ten sets of garments.
⁶He brought the letter to the king of Israel, which read,
"When this letter reaches you,
know that I have sent to you my servant Naaman,
that you may cure him of his leprosy."
⁷When the king of Israel read the letter, he tore his clothes and said,
"Am I God, to give death or life,
that this man sends word to me to cure a man of his leprosy?
Just look and see how he is trying to pick a quarrel with me."

⁸But when Elisha the man of God heard that the king of Israel had torn his
        clothes,
he sent a message to the king, "Why have you torn your clothes?
Let him come to me, that he may learn that there is a prophet in Israel."
⁹So Naaman came with his horses and chariots,
and halted at the entrance of Elisha's house.

[10]Elisha sent a messenger to him, saying,
"Go, wash in the Jordan seven times,
and your flesh shall be restored and you shall be clean."
[11]But Naaman became angry and went away, saying,
"I thought that for me he would surely come out,
and stand and call on the name of the LORD his God,
and would wave his hand over the spot, and cure the leprosy!
[12]Are not Abana and Pharpar, the rivers of Damascus,
better than all the waters of Israel?
Could I not wash in them, and be clean?"
He turned and went away in a rage.
[13]But his servants approached and said to him,
"Father, if the prophet had commanded you to do something difficult,
would you not have done it?
How much more, when all he said to you was, 'Wash, and be clean'?"
[14]So he went down and immersed himself seven times in the Jordan,
according to the word of the man of God;
his flesh was restored like the flesh of a young boy, and he was clean.

The word of the Lord.

PSALMODY: PSALM 30

SECOND READING: 1 CORINTHIANS 9:24–27

A reading from First Corinthians:

[24]Do you not know that in a race the runners all compete,
but only one receives the prize?
Run in such a way that you may win it.
[25]Athletes exercise self-control in all things;
they do it to receive a perishable wreath,
but we an imperishable one.
[26]So I do not run aimlessly,
nor do I box as though beating the air;
[27]but I punish my body and enslave it,
so that after proclaiming to others I myself should not be disqualified.

The word of the Lord.

GOSPEL: MARK 1:40–45

The Holy Gospel according to Mark, the first chapter.

[40]A leper came to Jesus begging him, and kneeling he said to him,
"If you choose, you can make me clean."
[41]Moved with pity, Jesus stretched out his hand and touched him,
and said to him, "I do choose. Be made clean!"
[42]Immediately the leprosy left him, and he was made clean.
[43]After sternly warning him he sent him away at once,
[44]saying to him, "See that you say nothing to anyone;
but go, show yourself to the priest,
and offer for your cleansing what Moses commanded, as a testimony to them."

[45]But he went out and began to proclaim it freely,
and to spread the word,
so that Jesus could no longer go into a town openly,
but stayed out in the country;
and people came to him from every quarter.

The Gospel of the Lord.

Seventh Sunday after the Epiphany

PROPER 2

FEBRUARY 20, 2000   FEBRUARY 23, 2003

FIRST READING: Isaiah 43:18–25

A reading from Isaiah:

[18]Do not remember the former things,
    or consider the things of old.
[19]I am about to do a new thing;
    now it springs forth, do you not perceive it?
I will make a way in the wilderness
    and rivers in the desert.
[20]The wild animals will honor me,
    the jackals and the ostriches;
for I give water in the wilderness,
    rivers in the desert,
to give drink to my chosen people,
    [21]the people whom I formed for myself
so that they might declare my praise.

[22]Yet you did not call upon me, O Jacob;
    but you have been weary of me, O Israel!
[23]You have not brought me your sheep for burnt offerings,
    or honored me with your sacrifices.
I have not burdened you with offerings,
    or wearied you with frankincense.
[24]You have not bought me sweet cane with money,
    or satisfied me with the fat of your sacrifices.
But you have burdened me with your sins;
    you have wearied me with your iniquities.

[25]I, I am He
    who blots out your transgressions for my own sake,
    and I will not remember your sins.

The word of the Lord.

PSALMODY: Psalm 41

SECOND READING: 2 Corinthians 1:18–22

A reading from Second Corinthians:

[18]As surely as God is faithful,
our word to you has not been "Yes and No."
[19]For the Son of God, Jesus Christ,
whom we proclaimed among you, Silvanus and Timothy and I,
was not "Yes and No";
but in him it is always "Yes."
[20]For in him every one of God's promises is a "Yes."
For this reason it is through him that we say the "Amen," to the glory of God.
[21]But it is God who establishes us with you in Christ and has anointed us,
[22]by putting his seal on us and giving us his Spirit in our hearts
        as a first installment.

The word of the Lord.

GOSPEL: MARK 2:1–12

The Holy Gospel according to Mark, the second chapter.

[1]When Jesus returned to Capernaum after some days,
it was reported that he was at home.
[2]So many gathered around that there was no longer room for them,
not even in front of the door;
and he was speaking the word to them.
[3]Then some people came,
bringing to him a paralyzed man, carried by four of them.
[4]And when they could not bring him to Jesus because of the crowd,
they removed the roof above him;
and after having dug through it,
they let down the mat on which the paralytic lay.
[5]When Jesus saw their faith, he said to the paralytic,
"Son, your sins are forgiven."

[6]Now some of the scribes were sitting there, questioning in their hearts,
[7]"Why does this fellow speak in this way?
It is blasphemy!
Who can forgive sins but God alone?"
[8]At once Jesus perceived in his spirit
that they were discussing these questions among themselves;
and he said to them, "Why do you raise such questions in your hearts?
[9]Which is easier, to say to the paralytic, 'Your sins are forgiven,'
or to say, 'Stand up and take your mat and walk'?
[10]But so that you may know that the Son of Man has authority on earth
        to forgive sins"—
he said to the paralytic—
[11]"I say to you, stand up, take your mat and go to your home."
[12]And he stood up,
and immediately took the mat and went out before all of them;
so that they were all amazed and glorified God, saying,
"We have never seen anything like this!"

The Gospel of the Lord.

EIGHTH SUNDAY AFTER THE EPIPHANY

PROPER 3

FEBRUARY 27, 2000

FIRST READING: HOSEA 2:14–20

A reading from Hosea:

> ¹⁴I will now allure her, says the LORD,
>> and bring her into the wilderness,
>> and speak tenderly to her.
> ¹⁵From there I will give her her vineyards,
>> and make the Valley of Achor a door of hope.
> There she shall respond as in the days of her youth,
>> as at the time when she came out of the land of Egypt.

> ¹⁶On that day, says the LORD, you will call me, "My husband,"
> and no longer will you call me, "My Baal."
> ¹⁷For I will remove the names of the Baals from her mouth,
> and they shall be mentioned by name no more.
> ¹⁸I will make for you a covenant on that day with the wild animals,
>> the birds of the air, and the creeping things of the ground;
> and I will abolish the bow, the sword, and war from the land;
> and I will make you lie down in safety.
> ¹⁹And I will take you for my wife forever;
> I will take you for my wife in righteousness and in justice,
> in steadfast love, and in mercy.
> ²⁰I will take you for my wife in faithfulness;
> and you shall know the LORD.

The word of the Lord.

PSALMODY: PSALM 103:1–13, 22

SECOND READING: 2 Corinthians 3:1–6

A reading from Second Corinthians:

[1]Are we beginning to commend ourselves again?
Surely we do not need, as some do,
letters of recommendation to you or from you, do we?
[2]You yourselves are our letter,
written on our hearts, to be known and read by all;
[3]and you show that you are a letter of Christ,
prepared by us, written not with ink but with the Spirit of the living God,
not on tablets of stone but on tablets of human hearts.
[4]Such is the confidence that we have through Christ toward God.
[5]Not that we are competent of ourselves to claim anything as coming from us;
our competence is from God,
[6]who has made us competent to be ministers of a new covenant,
not of letter but of spirit;
for the letter kills, but the Spirit gives life.

The word of the Lord.

The Holy Gospel according to Mark, the second chapter.

[13]Jesus went out again beside the sea;
the whole crowd gathered around him, and he taught them.
[14]As he was walking along,
he saw Levi son of Alphaeus sitting at the tax booth,
and he said to him, "Follow me."
And he got up and followed him.

[15]And as he sat at dinner in Levi's house,
many tax collectors and sinners were also sitting with Jesus and his disciples—
for there were many who followed him.
[16]When the scribes of the Pharisees saw that he was eating with sinners and
        tax collectors,
they said to his disciples,
"Why does he eat with tax collectors and sinners?"
[17]When Jesus heard this, he said to them,
"Those who are well have no need of a physician, but those who are sick;
I have come to call not the righteous but sinners."

[18]Now John's disciples and the Pharisees were fasting;
and people came and said to him,
"Why do John's disciples and the disciples of the Pharisees fast,
but your disciples do not fast?"
[19]Jesus said to them,
"The wedding guests cannot fast while the bridegroom is with them, can they?
As long as they have the bridegroom with them, they cannot fast.
[20]The days will come when the bridegroom is taken away from them,
and then they will fast on that day.

[21]"No one sews a piece of unshrunk cloth on an old cloak;
otherwise, the patch pulls away from it, the new from the old, and a worse tear
        is made.
[22]And no one puts new wine into old wineskins;
otherwise, the wine will burst the skins,
and the wine is lost, and so are the skins;
but one puts new wine into fresh wineskins."

The Gospel of the Lord.

THE TRANSFIGURATION OF OUR LORD
Last Sunday after the Epiphany

FEBRUARY 9, 1997   MARCH 5, 2000   MARCH 2, 2003

FIRST READING: 2 KINGS 2:1–12

A reading from Second Kings:

[1]Now when the LORD was about to take Elijah up to heaven by a whirlwind,
Elijah and Elisha were on their way from Gilgal.
[2]Elijah said to Elisha,
"Stay here; for the LORD has sent me as far as Bethel."
But Elisha said,
"As the LORD lives, and as you yourself live, I will not leave you."
So they went down to Bethel.
[3]The company of prophets who were in Bethel came out to Elisha,
and said to him,
"Do you know that today the LORD will take your master away from you?"
And he said, "Yes, I know; keep silent."

[4]Elijah said to him, "Elisha, stay here; for the LORD has sent me to Jericho."
But he said, "As the LORD lives, and as you yourself live, I will not leave you."
So they came to Jericho.
[5]The company of prophets who were at Jericho drew near to Elisha, and said
to him,
"Do you know that today the LORD will take your master away from you?"
And he answered, "Yes, I know; be silent."

[6]Then Elijah said to him, "Stay here; for the LORD has sent me to the Jordan."
But he said, "As the LORD lives, and as you yourself live, I will not leave you."
So the two of them went on.
[7]Fifty men of the company of prophets also went,
and stood at some distance from them, as they both were standing
by the Jordan.
[8]Then Elijah took his mantle and rolled it up, and struck the water;
the water was parted to the one side and to the other,
until the two of them crossed on dry ground.

[9]When they had crossed, Elijah said to Elisha,
"Tell me what I may do for you, before I am taken from you."
Elisha said, "Please let me inherit a double share of your spirit."

¹⁰He responded, "You have asked a hard thing;
yet, if you see me as I am being taken from you, it will be granted you;
if not, it will not."
¹¹As they continued walking and talking,
a chariot of fire and horses of fire separated the two of them,
and Elijah ascended in a whirlwind into heaven.
¹²Elisha kept watching and crying out, "Father, father!
The chariots of Israel and its horsemen!"
But when he could no longer see him,
he grasped his own clothes and tore them in two pieces.

The word of the Lord.

PSALMODY: PSALM 50:1–6

SECOND READING: 2 CORINTHIANS 4:3–6

A reading from Second Corinthians:

³Even if our gospel is veiled,
it is veiled to those who are perishing.
⁴In their case the god of this world has blinded the minds of the unbelievers,
to keep them from seeing the light of the gospel of the glory of Christ,
who is the image of God.
⁵For we do not proclaim ourselves;
we proclaim Jesus Christ as Lord and ourselves as your slaves for Jesus' sake.
⁶For it is the God who said, "Let light shine out of darkness,"
who has shone in our hearts
to give the light of the knowledge of the glory of God
in the face of Jesus Christ.

The word of the Lord.

GOSPEL: MARK 9:2–9

The Holy Gospel according to Mark, the ninth chapter.

[2]Six days later, Jesus took with him Peter and James and John,
and led them up a high mountain apart, by themselves.
And he was transfigured before them,
[3]and his clothes became dazzling white,
such as no one on earth could bleach them.
[4]And there appeared to them Elijah with Moses, who were talking with Jesus.
[5]Then Peter said to Jesus, "Rabbi, it is good for us to be here;
let us make three dwellings, one for you, one for Moses, and one for Elijah."
[6]He did not know what to say, for they were terrified.
[7]Then a cloud overshadowed them,
and from the cloud there came a voice,
"This is my Son, the Beloved; listen to him!"
[8]Suddenly when they looked around,
they saw no one with them any more, but only Jesus.

[9]As they were coming down the mountain,
he ordered them to tell no one about what they had seen,
until after the Son of Man had risen from the dead.

The Gospel of the Lord.

SEASON OF LENT

ASH WEDNESDAY

FEBRUARY 12, 1997   MARCH 8, 2000   MARCH 5, 2003

FIRST READING: JOEL 2:1–2, 12–17
Or Isaiah 58:1–12, following

A reading from Joel:

¹Blow the trumpet in Zion;
    sound the alarm on my holy mountain!
Let all the inhabitants of the land tremble,
    for the day of the LORD is coming, it is near—
²a day of darkness and gloom,
    a day of clouds and thick darkness!
Like blackness spread upon the mountains
    a great and powerful army comes;
their like has never been from of old,
    nor will be again after them
    in ages to come.

¹²Yet even now, says the LORD,
    return to me with all your heart,
with fasting, with weeping, and with mourning;
    ¹³rend your hearts and not your clothing.
Return to the LORD, your God,
    for he is gracious and merciful,
slow to anger, and abounding in steadfast love,
    and relents from punishing.
¹⁴Who knows whether he will not turn and relent,
    and leave a blessing behind him,
a grain offering and a drink offering
    for the LORD, your God?

¹⁵Blow the trumpet in Zion;
    sanctify a fast;
call a solemn assembly;
    ¹⁶gather the people.
Sanctify the congregation;
    assemble the aged;
gather the children,

even infants at the breast.
Let the bridegroom leave his room,
     and the bride her canopy.

[17]Between the vestibule and the altar
     let the priests, the ministers of the LORD, weep.
Let them say, "Spare your people, O LORD,
     and do not make your heritage a mockery,
     a byword among the nations.
Why should it be said among the peoples,
     'Where is their God?' "

The word of the Lord.

OR: ISAIAH 58:1–12

A reading from Isaiah:

[1]Shout out, do not hold back!
     Lift up your voice like a trumpet!
Announce to my people their rebellion,
     to the house of Jacob their sins.
[2]Yet day after day they seek me
     and delight to know my ways,
as if they were a nation that practiced righteousness
     and did not forsake the ordinance of their God;
they ask of me righteous judgments,
     they delight to draw near to God.

[3]"Why do we fast, but you do not see?
     Why humble ourselves, but you do not notice?"
Look, you serve your own interest on your fast day,
     and oppress all your workers.
[4]Look, you fast only to quarrel and to fight
     and to strike with a wicked fist.
Such fasting as you do today
     will not make your voice heard on high.

[5]Is such the fast that I choose,
     a day to humble oneself?
Is it to bow down the head like a bulrush,
     and to lie in sackcloth and ashes?
Will you call this a fast,
     a day acceptable to the LORD?

[6]Is not this the fast that I choose:
     to loose the bonds of injustice,

to undo the thongs of the yoke,
to let the oppressed go free,
and to break every yoke?
⁷Is it not to share your bread with the hungry,
and bring the homeless poor into your house;
when you see the naked, to cover them,
and not to hide yourself from your own kin?
⁸Then your light shall break forth like the dawn,
and your healing shall spring up quickly;
your vindicator shall go before you,
the glory of the LORD shall be your rear guard.
⁹Then you shall call, and the LORD will answer;
you shall cry for help, and he will say, Here I am.

If you remove the yoke from among you,
the pointing of the finger, the speaking of evil,
¹⁰if you offer your food to the hungry
and satisfy the needs of the afflicted,
then your light shall rise in the darkness
and your gloom be like the noonday.
¹¹The LORD will guide you continually,
and satisfy your needs in parched places,
and make your bones strong;
and you shall be like a watered garden,
like a spring of water,
whose waters never fail.
¹²Your ancient ruins shall be rebuilt;
you shall raise up the foundations of many generations;
you shall be called the repairer of the breach,
the restorer of streets to live in.

The word of the Lord.

PSALMODY: PSALM 51:1–17   *Psalm 51:1–18* LBW/BCP

SECOND READING: 2 Corinthians 5:20b—6:10

A reading from Second Corinthians:

20bWe entreat you on behalf of Christ,
be reconciled to God.
21For our sake he made him to be sin who knew no sin,
so that in him we might become the righteousness of God.

6:1As we work together with him,
we urge you also not to accept the grace of God in vain.
2For he says,
   "At an acceptable time I have listened to you,
      and on a day of salvation I have helped you."
See, now is the acceptable time;
see, now is the day of salvation!

3We are putting no obstacle in anyone's way,
so that no fault may be found with our ministry,
4but as servants of God we have commended ourselves in every way:
through great endurance,
in afflictions, hardships, calamities,
5beatings, imprisonments, riots,
labors, sleepless nights, hunger;
6by purity, knowledge, patience,
kindness, holiness of spirit, genuine love,
7truthful speech, and the power of God;
with the weapons of righteousness for the right hand and for the left;
8in honor and dishonor,
in ill repute and good repute.
We are treated as impostors, and yet are true;
9as unknown, and yet are well known;
as dying, and see—we are alive;
as punished, and yet not killed;
10as sorrowful, yet always rejoicing;
as poor, yet making many rich;
as having nothing, and yet possessing everything.

The word of the Lord.

GOSPEL: Matthew 6:1–6, 16–21

The Holy Gospel according to Matthew, the sixth chapter.

Jesus said to the disciples:
[1]"Beware of practicing your piety before others
in order to be seen by them;
for then you have no reward from your Father in heaven.
[2]So whenever you give alms, do not sound a trumpet before you,
as the hypocrites do in the synagogues and in the streets,
so that they may be praised by others.
Truly I tell you,
they have received their reward.
[3]But when you give alms,
do not let your left hand know what your right hand is doing,
[4]so that your alms may be done in secret;
and your Father who sees in secret will reward you.

[5]"And whenever you pray, do not be like the hypocrites;
for they love to stand and pray in the synagogues and at the street corners,
so that they may be seen by others.
Truly I tell you,
they have received their reward.
[6]But whenever you pray,
go into your room and shut the door
and pray to your Father who is in secret;
and your Father who sees in secret will reward you.

[16]"And whenever you fast, do not look dismal, like the hypocrites,
for they disfigure their faces so as to show others that they are fasting.
Truly I tell you,
they have received their reward.
[17]But when you fast,
put oil on your head and wash your face,
[18]so that your fasting may be seen not by others
but by your Father who is in secret;
and your Father who sees in secret will reward you.

[19]"Do not store up for yourselves treasures on earth,
where moth and rust consume
and where thieves break in and steal;
[20]but store up for yourselves treasures in heaven,
where neither moth nor rust consumes
and where thieves do not break in and steal.
[21]For where your treasure is,
there your heart will be also."

The Gospel of the Lord.

FIRST SUNDAY IN LENT

FEBRUARY 16, 1997   MARCH 12, 2000   MARCH 9, 2003

FIRST READING: GENESIS 9:8–17

A reading from Genesis:

⁸God said to Noah and to his sons with him,
⁹"As for me, I am establishing my covenant with you and your descendants
      after you,
¹⁰and with every living creature that is with you,
the birds, the domestic animals, and every animal of the earth with you,
as many as came out of the ark.
¹¹I establish my covenant with you,
that never again shall all flesh be cut off by the waters of a flood,
and never again shall there be a flood to destroy the earth."
¹²God said, "This is the sign of the covenant
that I make between me and you and every living creature that is with you,
for all future generations:
¹³I have set my bow in the clouds,
and it shall be a sign of the covenant between me and the earth.
¹⁴When I bring clouds over the earth and the bow is seen in the clouds,
¹⁵I will remember my covenant that is between me and you
and every living creature of all flesh;
and the waters shall never again become a flood to destroy all flesh.
¹⁶When the bow is in the clouds, I will see it and remember the everlasting
      covenant
between God and every living creature of all flesh that is on the earth."
¹⁷God said to Noah,
"This is the sign of the covenant that I have established
between me and all flesh that is on the earth."

The word of the Lord.

PSALMODY: PSALM 25:1–10   *Psalm 25:1–9* LBW/BCP

SECOND READING: 1 Peter 3:18–22

A reading from First Peter:

[18]Christ also suffered for sins once for all,
the righteous for the unrighteous,
in order to bring you to God.
He was put to death in the flesh, but made alive in the spirit,
[19]in which also he went and made a proclamation to the spirits in prison,
[20]who in former times did not obey,
when God waited patiently in the days of Noah,
during the building of the ark,
in which a few, that is, eight persons, were saved through water.
[21]And baptism, which this prefigured, now saves you—
not as a removal of dirt from the body,
but as an appeal to God for a good conscience,
through the resurrection of Jesus Christ,
[22]who has gone into heaven and is at the right hand of God,
with angels, authorities, and powers made subject to him.

The word of the Lord.

GOSPEL: Mark 1:9–15

The Holy Gospel according to Mark, the first chapter.

[9]In those days Jesus came from Nazareth of Galilee
and was baptized by John in the Jordan.
[10]And just as he was coming up out of the water,
he saw the heavens torn apart and the Spirit descending like a dove on him.
[11]And a voice came from heaven,
"You are my Son, the Beloved; with you I am well pleased."

[12]And the Spirit immediately drove him out into the wilderness.
[13]He was in the wilderness forty days, tempted by Satan;
and he was with the wild beasts; and the angels waited on him.

[14]Now after John was arrested, Jesus came to Galilee,
proclaiming the good news of God, [15]and saying,
"The time is fulfilled, and the kingdom of God has come near;
repent, and believe in the good news."

The Gospel of the Lord.

SECOND SUNDAY IN LENT

FEBRUARY 23, 1997   MARCH 19, 2000   MARCH 16, 2003

FIRST READING: GENESIS 17:1–7, 15–16

A reading from Genesis:

¹When Abram was ninety-nine years old,
the LORD appeared to Abram, and said to him,
"I am God Almighty; walk before me, and be blameless.
²And I will make my covenant between me and you,
and will make you exceedingly numerous."
³Then Abram fell on his face;
and God said to him, ⁴"As for me, this is my covenant with you:
You shall be the ancestor of a multitude of nations.
⁵No longer shall your name be Abram, but your name shall be Abraham;
for I have made you the ancestor of a multitude of nations.
⁶I will make you exceedingly fruitful;
and I will make nations of you, and kings shall come from you.
⁷I will establish my covenant between me and you,
and your offspring after you throughout their generations,
for an everlasting covenant,
to be God to you and to your offspring after you."

¹⁵God said to Abraham,
"As for Sarah your wife, you shall not call her Sarai,
but Sarah shall be her name.
¹⁶I will bless her, and moreover I will give you a son by her.
I will bless her, and she shall give rise to nations;
kings of peoples shall come from her."

The word of the Lord.

PSALMODY: PSALM 22:23–31   *Psalm 22:22–30* LBW/BCP

SECOND READING: ROMANS 4:13–25

A reading from Romans:

¹³The promise that he would inherit the world
did not come to Abraham or to his descendants through the law
but through the righteousness of faith.
¹⁴If it is the adherents of the law who are to be the heirs,
faith is null and the promise is void.
¹⁵For the law brings wrath;
but where there is no law, neither is there violation.

¹⁶For this reason it depends on faith,
in order that the promise may rest on grace and be guaranteed to all his
        descendants,
not only to the adherents of the law
but also to those who share the faith of Abraham
(for he is the father of all of us, ¹⁷as it is written,
"I have made you the father of many nations")—
in the presence of the God in whom he believed,
who gives life to the dead and calls into existence the things that do not exist.
¹⁸Hoping against hope,
he believed that he would become "the father of many nations,"
according to what was said, "So numerous shall your descendants be."
¹⁹He did not weaken in faith when he considered his own body,
which was already as good as dead
(for he was about a hundred years old),
or when he considered the barrenness of Sarah's womb.
²⁰No distrust made him waver concerning the promise of God,
but he grew strong in his faith as he gave glory to God,
²¹being fully convinced that God was able to do what he had promised.
²²Therefore his faith "was reckoned to him as righteousness."
²³Now the words, "it was reckoned to him,"
were written not for his sake alone, ²⁴but for ours also.
It will be reckoned to us who believe in him
who raised Jesus our Lord from the dead,
²⁵who was handed over to death for our trespasses
and was raised for our justification.

The word of the Lord.

GOSPEL: MARK 8:31–38

The Holy Gospel according to Mark, the eighth chapter.

[31]Jesus began to teach them that the Son of Man must undergo great suffering,
and be rejected by the elders, the chief priests, and the scribes,
and be killed, and after three days rise again.
[32]He said all this quite openly.
And Peter took him aside and began to rebuke him.
[33]But turning and looking at his disciples, he rebuked Peter and said,
"Get behind me, Satan!
For you are setting your mind not on divine things but on human things."

[34]He called the crowd with his disciples, and said to them,
"If any want to become my followers,
let them deny themselves and take up their cross and follow me.
[35]For those who want to save their life will lose it,
and those who lose their life for my sake, and for the sake of the gospel,
will save it.
[36]For what will it profit them to gain the whole world and forfeit their life?
[37]Indeed, what can they give in return for their life?
[38]Those who are ashamed of me and of my words in this adulterous and sinful
      generation,
of them the Son of Man will also be ashamed
when he comes in the glory of his Father with the holy angels."

The Gospel of the Lord.

THIRD SUNDAY IN LENT

MARCH 2, 1997   MARCH 26, 2000   MARCH 23, 2003

FIRST READING: EXODUS 20:1–17

A reading from Exodus:

¹God spoke all these words:
²I am the LORD your God, who brought you out of the land of Egypt,
out of the house of slavery;
³you shall have no other gods before me.

⁴You shall not make for yourself an idol,
whether in the form of anything that is in heaven above,
or that is on the earth beneath, or that is in the water under the earth.
⁵You shall not bow down to them or worship them;
for I the LORD your God am a jealous God,
punishing children for the iniquity of parents,
to the third and the fourth generation of those who reject me,
⁶but showing steadfast love to the thousandth generation
of those who love me and keep my commandments.

⁷You shall not make wrongful use of the name of the LORD your God,
for the LORD will not acquit anyone who misuses his name.

⁸Remember the sabbath day, and keep it holy.
⁹Six days you shall labor and do all your work.
¹⁰But the seventh day is a sabbath to the LORD your God;
you shall not do any work—
you, your son or your daughter, your male or female slave, your livestock,
or the alien resident in your towns.
¹¹For in six days the LORD made heaven and earth, the sea,
        and all that is in them,
but rested the seventh day;
therefore the LORD blessed the sabbath day and consecrated it.

¹²Honor your father and your mother,
so that your days may be long in the land that the LORD your God is giving you.
¹³You shall not murder.
¹⁴You shall not commit adultery.

¹⁵You shall not steal.

¹⁶You shall not bear false witness against your neighbor.

¹⁷You shall not covet your neighbor's house;

you shall not covet your neighbor's wife,

or male or female slave, or ox, or donkey, or anything that belongs to your
neighbor.

The word of the Lord.

PSALMODY: Psalm 19

SECOND READING: 1 Corinthians 1:18–25

A reading from First Corinthians:

¹⁸The message about the cross is foolishness to those who are perishing,
but to us who are being saved it is the power of God.
¹⁹For it is written,
"I will destroy the wisdom of the wise,
and the discernment of the discerning I will thwart."
²⁰Where is the one who is wise?
Where is the scribe?
Where is the debater of this age?
Has not God made foolish the wisdom of the world?

²¹For since, in the wisdom of God,
the world did not know God through wisdom,
God decided, through the foolishness of our proclamation,
to save those who believe.
²²For Jews demand signs and Greeks desire wisdom,
²³but we proclaim Christ crucified,
a stumbling block to Jews and foolishness to Gentiles,
²⁴but to those who are the called, both Jews and Greeks,
Christ the power of God and the wisdom of God.
²⁵For God's foolishness is wiser than human wisdom,
and God's weakness is stronger than human strength.

The word of the Lord.

GOSPEL: JOHN 2:13–22

The Holy Gospel according to John, the second chapter.

13The Passover of the Jews was near, and Jesus went up to Jerusalem.
14In the temple he found people selling cattle, sheep, and doves,
and the money changers seated at their tables.
15Making a whip of cords, he drove all of them out of the temple,
both the sheep and the cattle.
He also poured out the coins of the money changers and overturned their
          tables.
16He told those who were selling the doves,
"Take these things out of here!
Stop making my Father's house a marketplace!"
17His disciples remembered that it was written,
"Zeal for your house will consume me."
18The Jews then said to him,
"What sign can you show us for doing this?"
19Jesus answered them,
"Destroy this temple, and in three days I will raise it up."
20The Jews then said,
"This temple has been under construction for forty-six years,
and will you raise it up in three days?"
21But he was speaking of the temple of his body.

22After he was raised from the dead,
his disciples remembered that he had said this;
and they believed the scripture and the word that Jesus had spoken.

The Gospel of the Lord.

FOURTH SUNDAY IN LENT

MARCH 9, 1997   APRIL 2, 2000   MARCH 30, 2003

FIRST READING: NUMBERS 21:4–9

A reading from Numbers:

⁴From Mount Hor the Israelites set out by the way to the Red Sea,
to go around the land of Edom;
but the people became impatient on the way.
⁵The people spoke against God and against Moses,
"Why have you brought us up out of Egypt to die in the wilderness?
For there is no food and no water,
and we detest this miserable food."
⁶Then the LORD sent poisonous serpents among the people,
and they bit the people, so that many Israelites died.
⁷The people came to Moses and said,
"We have sinned by speaking against the LORD and against you;
pray to the LORD to take away the serpents from us."

So Moses prayed for the people.
⁸And the LORD said to Moses,
"Make a poisonous serpent, and set it on a pole;
and everyone who is bitten shall look at it and live."
⁹So Moses made a serpent of bronze, and put it upon a pole;
and whenever a serpent bit someone,
that person would look at the serpent of bronze and live.

The word of the Lord.

PSALMODY: PSALM 107:1–3, 17–22

SECOND READING: EPHESIANS 2:1–10

A reading from Ephesians:

¹You were dead through the trespasses and sins ²in which you once lived,
following the course of this world,
following the ruler of the power of the air,
the spirit that is now at work among those who are disobedient.
³All of us once lived among them in the passions of our flesh,

following the desires of flesh and senses,
and we were by nature children of wrath, like everyone else.

[4]But God, who is rich in mercy,
out of the great love with which he loved us
[5]even when we were dead through our trespasses,
made us alive together with Christ—
by grace you have been saved—
[6]and raised us up with him
and seated us with him in the heavenly places in Christ Jesus,
[7]so that in the ages to come
he might show the immeasurable riches of his grace
in kindness toward us in Christ Jesus.
[8]For by grace you have been saved through faith,
and this is not your own doing;
it is the gift of God—
[9]not the result of works, so that no one may boast.
[10]For we are what he has made us,
created in Christ Jesus for good works,
which God prepared beforehand to be our way of life.

The word of the Lord.

GOSPEL: JOHN 3:14–21

The Holy Gospel according to John, the third chapter.

Jesus said:
[14]"Just as Moses lifted up the serpent in the wilderness,
so must the Son of Man be lifted up,
[15]that whoever believes in him may have eternal life.
[16]For God so loved the world that he gave his only Son,
so that everyone who believes in him may not perish but may have eternal life.

[17]"Indeed, God did not send the Son into the world to condemn the world,
but in order that the world might be saved through him.
[18]Those who believe in him are not condemned;
but those who do not believe are condemned already,
because they have not believed in the name of the only Son of God.
[19]And this is the judgment, that the light has come into the world,
and people loved darkness rather than light because their deeds were evil.
[20]For all who do evil hate the light and do not come to the light,
so that their deeds may not be exposed.
[21]But those who do what is true come to the light,
so that it may be clearly seen that their deeds have been done in God."

The Gospel of the Lord.

FIFTH SUNDAY IN LENT

MARCH 16, 1997   APRIL 9, 2000   APRIL 6, 2003

FIRST READING: JEREMIAH 31:31–34

A reading from Jeremiah:

³¹The days are surely coming, says the LORD,
when I will make a new covenant with the house of Israel and the house of
    Judah.
³²It will not be like the covenant that I made with their ancestors
when I took them by the hand to bring them out of the land of Egypt—
a covenant that they broke, though I was their husband, says the LORD.

³³But this is the covenant that I will make with the house of Israel
after those days, says the LORD:
I will put my law within them,
and I will write it on their hearts;
and I will be their God,
and they shall be my people.
³⁴No longer shall they teach one another,
or say to each other, "Know the LORD,"
for they shall all know me,
from the least of them to the greatest, says the LORD;
for I will forgive their iniquity,
and remember their sin no more.

The word of the Lord.

PSALMODY: PSALM 51:1–12* or PSALM 119:9–16   *Psalm 51:1–13 LBW/BCP*

SECOND READING: HEBREWS 5:5–10

A reading from Hebrews:

[5]Christ did not glorify himself in becoming a high priest,
but was appointed by the one who said to him,
> "You are my Son,
>> today I have begotten you";

[6]as he says also in another place,
> "You are a priest forever,
>> according to the order of Melchizedek."

[7]In the days of his flesh,
Jesus offered up prayers and supplications, with loud cries and tears,
to the one who was able to save him from death,
and he was heard because of his reverent submission.
[8]Although he was a Son,
he learned obedience through what he suffered;
[9]and having been made perfect,
he became the source of eternal salvation for all who obey him,
[10]having been designated by God a high priest according to the order
of Melchizedek.

The word of the Lord.

The Holy Gospel according to John, the twelfth chapter.

²⁰Now among those who went up to worship at the festival were some Greeks.
²¹They came to Philip, who was from Bethsaida in Galilee,
and said to him, "Sir, we wish to see Jesus."
²²Philip went and told Andrew;
then Andrew and Philip went and told Jesus.
²³Jesus answered them,
"The hour has come for the Son of Man to be glorified.
²⁴Very truly, I tell you,
unless a grain of wheat falls into the earth and dies,
it remains just a single grain;
but if it dies, it bears much fruit.
²⁵Those who love their life lose it,
and those who hate their life in this world will keep it for eternal life.
²⁶Whoever serves me must follow me,
and where I am, there will my servant be also.
Whoever serves me, the Father will honor.

²⁷"Now my soul is troubled.
And what should I say—'Father, save me from this hour'?
No, it is for this reason that I have come to this hour.
²⁸Father, glorify your name."
Then a voice came from heaven,
"I have glorified it, and I will glorify it again."
²⁹The crowd standing there heard it and said that it was thunder.
Others said, "An angel has spoken to him."
³⁰Jesus answered, "This voice has come for your sake, not for mine.
³¹Now is the judgment of this world;
now the ruler of this world will be driven out.
³²And I, when I am lifted up from the earth,
will draw all people to myself."
³³He said this to indicate the kind of death he was to die.

The Gospel of the Lord.

HOLY WEEK

SUNDAY OF THE PASSION/PALM SUNDAY
Liturgy of the Palms

MARCH 23, 1997   APRIL 16, 2000   APRIL 13, 2003

PROCESSIONAL GOSPEL: MARK 11:1–11
Or John 12:12–16, following

The Holy Gospel according to Mark, the eleventh chapter.

¹When they were approaching Jerusalem,
at Bethphage and Bethany, near the Mount of Olives,
Jesus sent two of his disciples ²and said to them,
"Go into the village ahead of you,
and immediately as you enter it,
you will find tied there a colt that has never been ridden;
untie it and bring it.
³If anyone says to you, 'Why are you doing this?'
just say this, 'The Lord needs it and will send it back here immediately.' "
⁴They went away and found a colt tied near a door, outside in the street.
As they were untying it, ⁵some of the bystanders said to them,
"What are you doing, untying the colt?"
⁶They told them what Jesus had said; and they allowed them to take it.

⁷Then they brought the colt to Jesus and threw their cloaks on it;
and he sat on it.
⁸Many people spread their cloaks on the road,
and others spread leafy branches that they had cut in the fields.
⁹Then those who went ahead and those who followed were shouting,
    "Hosanna!
        Blessed is the one who comes in the name of the Lord!
        ¹⁰Blessed is the coming kingdom of our ancestor David!
    Hosanna in the highest heaven!"

¹¹Then he entered Jerusalem and went into the temple;
and when he had looked around at everything, as it was already late,
he went out to Bethany with the twelve.

The Gospel of the Lord.

OR: JOHN 12:12–16

The Holy Gospel according to John, the twelfth chapter.

¹²The next day the great crowd that had come to the festival
heard that Jesus was coming to Jerusalem.
¹³So they took branches of palm trees and went out to meet him, shouting,
    "Hosanna!
    Blessed is the one who comes in the name of the Lord—
        the King of Israel!"
¹⁴Jesus found a young donkey and sat on it; as it is written:
    ¹⁵"Do not be afraid, daughter of Zion.
    Look, your king is coming,
        sitting on a donkey's colt!"
¹⁶His disciples did not understand these things at first;
but when Jesus was glorified,
then they remembered that these things had been written of him
and had been done to him.

The Gospel of the Lord.

PSALMODY: PSALM 118:1–2, 19–29

SUNDAY OF THE PASSION/PALM SUNDAY
Liturgy of the Passion

MARCH 23, 1997   APRIL 16, 2000   APRIL 13, 2003

FIRST READING: ISAIAH 50:4–9a

A reading from Isaiah:

⁴The Lord GOD has given me
      the tongue of a teacher,
that I may know how to sustain
      the weary with a word.
Morning by morning he wakens—
      wakens my ear
      to listen as those who are taught.
⁵The Lord GOD has opened my ear,
      and I was not rebellious,
      I did not turn backward.
⁶I gave my back to those who struck me,
      and my cheeks to those who pulled out the beard;
I did not hide my face
      from insult and spitting.

⁷The Lord GOD helps me;
      therefore I have not been disgraced;
therefore I have set my face like flint,
      and I know that I shall not be put to shame;
      ⁸he who vindicates me is near.
Who will contend with me?
      Let us stand up together.
Who are my adversaries?
      Let them confront me.
⁹It is the Lord GOD who helps me;
      who will declare me guilty?

The word of the Lord.

PSALMODY: PSALM 31:9–16

SECOND READING: PHILIPPIANS 2:5–11

A reading from Philippians:

⁵Let the same mind be in you that was in Christ Jesus,
    ⁶who, though he was in the form of God,
        did not regard equality with God
        as something to be exploited,
    ⁷but emptied himself,
        taking the form of a slave,
        being born in human likeness.
And being found in human form,
    ⁸he humbled himself
        and became obedient to the point of death—
        even death on a cross.

⁹Therefore God also highly exalted him
    and gave him the name
    that is above every name,
¹⁰so that at the name of Jesus
    every knee should bend,
    in heaven and on earth and under the earth,
¹¹and every tongue should confess
    that Jesus Christ is Lord,
    to the glory of God the Father.

The word of the Lord.

GOSPEL: MARK 14:1—15:47

Or Mark 15:1–39 [40–47], following on p. 97

The Passion of our Lord Jesus Christ according to Mark.

[1]It was two days before the Passover and the festival of Unleavened Bread.
The chief priests and the scribes were looking for a way to arrest Jesus by
      stealth and kill him;
[2]for they said, "Not during the festival,
or there may be a riot among the people."

[3]While he was at Bethany in the house of Simon the leper,
as he sat at the table,
a woman came with an alabaster jar of very costly ointment of nard,
and she broke open the jar and poured the ointment on his head.
[4]But some were there who said to one another in anger,
"Why was the ointment wasted in this way?
[5]For this ointment could have been sold for more than three hundred denarii,
and the money given to the poor."
And they scolded her.
[6]But Jesus said, "Let her alone; why do you trouble her?
She has performed a good service for me.
[7]For you always have the poor with you,
and you can show kindness to them whenever you wish;
but you will not always have me.
[8]She has done what she could;
she has anointed my body beforehand for its burial.
[9]Truly I tell you,
wherever the good news is proclaimed in the whole world,
what she has done will be told in remembrance of her."

[10]Then Judas Iscariot, who was one of the twelve,
went to the chief priests in order to betray him to them.
[11]When they heard it, they were greatly pleased,
and promised to give him money.
So he began to look for an opportunity to betray him.

[12]On the first day of Unleavened Bread,
when the Passover lamb is sacrificed, his disciples said to him,
"Where do you want us to go
and make the preparations for you to eat the Passover?"
[13]So he sent two of his disciples, saying to them,
"Go into the city, and a man carrying a jar of water will meet you;
follow him, [14]and wherever he enters,
say to the owner of the house, 'The Teacher asks,
Where is my guest room where I may eat the Passover with my disciples?'
[15]He will show you a large room upstairs, furnished and ready.
Make preparations for us there."

¹⁶So the disciples set out and went to the city,
and found everything as he had told them;
and they prepared the Passover meal.

¹⁷When it was evening, he came with the twelve.
¹⁸And when they had taken their places and were eating, Jesus said,
"Truly I tell you, one of you will betray me,
one who is eating with me."
¹⁹They began to be distressed and to say to him one after another,
"Surely, not I?"
²⁰He said to them,
"It is one of the twelve,
one who is dipping bread into the bowl with me.
²¹For the Son of Man goes as it is written of him,
but woe to that one by whom the Son of Man is betrayed!
It would have been better for that one not to have been born."

²²While they were eating, he took a loaf of bread,
and after blessing it he broke it, gave it to them,
and said, "Take; this is my body."
²³Then he took a cup, and after giving thanks he gave it to them,
and all of them drank from it.
²⁴He said to them,
"This is my blood of the covenant, which is poured out for many.
²⁵Truly I tell you, I will never again drink of the fruit of the vine
until that day when I drink it new in the kingdom of God."

²⁶When they had sung the hymn, they went out to the Mount of Olives.
²⁷And Jesus said to them, "You will all become deserters;
for it is written,
'I will strike the shepherd,
and the sheep will be scattered.'
²⁸But after I am raised up, I will go before you to Galilee."
²⁹Peter said to him, "Even though all become deserters, I will not."
³⁰Jesus said to him, "Truly I tell you, this day, this very night,
before the cock crows twice,
you will deny me three times."
³¹But he said vehemently,
"Even though I must die with you, I will not deny you."
And all of them said the same.

³²They went to a place called Gethsemane; and he said to his disciples,
"Sit here while I pray."
³³He took with him Peter and James and John,
and began to be distressed and agitated.
³⁴And he said to them, "I am deeply grieved, even to death;
remain here, and keep awake."
³⁵And going a little farther,

he threw himself on the ground and prayed that,
if it were possible, the hour might pass from him.
[36]He said, "Abba, Father, for you all things are possible;
remove this cup from me;
yet, not what I want, but what you want."
[37]He came and found them sleeping; and he said to Peter,
"Simon, are you asleep?
Could you not keep awake one hour?
[38]Keep awake and pray that you may not come into the time of trial;
the spirit indeed is willing, but the flesh is weak."
[39]And again he went away and prayed, saying the same words.
[40]And once more he came and found them sleeping,
for their eyes were very heavy;
and they did not know what to say to him.
[41]He came a third time and said to them,
"Are you still sleeping and taking your rest? Enough!
The hour has come;
the Son of Man is betrayed into the hands of sinners.
[42]Get up, let us be going.
See, my betrayer is at hand."

[43]Immediately, while he was still speaking, Judas, one of the twelve, arrived;
and with him there was a crowd with swords and clubs,
from the chief priests, the scribes, and the elders.
[44]Now the betrayer had given them a sign, saying,
"The one I will kiss is the man;
arrest him and lead him away under guard."
[45]So when he came, he went up to him at once and said,
"Rabbi!" and kissed him.
[46]Then they laid hands on him and arrested him.
[47]But one of those who stood near drew his sword
and struck the slave of the high priest, cutting off his ear.
[48]Then Jesus said to them,
"Have you come out with swords and clubs
to arrest me as though I were a bandit?
[49]Day after day I was with you in the temple teaching,
and you did not arrest me.
But let the scriptures be fulfilled."
[50]All of them deserted him and fled.

[51]A certain young man was following him,
wearing nothing but a linen cloth.
They caught hold of him, [52]but he left the linen cloth and ran off naked.

[53]They took Jesus to the high priest;
and all the chief priests, the elders, and the scribes were assembled.
[54]Peter had followed him at a distance,
right into the courtyard of the high priest;

and he was sitting with the guards, warming himself at the fire.
[55]Now the chief priests and the whole council
were looking for testimony against Jesus to put him to death;
but they found none.
[56]For many gave false testimony against him,
and their testimony did not agree.
[57]Some stood up and gave false testimony against him, saying,
[58]"We heard him say,
'I will destroy this temple that is made with hands,
and in three days I will build another, not made with hands.' "
[59]But even on this point their testimony did not agree.
[60]Then the high priest stood up before them and asked Jesus,
"Have you no answer?
What is it that they testify against you?"
[61]But he was silent and did not answer.
Again the high priest asked him,
"Are you the Messiah, the Son of the Blessed One?"
[62]Jesus said, "I am; and
'you will see the Son of Man
seated at the right hand of the Power,'
and 'coming with the clouds of heaven.' "
[63]Then the high priest tore his clothes and said,
"Why do we still need witnesses?
[64]You have heard his blasphemy!
What is your decision?"
All of them condemned him as deserving death.
[65]Some began to spit on him, to blindfold him, and to strike him,
saying to him, "Prophesy!"
The guards also took him over and beat him.

[66]While Peter was below in the courtyard,
one of the servant-girls of the high priest came by.
[67]When she saw Peter warming himself, she stared at him and said,
"You also were with Jesus, the man from Nazareth."
[68]But he denied it, saying,
"I do not know or understand what you are talking about."
And he went out into the forecourt.
Then the cock crowed.
[69]And the servant-girl, on seeing him, began again to say to the bystanders,
"This man is one of them."
[70]But again he denied it.
Then after a little while the bystanders again said to Peter,
"Certainly you are one of them; for you are a Galilean."
[71]But he began to curse, and he swore an oath,
"I do not know this man you are talking about."
[72]At that moment the cock crowed for the second time.
Then Peter remembered that Jesus had said to him,
"Before the cock crows twice, you will deny me three times."

And he broke down and wept.

¹⁵:¹As soon as it was morning, the chief priests held a consultation
with the elders and scribes and the whole council.
They bound Jesus, led him away, and handed him over to Pilate.
²Pilate asked him, "Are you the King of the Jews?"
He answered him, "You say so."
³Then the chief priests accused him of many things.
⁴Pilate asked him again, "Have you no answer?
See how many charges they bring against you."
⁵But Jesus made no further reply, so that Pilate was amazed.

⁶Now at the festival he used to release a prisoner for them,
anyone for whom they asked.
⁷Now a man called Barabbas was in prison
with the rebels who had committed murder during the insurrection.
⁸So the crowd came and began to ask Pilate to do for them according to his
         custom.
⁹Then he answered them,
"Do you want me to release for you the King of the Jews?"
¹⁰For he realized that it was out of jealousy that the chief priests had handed
         him over.
¹¹But the chief priests stirred up the crowd
to have him release Barabbas for them instead.
¹²Pilate spoke to them again,
"Then what do you wish me to do with the man you call the King of the Jews?"
¹³They shouted back, "Crucify him!"
¹⁴Pilate asked them, "Why, what evil has he done?"
But they shouted all the more, "Crucify him!"
¹⁵So Pilate, wishing to satisfy the crowd, released Barabbas for them;
and after flogging Jesus, he handed him over to be crucified.

¹⁶Then the soldiers led him into the courtyard of the palace
(that is, the governor's headquarters);
and they called together the whole cohort.
¹⁷And they clothed him in a purple cloak;
and after twisting some thorns into a crown, they put it on him.
¹⁸And they began saluting him, "Hail, King of the Jews!"
¹⁹They struck his head with a reed,
spat upon him, and knelt down in homage to him.
²⁰After mocking him, they stripped him of the purple cloak
and put his own clothes on him.
Then they led him out to crucify him.

²¹They compelled a passer-by, who was coming in from the country,
to carry his cross;
it was Simon of Cyrene, the father of Alexander and Rufus.
²²Then they brought Jesus to the place called Golgotha
(which means the place of a skull).

²³And they offered him wine mixed with myrrh; but he did not take it.
²⁴And they crucified him,
and divided his clothes among them,
casting lots to decide what each should take.

²⁵It was nine o'clock in the morning when they crucified him.
²⁶The inscription of the charge against him read,
"The King of the Jews."
²⁷And with him they crucified two bandits, one on his right and one on his left.
²⁹Those who passed by derided him, shaking their heads and saying,
"Aha! You who would destroy the temple and build it in three days,
³⁰save yourself, and come down from the cross!"
³¹In the same way the chief priests, along with the scribes,
were also mocking him among themselves and saying,
"He saved others; he cannot save himself.
³²Let the Messiah, the King of Israel, come down from the cross now,
so that we may see and believe."
Those who were crucified with him also taunted him.

³³When it was noon,
darkness came over the whole land until three in the afternoon.
³⁴At three o'clock Jesus cried out with a loud voice,
"Eloi, Eloi, lema sabachthani?"
which means, "My God, my God, why have you forsaken me?"
³⁵When some of the bystanders heard it, they said,
"Listen, he is calling for Elijah."
³⁶And someone ran, filled a sponge with sour wine,
put it on a stick, and gave it to him to drink, saying,
"Wait, let us see whether Elijah will come to take him down."
³⁷Then Jesus gave a loud cry and breathed his last.
³⁸And the curtain of the temple was torn in two, from top to bottom.
³⁹Now when the centurion, who stood facing him,
saw that in this way he breathed his last, he said,
"Truly this man was God's Son!"

⁴⁰There were also women looking on from a distance;
among them were Mary Magdalene,
and Mary the mother of James the younger and of Joses, and Salome.
⁴¹These used to follow him and provided for him when he was in Galilee;
and there were many other women who had come up with him to Jerusalem.

⁴²When evening had come,
and since it was the day of Preparation, that is, the day before the sabbath,
⁴³Joseph of Arimathea, a respected member of the council,
who was also himself waiting expectantly for the kingdom of God,
went boldly to Pilate and asked for the body of Jesus.
⁴⁴Then Pilate wondered if he were already dead;
and summoning the centurion,

he asked him whether he had been dead for some time.
⁴⁵When he learned from the centurion that he was dead,
he granted the body to Joseph.
⁴⁶Then Joseph bought a linen cloth,
and taking down the body, wrapped it in the linen cloth,
and laid it in a tomb that had been hewn out of the rock.
He then rolled a stone against the door of the tomb.
⁴⁷Mary Magdalene and Mary the mother of Joses saw where the body was
    laid.

The Gospel of the Lord.

OR: MARK 15:1–39 [40–47]

The Passion of our Lord Jesus Christ according to Mark.

¹As soon as it was morning, the chief priests held a consultation
with the elders and scribes and the whole council.
They bound Jesus, led him away, and handed him over to Pilate.
²Pilate asked him, "Are you the King of the Jews?"
He answered him, "You say so."
³Then the chief priests accused him of many things.
⁴Pilate asked him again, "Have you no answer?
See how many charges they bring against you."
⁵But Jesus made no further reply, so that Pilate was amazed.

⁶Now at the festival he used to release a prisoner for them,
anyone for whom they asked.
⁷Now a man called Barabbas was in prison
with the rebels who had committed murder during the insurrection.
⁸So the crowd came and began to ask Pilate to do for them according to his
    custom.
⁹Then he answered them,
"Do you want me to release for you the King of the Jews?"
¹⁰For he realized that it was out of jealousy that the chief priests had handed
    him over.
¹¹But the chief priests stirred up the crowd
to have him release Barabbas for them instead.
¹²Pilate spoke to them again,
"Then what do you wish me to do with the man you call the King of the Jews?"
¹³They shouted back, "Crucify him!"
¹⁴Pilate asked them, "Why, what evil has he done?"
But they shouted all the more, "Crucify him!"
¹⁵So Pilate, wishing to satisfy the crowd, released Barabbas for them;
and after flogging Jesus, he handed him over to be crucified.

¹⁶Then the soldiers led him into the courtyard of the palace
(that is, the governor's headquarters);

and they called together the whole cohort.
¹⁷And they clothed him in a purple cloak;
and after twisting some thorns into a crown, they put it on him.
¹⁸And they began saluting him, "Hail, King of the Jews!"
¹⁹They struck his head with a reed,
spat upon him, and knelt down in homage to him.
²⁰After mocking him, they stripped him of the purple cloak
and put his own clothes on him.
Then they led him out to crucify him.

²¹They compelled a passer-by, who was coming in from the country,
to carry his cross;
it was Simon of Cyrene, the father of Alexander and Rufus.
²²Then they brought Jesus to the place called Golgotha
(which means the place of a skull).
²³And they offered him wine mixed with myrrh; but he did not take it.
²⁴And they crucified him,
and divided his clothes among them,
casting lots to decide what each should take.

²⁵It was nine o'clock in the morning when they crucified him.
²⁶The inscription of the charge against him read,
"The King of the Jews."
²⁷And with him they crucified two bandits, one on his right and one on his left.
²⁹Those who passed by derided him, shaking their heads and saying,
"Aha! You who would destroy the temple and build it in three days,
³⁰save yourself, and come down from the cross!"
³¹In the same way the chief priests, along with the scribes,
were also mocking him among themselves and saying,
"He saved others; he cannot save himself.
³²Let the Messiah, the King of Israel, come down from the cross now,
so that we may see and believe."
Those who were crucified with him also taunted him.

³³When it was noon,
darkness came over the whole land until three in the afternoon.
³⁴At three o'clock Jesus cried out with a loud voice,
"Eloi, Eloi, lema sabachthani?"
which means, "My God, my God, why have you forsaken me?"
³⁵When some of the bystanders heard it, they said,
"Listen, he is calling for Elijah."
³⁶And someone ran, filled a sponge with sour wine,
put it on a stick, and gave it to him to drink, saying,
"Wait, let us see whether Elijah will come to take him down."
³⁷Then Jesus gave a loud cry and breathed his last.
³⁸And the curtain of the temple was torn in two, from top to bottom.
³⁹Now when the centurion, who stood facing him,
saw that in this way he breathed his last, he said,

"Truly this man was God's Son!"
[40There were also women looking on from a distance;
among them were Mary Magdalene,
and Mary the mother of James the younger and of Joses, and Salome.
41These used to follow him and provided for him when he was in Galilee;
and there were many other women who had come up with him to Jerusalem.

42When evening had come,
and since it was the day of Preparation, that is, the day before the sabbath,
43Joseph of Arimathea, a respected member of the council,
who was also himself waiting expectantly for the kingdom of God,
went boldly to Pilate and asked for the body of Jesus.
44Then Pilate wondered if he were already dead;
and summoning the centurion,
he asked him whether he had been dead for some time.
45When he learned from the centurion that he was dead,
he granted the body to Joseph.
46Then Joseph bought a linen cloth,
and taking down the body, wrapped it in the linen cloth,
and laid it in a tomb that had been hewn out of the rock.
He then rolled a stone against the door of the tomb.
47Mary Magdalene and Mary the mother of Joses saw where the body was
        laid.]

The Gospel of the Lord.

MONDAY IN HOLY WEEK

MARCH 24, 1997   APRIL 17, 2000   APRIL 14, 2003

FIRST READING: Isaiah 42:1–9

A reading from Isaiah:

¹Here is my servant, whom I uphold,
      my chosen, in whom my soul delights;
I have put my spirit upon him;
      he will bring forth justice to the nations.
²He will not cry or lift up his voice,
      or make it heard in the street;
³a bruised reed he will not break,
      and a dimly burning wick he will not quench;
      he will faithfully bring forth justice.
⁴He will not grow faint or be crushed
      until he has established justice in the earth;
      and the coastlands wait for his teaching.

⁵Thus says God, the LORD,
      who created the heavens and stretched them out,
      who spread out the earth and what comes from it,
who gives breath to the people upon it
      and spirit to those who walk in it:
⁶I am the LORD, I have called you in righteousness,
      I have taken you by the hand and kept you;
I have given you as a covenant to the people,
      a light to the nations,
      ⁷to open the eyes that are blind,
to bring out the prisoners from the dungeon,
      from the prison those who sit in darkness.
⁸I am the LORD, that is my name;
      my glory I give to no other,
      nor my praise to idols.
⁹See, the former things have come to pass,
      and new things I now declare;
before they spring forth,
      I tell you of them.

The word of the Lord.

PSALMODY: Psalm 36:5–11

SECOND READING: HEBREWS 9:11–15

A reading from Hebrews:

[11]When Christ came as a high priest of the good things that have come,
then through the greater and perfect tent
(not made with hands, that is, not of this creation),
[12]he entered once for all into the Holy Place,
not with the blood of goats and calves,
but with his own blood, thus obtaining eternal redemption.

[13]For if the blood of goats and bulls,
with the sprinkling of the ashes of a heifer,
sanctifies those who have been defiled so that their flesh is purified,
[14]how much more will the blood of Christ,
who through the eternal Spirit offered himself without blemish to God,
purify our conscience from dead works to worship the living God!

[15]For this reason he is the mediator of a new covenant,
so that those who are called may receive the promised eternal inheritance,
because a death has occurred
that redeems them from the transgressions under the first covenant.

The word of the Lord.

GOSPEL: JOHN 12:1–11

The Holy Gospel according to John, the twelfth chapter.

¹Six days before the Passover Jesus came to Bethany,
the home of Lazarus, whom he had raised from the dead.
²There they gave a dinner for him.
Martha served, and Lazarus was one of those at the table with him.
³Mary took a pound of costly perfume made of pure nard,
anointed Jesus' feet, and wiped them with her hair.
The house was filled with the fragrance of the perfume.

⁴But Judas Iscariot, one of his disciples
(the one who was about to betray him), said,
⁵"Why was this perfume not sold for three hundred denarii
and the money given to the poor?"
⁶(He said this not because he cared about the poor,
but because he was a thief;
he kept the common purse and used to steal what was put into it.)
⁷Jesus said,
"Leave her alone.
She bought it so that she might keep it for the day of my burial.
⁸You always have the poor with you,
but you do not always have me."

⁹When the great crowd of the Jews learned that he was there,
they came not only because of Jesus
but also to see Lazarus, whom he had raised from the dead.
¹⁰So the chief priests planned to put Lazarus to death as well,
¹¹since it was on account of him that many of the Jews were deserting
and were believing in Jesus.

The Gospel of the Lord.

TUESDAY IN HOLY WEEK

MARCH 25, 1997   APRIL 18, 2000   APRIL 15, 2003

FIRST READING: Isaiah 49:1–7

A reading from Isaiah:

¹Listen to me, O coastlands,
    pay attention, you peoples from far away!
The LORD called me before I was born,
    while I was in my mother's womb he named me.
²He made my mouth like a sharp sword,
    in the shadow of his hand he hid me;
he made me a polished arrow,
    in his quiver he hid me away.
³And he said to me, "You are my servant,
    Israel, in whom I will be glorified."
⁴But I said, "I have labored in vain,
    I have spent my strength for nothing and vanity;
yet surely my cause is with the LORD,
    and my reward with my God."

⁵And now the LORD says,
    who formed me in the womb to be his servant,
to bring Jacob back to him,
    and that Israel might be gathered to him,
for I am honored in the sight of the LORD,
    and my God has become my strength—
⁶he says,
"It is too light a thing that you should be my servant
    to raise up the tribes of Jacob
    and to restore the survivors of Israel;
I will give you as a light to the nations,
    that my salvation may reach to the end of the earth."

⁷Thus says the LORD,
    the Redeemer of Israel and his Holy One,
to one deeply despised, abhorred by the nations,
    the slave of rulers,

"Kings shall see and stand up,
    princes, and they shall prostrate themselves,
because of the Lord, who is faithful,
    the Holy One of Israel, who has chosen you."

The word of the Lord.

PSALMODY: Psalm 71:1–14

SECOND READING: 1 Corinthians 1:18–31

A reading from First Corinthians:

[18]The message about the cross is foolishness to those who are perishing,
but to us who are being saved it is the power of God.
[19]For it is written,
    "I will destroy the wisdom of the wise,
        and the discernment of the discerning I will thwart."
[20]Where is the one who is wise?
Where is the scribe?
Where is the debater of this age?
Has not God made foolish the wisdom of the world?

[21]For since, in the wisdom of God,
the world did not know God through wisdom,
God decided, through the foolishness of our proclamation,
to save those who believe.
[22]For Jews demand signs and Greeks desire wisdom,
[23]but we proclaim Christ crucified,
a stumbling block to Jews and foolishness to Gentiles,
[24]but to those who are the called, both Jews and Greeks,
Christ the power of God and the wisdom of God.
[25]For God's foolishness is wiser than human wisdom,
and God's weakness is stronger than human strength.

[26]Consider your own call, brothers and sisters:
not many of you were wise by human standards,
not many were powerful,
not many were of noble birth.
[27]But God chose what is foolish in the world to shame the wise;
God chose what is weak in the world to shame the strong;
[28]God chose what is low and despised in the world,
things that are not,
to reduce to nothing things that are,
[29]so that no one might boast in the presence of God.

[30]He is the source of your life in Christ Jesus,
who became for us wisdom from God,
and righteousness and sanctification and redemption,
[31]in order that, as it is written,
"Let the one who boasts, boast in the Lord."

The word of the Lord.

GOSPEL: JOHN 12:20–36

The Holy Gospel according to John, the twelfth chapter.

[20]Now among those who went up to worship at the festival were some Greeks.
[21]They came to Philip, who was from Bethsaida in Galilee,
and said to him, "Sir, we wish to see Jesus."
[22]Philip went and told Andrew;
then Andrew and Philip went and told Jesus.
[23]Jesus answered them,
"The hour has come for the Son of Man to be glorified.
[24]Very truly, I tell you,
unless a grain of wheat falls into the earth and dies,
it remains just a single grain;
but if it dies, it bears much fruit.
[25]Those who love their life lose it,
and those who hate their life in this world will keep it for eternal life.
[26]Whoever serves me must follow me,
and where I am, there will my servant be also.
Whoever serves me, the Father will honor.

[27]"Now my soul is troubled.
And what should I say—'Father, save me from this hour'?
No, it is for this reason that I have come to this hour.
[28]Father, glorify your name."
Then a voice came from heaven,
"I have glorified it, and I will glorify it again."
[29]The crowd standing there heard it and said that it was thunder.
Others said, "An angel has spoken to him."
[30]Jesus answered,
"This voice has come for your sake, not for mine.
[31]Now is the judgment of this world;
now the ruler of this world will be driven out.
[32]And I, when I am lifted up from the earth,
will draw all people to myself."
[33]He said this to indicate the kind of death he was to die.
[34]The crowd answered him,
"We have heard from the law that the Messiah remains forever.
How can you say that the Son of Man must be lifted up?
Who is this Son of Man?"

[35]Jesus said to them,
"The light is with you for a little longer.
Walk while you have the light,
so that the darkness may not overtake you.
If you walk in the darkness, you do not know where you are going.
[36]While you have the light, believe in the light,
so that you may become children of light."

After Jesus had said this, he departed and hid from them.

The Gospel of the Lord.

WEDNESDAY IN HOLY WEEK

MARCH 26, 1997   APRIL 19, 2000   APRIL 16, 2003

FIRST READING: ISAIAH 50:4–9a

A reading from Isaiah:

⁴The Lord GOD has given me
    the tongue of a teacher,
that I may know how to sustain
    the weary with a word.
Morning by morning he wakens—
    wakens my ear
    to listen as those who are taught.
⁵The Lord GOD has opened my ear,
    and I was not rebellious,
    I did not turn backward.
⁶I gave my back to those who struck me,
    and my cheeks to those who pulled out the beard;
I did not hide my face
    from insult and spitting.

⁷The Lord GOD helps me;
    therefore I have not been disgraced;
therefore I have set my face like flint,
    and I know that I shall not be put to shame;
    ⁸he who vindicates me is near.
Who will contend with me?
    Let us stand up together.
Who are my adversaries?
    Let them confront me.
⁹It is the Lord GOD who helps me;
    who will declare me guilty?

The word of the Lord.

PSALMODY: PSALM 70

SECOND READING: HEBREWS 12:1–3

A reading from Hebrews:

¹Since we are surrounded by so great a cloud of witnesses,
let us also lay aside every weight and the sin that clings so closely,

and let us run with perseverance the race that is set before us,
²looking to Jesus the pioneer and perfecter of our faith,
who for the sake of the joy that was set before him
endured the cross, disregarding its shame,
and has taken his seat at the right hand of the throne of God.

³Consider him who endured such hostility against himself from sinners,
so that you may not grow weary or lose heart.

The word of the Lord.

GOSPEL: JOHN 13:21–32

The Holy Gospel according to John, the 13th chapter.

²¹Jesus was troubled in spirit, and declared,
"Very truly, I tell you, one of you will betray me."
²²The disciples looked at one another,
uncertain of whom he was speaking.

²³One of his disciples—the one whom Jesus loved—was reclining next to him;
²⁴Simon Peter therefore motioned to him to ask Jesus of whom he was speaking.
²⁵So while reclining next to Jesus, he asked him,
"Lord, who is it?"
²⁶Jesus answered,
"It is the one to whom I give this piece of bread
when I have dipped it in the dish."
So when he had dipped the piece of bread,
he gave it to Judas son of Simon Iscariot.
²⁷After he received the piece of bread, Satan entered into him.
Jesus said to him,
"Do quickly what you are going to do."
²⁸Now no one at the table knew why he said this to him.
²⁹Some thought that, because Judas had the common purse,
Jesus was telling him, "Buy what we need for the festival";
or, that he should give something to the poor.
³⁰So, after receiving the piece of bread, he immediately went out.
And it was night.

³¹When he had gone out, Jesus said,
"Now the Son of Man has been glorified,
and God has been glorified in him.
³²If God has been glorified in him,
God will also glorify him in himself and will glorify him at once."

The Gospel of the Lord.

THE THREE DAYS

MAUNDY THURSDAY

MARCH 27, 1997   APRIL 20, 2000   APRIL 17, 2003

FIRST READING: EXODUS 12:1–4 [5–10] 11–14

A reading from Exodus:

¹The LORD said to Moses and Aaron in the land of Egypt:
²This month shall mark for you the beginning of months;
it shall be the first month of the year for you.
³Tell the whole congregation of Israel
that on the tenth of this month they are to take a lamb for each family,
a lamb for each household.
⁴If a household is too small for a whole lamb,
it shall join its closest neighbor in obtaining one;
the lamb shall be divided in proportion to the number of people who eat of it.

[⁵Your lamb shall be without blemish, a year-old male;
you may take it from the sheep or from the goats.
⁶You shall keep it until the fourteenth day of this month;
then the whole assembled congregation of Israel shall slaughter it at twilight.
⁷They shall take some of the blood and put it on the two doorposts
and the lintel of the houses in which they eat it.
⁸They shall eat the lamb that same night;
they shall eat it roasted over the fire
with unleavened bread and bitter herbs.
⁹Do not eat any of it raw or boiled in water,
but roasted over the fire, with its head, legs, and inner organs.
¹⁰You shall let none of it remain until the morning;
anything that remains until the morning you shall burn.]

¹¹This is how you shall eat it:
your loins girded, your sandals on your feet, and your staff in your hand;
and you shall eat it hurriedly.
It is the passover of the LORD.
¹²For I will pass through the land of Egypt that night,
and I will strike down every firstborn in the land of Egypt,
both human beings and animals;
on all the gods of Egypt I will execute judgments:
I am the LORD.
¹³The blood shall be a sign for you on the houses where you live:
when I see the blood, I will pass over you,

and no plague shall destroy you when I strike the land of Egypt.
¹⁴This day shall be a day of remembrance for you.
You shall celebrate it as a festival to the LORD;
throughout your generations you shall observe it as a perpetual ordinance.

The word of the Lord.

PSALMODY: PSALM 116:1–2, 12–19   *Psalm 116:1, 10–17* LBW/BCP

SECOND READING: 1 CORINTHIANS 11:23–26

A reading from First Corinthians:

²³For I received from the Lord what I also handed on to you,
that the Lord Jesus on the night when he was betrayed
took a loaf of bread,
²⁴and when he had given thanks, he broke it and said,
"This is my body that is for you.
Do this in remembrance of me."
²⁵In the same way he took the cup also, after supper, saying,
"This cup is the new covenant in my blood.
Do this, as often as you drink it, in remembrance of me."

²⁶For as often as you eat this bread and drink the cup,
you proclaim the Lord's death until he comes.

The word of the Lord.

GOSPEL: JOHN 13:1–17, 31b–35

The Holy Gospel according to John, the 13th chapter.

¹Now before the festival of the Passover,
Jesus knew that his hour had come to depart from this world
and go to the Father.
Having loved his own who were in the world,
he loved them to the end.
²The devil had already put it into the heart of Judas son of Simon Iscariot
to betray him.

And during supper
³Jesus, knowing that the Father had given all things into his hands,
and that he had come from God and was going to God,
⁴got up from the table,
took off his outer robe, and tied a towel around himself.
⁵Then he poured water into a basin
and began to wash the disciples' feet
and to wipe them with the towel that was tied around him.

⁶He came to Simon Peter, who said to him,
"Lord, are you going to wash my feet?"
⁷Jesus answered,
"You do not know now what I am doing,
but later you will understand."
⁸Peter said to him,
"You will never wash my feet."
Jesus answered,
"Unless I wash you, you have no share with me."
⁹Simon Peter said to him,
"Lord, not my feet only but also my hands and my head!"
¹⁰Jesus said to him,
"One who has bathed does not need to wash, except for the feet,
but is entirely clean.
And you are clean, though not all of you."
¹¹For he knew who was to betray him;
for this reason he said, "Not all of you are clean."

¹²After he had washed their feet, had put on his robe,
and had returned to the table, he said to them,
"Do you know what I have done to you?
¹³You call me Teacher and Lord—
and you are right, for that is what I am.
¹⁴So if I, your Lord and Teacher, have washed your feet,
you also ought to wash one another's feet.
¹⁵For I have set you an example,
that you also should do as I have done to you.
¹⁶Very truly, I tell you,
servants are not greater than their master,
nor are messengers greater than the one who sent them.
¹⁷If you know these things,
you are blessed if you do them.

³¹ᵇ"Now the Son of Man has been glorified,
and God has been glorified in him.
³²If God has been glorified in him,
God will also glorify him in himself and will glorify him at once.
³³Little children, I am with you only a little longer.
You will look for me;
and as I said to the Jews so now I say to you,
'Where I am going, you cannot come.'

³⁴"I give you a new commandment,
that you love one another.
Just as I have loved you, you also should love one another.
³⁵By this everyone will know that you are my disciples,
if you have love for one another."

The Gospel of the Lord.

GOOD FRIDAY

MARCH 28, 1997   APRIL 21, 2000   APRIL 18, 2003

FIRST READING: ISAIAH 52:13—53:12

A reading from Isaiah:

¹³See, my servant shall prosper;
> he shall be exalted and lifted up,
> and shall be very high.
¹⁴Just as there were many who were astonished at him
> —so marred was his appearance, beyond human semblance,
> and his form beyond that of mortals—
¹⁵so he shall startle many nations;
> kings shall shut their mouths because of him;
for that which had not been told them they shall see,
> and that which they had not heard they shall contemplate.

^{53:1}Who has believed what we have heard?
> And to whom has the arm of the LORD been revealed?
²For he grew up before him like a young plant,
> and like a root out of dry ground;
he had no form or majesty that we should look at him,
> nothing in his appearance that we should desire him.
³He was despised and rejected by others;
> a man of suffering and acquainted with infirmity;
and as one from whom others hide their faces
> he was despised, and we held him of no account.

⁴Surely he has borne our infirmities
> and carried our diseases;
yet we accounted him stricken,
> struck down by God, and afflicted.
⁵But he was wounded for our transgressions,
> crushed for our iniquities;
upon him was the punishment that made us whole,
> and by his bruises we are healed.
⁶All we like sheep have gone astray;
> we have all turned to our own way,
and the LORD has laid on him
> the iniquity of us all.

⁷He was oppressed, and he was afflicted,
  yet he did not open his mouth;
like a lamb that is led to the slaughter,
  and like a sheep that before its shearers is silent,
  so he did not open his mouth.
⁸By a perversion of justice he was taken away.
  Who could have imagined his future?
For he was cut off from the land of the living,
  stricken for the transgression of my people.
⁹They made his grave with the wicked
  and his tomb with the rich,
although he had done no violence,
  and there was no deceit in his mouth.

¹⁰Yet it was the will of the LORD to crush him with pain.
When you make his life an offering for sin,
  he shall see his offspring, and shall prolong his days;
through him the will of the LORD shall prosper.
  ¹¹Out of his anguish he shall see light;
he shall find satisfaction through his knowledge.
  The righteous one, my servant, shall make many righteous,
  and he shall bear their iniquities.
¹²Therefore I will allot him a portion with the great,
  and he shall divide the spoil with the strong;
because he poured out himself to death,
  and was numbered with the transgressors;
yet he bore the sin of many,
  and made intercession for the transgressors.

The word of the Lord.

PSALMODY: PSALM 22

SECOND READING: HEBREWS 10:16–25
Or Hebrews 4:14–16; 5:7–9, following

A reading from Hebrews:

¹⁶"This is the covenant that I will make with them
  after those days, says the Lord:
I will put my laws in their hearts,
  and I will write them on their minds,"
¹⁷he also adds,
  "I will remember their sins and their lawless deeds no more."
¹⁸Where there is forgiveness of these,
there is no longer any offering for sin.

[19]Therefore, my friends,
since we have confidence to enter the sanctuary by the blood of Jesus,
[20]by the new and living way that he opened for us through the curtain
(that is, through his flesh),
[21]and since we have a great priest over the house of God,
[22]let us approach with a true heart in full assurance of faith,
with our hearts sprinkled clean from an evil conscience
and our bodies washed with pure water.
[23]Let us hold fast to the confession of our hope without wavering,
for he who has promised is faithful.
[24]And let us consider how to provoke one another to love and good deeds,
[25]not neglecting to meet together, as is the habit of some,
but encouraging one another,
and all the more as you see the Day approaching.

The word of the Lord.

OR: HEBREWS 4:14–16; 5:7–9

A reading from Hebrews:

[14]Since, then, we have a great high priest who has passed
        through the heavens,
Jesus, the Son of God,
let us hold fast to our confession.
[15]For we do not have a high priest who is unable to sympathize with our
        weaknesses,
but we have one who in every respect has been tested as we are,
yet without sin.
[16]Let us therefore approach the throne of grace with boldness,
so that we may receive mercy and find grace
to help in time of need.

[5:7]In the days of his flesh, Jesus offered up prayers and supplications,
with loud cries and tears,
to the one who was able to save him from death,
and he was heard because of his reverent submission.
[8]Although he was a Son,
he learned obedience through what he suffered;
[9]and having been made perfect,
he became the source of eternal salvation for all who obey him.

The word of the Lord.

GOSPEL: JOHN 18:1—19:42

The Passion of our Lord Jesus Christ according to John.

¹Jesus went out with his disciples across the Kidron valley
to a place where there was a garden, which he and his disciples entered.
²Now Judas, who betrayed him, also knew the place,
because Jesus often met there with his disciples.
³So Judas brought a detachment of soldiers together
with police from the chief priests and the Pharisees,
and they came there with lanterns and torches and weapons.
⁴Then Jesus, knowing all that was to happen to him,
came forward and asked them,
"Whom are you looking for?"
⁵They answered, "Jesus of Nazareth."
Jesus replied, "I am he."
Judas, who betrayed him, was standing with them.
⁶When Jesus said to them, "I am he,"
they stepped back and fell to the ground.
⁷Again he asked them, "Whom are you looking for?"
And they said, "Jesus of Nazareth."
⁸Jesus answered, "I told you that I am he.
So if you are looking for me, let these men go."
⁹This was to fulfill the word that he had spoken,
"I did not lose a single one of those whom you gave me."
¹⁰Then Simon Peter, who had a sword, drew it,
struck the high priest's slave, and cut off his right ear.
The slave's name was Malchus.
¹¹Jesus said to Peter,
"Put your sword back into its sheath.
Am I not to drink the cup that the Father has given me?"

¹²So the soldiers, their officer, and the Jewish police
arrested Jesus and bound him.
¹³First they took him to Annas,
who was the father-in-law of Caiaphas, the high priest that year.
¹⁴Caiaphas was the one who had advised the Jews
that it was better to have one person die for the people.

¹⁵Simon Peter and another disciple followed Jesus.
Since that disciple was known to the high priest,
he went with Jesus into the courtyard of the high priest,
¹⁶but Peter was standing outside at the gate.
So the other disciple, who was known to the high priest,
went out, spoke to the woman who guarded the gate,
and brought Peter in.

¹⁷The woman said to Peter,
"You are not also one of this man's disciples, are you?"
He said, "I am not."
¹⁸Now the slaves and the police had made a charcoal fire because it was cold,
and they were standing around it and warming themselves.
Peter also was standing with them and warming himself.

¹⁹Then the high priest questioned Jesus about his disciples
        and about his teaching.
²⁰Jesus answered, "I have spoken openly to the world;
I have always taught in synagogues and in the temple,
where all the Jews come together.
I have said nothing in secret.
²¹Why do you ask me?
Ask those who heard what I said to them; they know what I said."
²²When he had said this,
one of the police standing nearby struck Jesus on the face, saying,
"Is that how you answer the high priest?"
²³Jesus answered, "If I have spoken wrongly, testify to the wrong.
But if I have spoken rightly, why do you strike me?"
²⁴Then Annas sent him bound to Caiaphas the high priest.

²⁵Now Simon Peter was standing and warming himself.
They asked him, "You are not also one of his disciples, are you?"
He denied it and said, "I am not."
²⁶One of the slaves of the high priest,
a relative of the man whose ear Peter had cut off, asked,
"Did I not see you in the garden with him?"
²⁷Again Peter denied it, and at that moment the cock crowed.

²⁸Then they took Jesus from Caiaphas to Pilate's headquarters.
It was early in the morning.
They themselves did not enter the headquarters,
so as to avoid ritual defilement
and to be able to eat the Passover.
²⁹So Pilate went out to them and said,
"What accusation do you bring against this man?"
³⁰They answered, "If this man were not a criminal,
we would not have handed him over to you."
³¹Pilate said to them,
"Take him yourselves and judge him according to your law."
The Jews replied,
"We are not permitted to put anyone to death."
³²(This was to fulfill what Jesus had said
when he indicated the kind of death he was to die.)

³³Then Pilate entered the headquarters again,
summoned Jesus, and asked him,
"Are you the King of the Jews?"

³⁴Jesus answered,

"Do you ask this on your own, or did others tell you about me?"
³⁵Pilate replied, "I am not a Jew, am I?

Your own nation and the chief priests have handed you over to me.
What have you done?"
³⁶Jesus answered,

"My kingdom is not from this world.
If my kingdom were from this world,
my followers would be fighting to keep me from being handed over
        to the Jews.
But as it is, my kingdom is not from here."
³⁷Pilate asked him, "So you are a king?"

Jesus answered,

"You say that I am a king. For this I was born,
and for this I came into the world, to testify to the truth.
Everyone who belongs to the truth listens to my voice."
³⁸Pilate asked him, "What is truth?"

After he had said this, he went out to the Jews again and told them,
"I find no case against him.
³⁹But you have a custom that I release someone for you at the Passover.

Do you want me to release for you the King of the Jews?"
⁴⁰They shouted in reply,

"Not this man, but Barabbas!"
Now Barabbas was a bandit.

^{19:1}Then Pilate took Jesus and had him flogged.
²And the soldiers wove a crown of thorns and put it on his head,

and they dressed him in a purple robe.
³They kept coming up to him, saying,

"Hail, King of the Jews!" and striking him on the face.
⁴Pilate went out again and said to them,

"Look, I am bringing him out to you
to let you know that I find no case against him."
⁵So Jesus came out, wearing the crown of thorns and the purple robe.

Pilate said to them, "Here is the man!"
⁶When the chief priests and the police saw him, they shouted,

"Crucify him! Crucify him!"
Pilate said to them,
"Take him yourselves and crucify him; I find no case against him."
⁷The Jews answered him,

"We have a law, and according to that law
he ought to die because he has claimed to be the Son of God."

⁸Now when Pilate heard this, he was more afraid than ever.
⁹He entered his headquarters again and asked Jesus,

"Where are you from?"
But Jesus gave him no answer.

¹⁰Pilate therefore said to him,
"Do you refuse to speak to me?
Do you not know that I have power to release you, and power to crucify you?"
¹¹Jesus answered him,
"You would have no power over me unless it had been given you from above;
therefore the one who handed me over to you is guilty of a greater sin."
¹²From then on Pilate tried to release him,
but the Jews cried out,
"If you release this man, you are no friend of the emperor.
Everyone who claims to be a king sets himself against the emperor."

¹³When Pilate heard these words, he brought Jesus outside
and sat on the judge's bench at a place called The Stone Pavement,
or in Hebrew Gabbatha.
¹⁴Now it was the day of Preparation for the Passover; and it was about noon.
He said to the Jews, "Here is your King!"
¹⁵They cried out,
"Away with him! Away with him! Crucify him!"
Pilate asked them, "Shall I crucify your King?"
The chief priests answered,
"We have no king but the emperor."
¹⁶Then he handed him over to them to be crucified.

So they took Jesus; ¹⁷and carrying the cross by himself,
he went out to what is called The Place of the Skull,
which in Hebrew is called Golgotha.
¹⁸There they crucified him,
and with him two others, one on either side, with Jesus between them.
¹⁹Pilate also had an inscription written and put on the cross.
It read, "Jesus of Nazareth, the King of the Jews."
²⁰Many of the Jews read this inscription,
because the place where Jesus was crucified was near the city;
and it was written in Hebrew, in Latin, and in Greek.
²¹Then the chief priests of the Jews said to Pilate,
"Do not write, 'The King of the Jews,' but,
'This man said, I am King of the Jews.' "
²²Pilate answered,
"What I have written I have written."
²³When the soldiers had crucified Jesus,
they took his clothes and divided them into four parts, one for each soldier.
They also took his tunic;
now the tunic was seamless, woven in one piece from the top.
²⁴So they said to one another,
"Let us not tear it, but cast lots for it to see who will get it."
This was to fulfill what the scripture says,
    "They divided my clothes among themselves,
        and for my clothing they cast lots."
²⁵And that is what the soldiers did.

Meanwhile, standing near the cross of Jesus were his mother,
and his mother's sister, Mary the wife of Clopas, and Mary Magdalene.
26When Jesus saw his mother
and the disciple whom he loved standing beside her,
he said to his mother, "Woman, here is your son."
27Then he said to the disciple, "Here is your mother."
And from that hour the disciple took her into his own home.

28After this, when Jesus knew that all was now finished,
he said (in order to fulfill the scripture),
"I am thirsty."
29A jar full of sour wine was standing there.
So they put a sponge full of the wine on a branch of hyssop
and held it to his mouth.
30When Jesus had received the wine, he said,
"It is finished."
Then he bowed his head and gave up his spirit.

31Since it was the day of Preparation,
the Jews did not want the bodies left on the cross during the sabbath,
especially because that sabbath was a day of great solemnity.
So they asked Pilate to have the legs of the crucified men broken
and the bodies removed.
32Then the soldiers came and broke the legs of the first
and of the other who had been crucified with him.
33But when they came to Jesus and saw that he was already dead,
they did not break his legs.
34Instead, one of the soldiers pierced his side with a spear,
and at once blood and water came out.
35(He who saw this has testified so that you also may believe.
His testimony is true, and he knows that he tells the truth.)
36These things occurred so that the scripture might be fulfilled,
"None of his bones shall be broken."
37And again another passage of scripture says,
"They will look on the one whom they have pierced."

38After these things, Joseph of Arimathea, who was a disciple of Jesus,
though a secret one because of his fear of the Jews,
asked Pilate to let him take away the body of Jesus.
Pilate gave him permission; so he came and removed his body.
39Nicodemus, who had at first come to Jesus by night, also came,
bringing a mixture of myrrh and aloes, weighing about a hundred pounds.
40They took the body of Jesus and wrapped it with the spices in linen cloths,
according to the burial custom of the Jews.
41Now there was a garden in the place where he was crucified,
and in the garden there was a new tomb in which no one had ever been laid.
42And so, because it was the Jewish day of Preparation,
and the tomb was nearby, they laid Jesus there.

The Gospel of the Lord.

Saturday in Holy Week

(for services other than the Vigil of Easter)

MARCH 29, 1997   APRIL 22, 2000   APRIL 19, 2003

FIRST READING: Job 14:1–14

Or Lamentations 3:1–9, 19–24, following

A reading from Job:

¹"A mortal, born of woman, few of days and full of trouble,
²comes up like a flower and withers,
    flees like a shadow and does not last.
³Do you fix your eyes on such a one?
    Do you bring me into judgment with you?
⁴Who can bring a clean thing out of an unclean?
    No one can.
⁵Since their days are determined,
    and the number of their months is known to you,
    and you have appointed the bounds that they cannot pass,
⁶look away from them, and desist,
    that they may enjoy, like laborers, their days.

⁷"For there is hope for a tree,
    if it is cut down, that it will sprout again,
    and that its shoots will not cease.
⁸Though its root grows old in the earth,
    and its stump dies in the ground,
⁹yet at the scent of water it will bud
    and put forth branches like a young plant.
¹⁰But mortals die, and are laid low;
    humans expire, and where are they?
¹¹As waters fail from a lake,
    and a river wastes away and dries up,
¹²so mortals lie down and do not rise again;
    until the heavens are no more, they will not awake
    or be roused out of their sleep.
¹³O that you would hide me in Sheol,
    that you would conceal me until your wrath is past,
    that you would appoint me a set time, and remember me!
¹⁴If mortals die, will they live again?
    All the days of my service I would wait
    until my release should come."

The word of the Lord.

OR: Lamentations 3:1–9, 19–24

A reading from Lamentations:

¹I am one who has seen affliction
 under the rod of God's wrath;
²he has driven and brought me
 into darkness without any light;
³against me alone he turns his hand,
 again and again, all day long.

⁴He has made my flesh and my skin waste away,
 and broken my bones;
⁵he has besieged and enveloped me
 with bitterness and tribulation;
⁶he has made me sit in darkness
 like the dead of long ago.

⁷He has walled me about so that I cannot escape;
 he has put heavy chains on me;
⁸though I call and cry for help,
 he shuts out my prayer;
⁹he has blocked my ways with hewn stones,
 he has made my paths crooked.

¹⁹The thought of my affliction and my homelessness
 is wormwood and gall!
²⁰My soul continually thinks of it
 and is bowed down within me.
²¹But this I call to mind,
 and therefore I have hope:

²²The steadfast love of the Lord never ceases,
 his mercies never come to an end;
²³they are new every morning;
 great is your faithfulness.
²⁴"The Lord is my portion," says my soul,
 "therefore I will hope in him."

The word of the Lord.

PSALMODY: Psalm 31:1–4, 15–16

SECOND READING: 1 PETER 4:1–8

A reading from First Peter:

[1]Since therefore Christ suffered in the flesh,
arm yourselves also with the same intention
(for whoever has suffered in the flesh has finished with sin),
[2]so as to live for the rest of your earthly life
no longer by human desires but by the will of God.
[3]You have already spent enough time in doing what the Gentiles like to do,
living in licentiousness, passions, drunkenness,
revels, carousing, and lawless idolatry.
[4]They are surprised that you no longer join them
in the same excesses of dissipation, and so they blaspheme.

[5]But they will have to give an accounting to him who stands ready
to judge the living and the dead.
[6]For this is the reason the gospel was proclaimed even to the dead,
so that, though they had been judged in the flesh as everyone is judged,
they might live in the spirit as God does.

[7]The end of all things is near;
therefore be serious and discipline yourselves for the sake of your prayers.
[8]Above all, maintain constant love for one another,
for love covers a multitude of sins.

The word of the Lord.

GOSPEL: MATTHEW 27:57–66

Or John 19:38–42, following

The Holy Gospel according to Matthew, the 27th chapter:

[57]When it was evening, there came a rich man from Arimathea, named Joseph,
who was also a disciple of Jesus.
[58]He went to Pilate and asked for the body of Jesus;
then Pilate ordered it to be given to him.
[59]So Joseph took the body and wrapped it in a clean linen cloth
[60]and laid it in his own new tomb, which he had hewn in the rock.
He then rolled a great stone to the door of the tomb and went away.
[61]Mary Magdalene and the other Mary were there, sitting opposite the tomb.

[62]The next day, that is, after the day of Preparation,
the chief priests and the Pharisees gathered before Pilate [63]and said,
"Sir, we remember what that impostor said while he was still alive,
'After three days I will rise again.'
[64]Therefore command the tomb to be made secure until the third day;
otherwise his disciples may go and steal him away,

and tell the people, 'He has been raised from the dead,'
and the last deception would be worse than the first."
[65]Pilate said to them,
"You have a guard of soldiers;
go, make it as secure as you can."
[66]So they went with the guard and made the tomb secure by sealing the stone.

The Gospel of the Lord.

OR: JOHN 19:38–42

The Holy Gospel according to John, the 19th chapter.

[38]Joseph of Arimathea, who was a disciple of Jesus,
though a secret one because of his fear of the Jews,
asked Pilate to let him take away the body of Jesus.
Pilate gave him permission; so he came and removed his body.
[39]Nicodemus, who had at first come to Jesus by night, also came,
bringing a mixture of myrrh and aloes, weighing about a hundred pounds.
[40]They took the body of Jesus
and wrapped it with the spices in linen cloths,
according to the burial custom of the Jews.
[41]Now there was a garden in the place where he was crucified,
and in the garden there was a new tomb in which no one had ever been laid.
[42]And so, because it was the Jewish day of Preparation,
and the tomb was nearby, they laid Jesus there.

The Gospel of the Lord.

The Resurrection of Our Lord
Vigil of Easter

MARCH 29, 1997   APRIL 22, 2000   APRIL 19, 2003

FIRST READING: Genesis 1:1—2:4a
Creation

A reading from Genesis:

[1]In the beginning when God created the heavens and the earth,
[2]the earth was a formless void and darkness covered the face of the deep,
while a wind from God swept over the face of the waters.
[3]Then God said,
"Let there be light"; and there was light.
[4]And God saw that the light was good;
and God separated the light from the darkness.
[5]God called the light Day,
and the darkness he called Night.
And there was evening and there was morning, the first day.

[6]And God said,
"Let there be a dome in the midst of the waters,
and let it separate the waters from the waters."
[7]So God made the dome
and separated the waters that were under the dome
from the waters that were above the dome.
And it was so.
[8]God called the dome Sky.
And there was evening and there was morning, the second day.

[9]And God said,
"Let the waters under the sky be gathered together into one place,
and let the dry land appear."
And it was so.
[10]God called the dry land Earth,
and the waters that were gathered together he called Seas.
And God saw that it was good.
[11]Then God said,
"Let the earth put forth vegetation:
plants yielding seed,
and fruit trees of every kind on earth that bear fruit with the seed in it."
And it was so.
[12]The earth brought forth vegetation:

plants yielding seed of every kind,
and trees of every kind bearing fruit with the seed in it.
And God saw that it was good.
[13]And there was evening and there was morning, the third day.

[14]And God said,
"Let there be lights in the dome of the sky
to separate the day from the night;
and let them be for signs and for seasons and for days and years,
[15]and let them be lights in the dome of the sky to give light upon the earth."
And it was so.
[16]God made the two great lights—
the greater light to rule the day
and the lesser light to rule the night—and the stars.
[17]God set them in the dome of the sky to give light upon the earth,
[18]to rule over the day and over the night,
and to separate the light from the darkness.
And God saw that it was good.
[19]And there was evening and there was morning, the fourth day.

[20]And God said,
"Let the waters bring forth swarms of living creatures,
and let birds fly above the earth across the dome of the sky."
[21]So God created the great sea monsters
and every living creature that moves,
of every kind, with which the waters swarm,
and every winged bird of every kind.
And God saw that it was good.
[22]God blessed them, saying,
"Be fruitful and multiply and fill the waters in the seas,
and let birds multiply on the earth."
[23]And there was evening and there was morning, the fifth day.

[24]And God said,
"Let the earth bring forth living creatures of every kind:
cattle and creeping things and wild animals of the earth of every kind."
And it was so.
[25]God made the wild animals of the earth of every kind,
and the cattle of every kind,
and everything that creeps upon the ground of every kind.
And God saw that it was good.

[26]Then God said,
"Let us make humankind in our image, according to our likeness;
and let them have dominion over the fish of the sea,
and over the birds of the air,
and over the cattle, and over all the wild animals of the earth,
and over every creeping thing that creeps upon the earth."

²⁷So God created humankind in his image,
    in the image of God he created them;
    male and female he created them.
²⁸God blessed them, and God said to them,
"Be fruitful and multiply,
and fill the earth and subdue it;
and have dominion over the fish of the sea
and over the birds of the air
and over every living thing that moves upon the earth."
²⁹God said,
"See, I have given you every plant yielding seed
that is upon the face of all the earth,
and every tree with seed in its fruit;
you shall have them for food.
³⁰And to every beast of the earth,
and to every bird of the air,
and to everything that creeps on the earth,
everything that has the breath of life,
I have given every green plant for food."
And it was so.
³¹God saw everything that he had made,
and indeed, it was very good.
And there was evening and there was morning, the sixth day.

²:¹Thus the heavens and the earth were finished, and all their multitude.
²And on the seventh day God finished the work that he had done,
and he rested on the seventh day from all the work that he had done.
³So God blessed the seventh day and hallowed it,
because on it God rested from all the work that he had done in creation.
⁴These are the generations of the heavens and the earth
    when they were created.

The word of the Lord.

RESPONSE: PSALM 136:1–9, 23–26

SECOND READING: Genesis 7:1–5, 11–18; 8:6–18; 9:8–13
The Flood

A reading from Genesis:

¹The Lord said to Noah,
"Go into the ark, you and all your household,
for I have seen that you alone are righteous before me in this generation.
²Take with you seven pairs of all clean animals,
the male and its mate;
and a pair of the animals that are not clean,
the male and its mate;
³and seven pairs of the birds of the air also, male and female,
to keep their kind alive on the face of all the earth.
⁴For in seven days I will send rain on the earth
for forty days and forty nights;
and every living thing that I have made
I will blot out from the face of the ground."
⁵And Noah did all that the Lord had commanded him.

¹¹In the six hundredth year of Noah's life,
in the second month, on the seventeenth day of the month,
on that day all the fountains of the great deep burst forth,
and the windows of the heavens were opened.
¹²The rain fell on the earth forty days and forty nights.
¹³On the very same day Noah with his sons,
Shem and Ham and Japheth,
and Noah's wife and the three wives of his sons entered the ark,
¹⁴they and every wild animal of every kind,
and all domestic animals of every kind,
and every creeping thing that creeps on the earth,
and every bird of every kind—every bird, every winged creature.
¹⁵They went into the ark with Noah,
two and two of all flesh in which there was the breath of life.
¹⁶And those that entered, male and female of all flesh,
went in as God had commanded him;
and the Lord shut him in.

¹⁷The flood continued forty days on the earth;
and the waters increased,
and bore up the ark, and it rose high above the earth.
¹⁸The waters swelled and increased greatly on the earth;
and the ark floated on the face of the waters.

⁸:⁶At the end of forty days
Noah opened the window of the ark that he had made
⁷and sent out the raven;
and it went to and fro until the waters were dried up from the earth.
⁸Then he sent out the dove from him,
to see if the waters had subsided from the face of the ground;
⁹but the dove found no place to set its foot,

and it returned to him to the ark,
for the waters were still on the face of the whole earth.
So he put out his hand and took it
and brought it into the ark with him.
¹⁰He waited another seven days,
and again he sent out the dove from the ark;
¹¹and the dove came back to him in the evening,
and there in its beak was a freshly plucked olive leaf;
so Noah knew that the waters had subsided from the earth.
¹²Then he waited another seven days, and sent out the dove;
and it did not return to him any more.

¹³In the six hundred first year,
in the first month, on the first day of the month,
the waters were dried up from the earth;
and Noah removed the covering of the ark,
and looked, and saw that the face of the ground was drying.
¹⁴In the second month, on the twenty-seventh day of the month,
the earth was dry.
¹⁵Then God said to Noah,
¹⁶"Go out of the ark, you and your wife,
and your sons and your sons' wives with you.
¹⁷Bring out with you every living thing that is with you of all flesh—
birds and animals and every creeping thing that creeps on the earth—
so that they may abound on the earth,
and be fruitful and multiply on the earth."
¹⁸So Noah went out with his sons and his wife and his sons' wives.

⁹:⁸Then God said to Noah and to his sons with him,
⁹"As for me,
I am establishing my covenant with you and your descendants after you,
¹⁰and with every living creature that is with you,
the birds, the domestic animals,
and every animal of the earth with you,
as many as came out of the ark.
¹¹I establish my covenant with you,
that never again shall all flesh be cut off by the waters of a flood,
and never again shall there be a flood to destroy the earth."
¹²God said,
"This is the sign of the covenant that I make
between me and you and every living creature that is with you,
for all future generations:
¹³I have set my bow in the clouds,
and it shall be a sign of the covenant between me and the earth."

The word of the Lord.

RESPONSE: PSALM 46

THIRD READING: GENESIS 22:1–18
The Testing of Abraham

A reading from Genesis:

¹God tested Abraham.
He said to him, "Abraham!"
And he said, "Here I am."
²God said,
"Take your son, your only son Isaac, whom you love,
and go to the land of Moriah, and offer him there as a burnt offering
on one of the mountains that I shall show you."

³So Abraham rose early in the morning,
saddled his donkey, and took two of his young men with him,
and his son Isaac;
he cut the wood for the burnt offering,
and set out and went to the place in the distance that God had shown him.
⁴On the third day Abraham looked up and saw the place far away.
⁵Then Abraham said to his young men,
"Stay here with the donkey;
the boy and I will go over there;
we will worship, and then we will come back to you."

⁶Abraham took the wood of the burnt offering
and laid it on his son Isaac,
and he himself carried the fire and the knife.
So the two of them walked on together.
⁷Isaac said to his father Abraham, "Father!"
And he said, "Here I am, my son."
He said, "The fire and the wood are here,
but where is the lamb for a burnt offering?"
⁸Abraham said,
"God himself will provide the lamb for a burnt offering, my son."
So the two of them walked on together.

⁹When they came to the place that God had shown him,
Abraham built an altar there and laid the wood in order.
He bound his son Isaac,
and laid him on the altar, on top of the wood.
¹⁰Then Abraham reached out his hand
and took the knife to kill his son.
¹¹But the angel of the LORD called to him from heaven, and said,
"Abraham, Abraham!"
And he said, "Here I am."
¹²He said,
"Do not lay your hand on the boy or do anything to him;
for now I know that you fear God,
since you have not withheld your son, your only son, from me."

[13]And Abraham looked up and saw a ram, caught in a thicket by its horns.
Abraham went and took the ram
and offered it up as a burnt offering instead of his son.
[14]So Abraham called that place "The LORD will provide";
as it is said to this day,
"On the mount of the LORD it shall be provided."

[15]The angel of the LORD called to Abraham a second time from heaven,
[16]and said,
"By myself I have sworn, says the LORD:
Because you have done this,
and have not withheld your son, your only son,
[17]I will indeed bless you,
and I will make your offspring as numerous as the stars of heaven
and as the sand that is on the seashore.
And your offspring shall possess the gate of their enemies,
[18]and by your offspring shall all the nations of the earth
gain blessing for themselves,
because you have obeyed my voice."

The word of the Lord.

RESPONSE: PSALM 16

FOURTH READING: Exodus 14:10–31; 15:20–21
Israel's Deliverance at the Red Sea

A reading from Exodus:

¹⁰As Pharaoh drew near, the Israelites looked back,
and there were the Egyptians advancing on them.
In great fear the Israelites cried out to the LORD.
¹¹They said to Moses,
"Was it because there were no graves in Egypt
that you have taken us away to die in the wilderness?
What have you done to us, bringing us out of Egypt?
¹²Is this not the very thing we told you in Egypt,
'Let us alone and let us serve the Egyptians'?
For it would have been better for us to serve the Egyptians
than to die in the wilderness."
¹³But Moses said to the people,
"Do not be afraid, stand firm,
and see the deliverance that the LORD will accomplish for you today;
for the Egyptians whom you see today you shall never see again.
¹⁴The LORD will fight for you,
 and you have only to keep still."

¹⁵Then the LORD said to Moses,
"Why do you cry out to me?
Tell the Israelites to go forward.
¹⁶But you lift up your staff,
and stretch out your hand over the sea and divide it,
that the Israelites may go into the sea on dry ground.
¹⁷Then I will harden the hearts of the Egyptians
so that they will go in after them;
and so I will gain glory for myself over Pharaoh and all his army,
his chariots, and his chariot drivers.
¹⁸And the Egyptians shall know that I am the LORD,
when I have gained glory for myself over Pharaoh,
his chariots, and his chariot drivers."

¹⁹The angel of God who was going before the Israelite army moved
and went behind them;
and the pillar of cloud moved from in front of them
and took its place behind them.
²⁰It came between the army of Egypt and the army of Israel.
And so the cloud was there with the darkness,
and it lit up the night;
one did not come near the other all night.

²¹Then Moses stretched out his hand over the sea.
The LORD drove the sea back by a strong east wind all night,
and turned the sea into dry land;

and the waters were divided.
²²The Israelites went into the sea on dry ground,
the waters forming a wall for them on their right and on their left.
²³The Egyptians pursued, and went into the sea after them,
all of Pharaoh's horses, chariots, and chariot drivers.
²⁴At the morning watch
the LORD in the pillar of fire and cloud looked down upon the Egyptian army,
and threw the Egyptian army into panic.
²⁵He clogged their chariot wheels so that they turned with difficulty.
The Egyptians said,
"Let us flee from the Israelites,
for the LORD is fighting for them against Egypt."

²⁶Then the LORD said to Moses,
"Stretch out your hand over the sea,
so that the water may come back upon the Egyptians,
upon their chariots and chariot drivers."
²⁷So Moses stretched out his hand over the sea,
and at dawn the sea returned to its normal depth.
As the Egyptians fled before it,
the LORD tossed the Egyptians into the sea.
²⁸The waters returned and covered the chariots and the chariot drivers,
the entire army of Pharaoh that had followed them into the sea;
not one of them remained.
²⁹But the Israelites walked on dry ground through the sea,
the waters forming a wall for them on their right and on their left.

³⁰Thus the LORD saved Israel that day from the Egyptians;
and Israel saw the Egyptians dead on the seashore.
³¹Israel saw the great work that the LORD did against the Egyptians.
So the people feared the LORD
and believed in the LORD and in his servant Moses.

^{15:20}Then the prophet Miriam, Aaron's sister, took a tambourine in her hand;
and all the women went out after her with tambourines and with dancing.
²¹And Miriam sang to them:
  "Sing to the LORD, for he has triumphed gloriously;
  horse and rider he has thrown into the sea."

The word of the Lord.

RESPONSE: EXODUS 15:1b–13, 17–18

FIFTH READING: ISAIAH 55:1–11
Salvation Freely Offered to All

A reading from Isaiah:

¹Ho, everyone who thirsts,
    come to the waters;
and you that have no money,
    come, buy and eat!
Come, buy wine and milk
    without money and without price.
²Why do you spend your money for that which is not bread,
    and your labor for that which does not satisfy?
Listen carefully to me, and eat what is good,
    and delight yourselves in rich food.

³Incline your ear, and come to me;
    listen, so that you may live.
I will make with you an everlasting covenant,
    my steadfast, sure love for David.
⁴See, I made him a witness to the peoples,
    a leader and commander for the peoples.
⁵See, you shall call nations that you do not know,
    and nations that do not know you shall run to you,
because of the LORD your God, the Holy One of Israel,
    for he has glorified you.

⁶Seek the LORD while he may be found,
    call upon him while he is near;
⁷let the wicked forsake their way,
    and the unrighteous their thoughts;
let them return to the LORD, that he may have mercy on them,
    and to our God, for he will abundantly pardon.
⁸For my thoughts are not your thoughts,
    nor are your ways my ways, says the LORD.
⁹For as the heavens are higher than the earth,
    so are my ways higher than your ways
    and my thoughts than your thoughts.

¹⁰For as the rain and the snow come down from heaven,
    and do not return there until they have watered the earth,
making it bring forth and sprout,
    giving seed to the sower and bread to the eater,
¹¹so shall my word be that goes out from my mouth;
    it shall not return to me empty,
but it shall accomplish that which I purpose,
    and succeed in the thing for which I sent it.

The word of the Lord.

RESPONSE: ISAIAH 12:2–6

The Wisdom of God   *Alternate Reading: Baruch 3:9–15, 32—4:4 (p. 404)*

A reading from Proverbs:

¹Does not wisdom call,
      and does not understanding raise her voice?
²On the heights, beside the way,
      at the crossroads she takes her stand;
³beside the gates in front of the town,
      at the entrance of the portals she cries out:
⁴"To you, O people, I call,
      and my cry is to all that live.
⁵O simple ones, learn prudence;
      acquire intelligence, you who lack it.
⁶Hear, for I will speak noble things,
      and from my lips will come what is right;
⁷for my mouth will utter truth;
      wickedness is an abomination to my lips.
⁸All the words of my mouth are righteous;
      there is nothing twisted or crooked in them.

¹⁹My fruit is better than gold, even fine gold,
      and my yield than choice silver.
²⁰I walk in the way of righteousness,
      along the paths of justice,
²¹endowing with wealth those who love me,
      and filling their treasuries.
      ^{9:4b}To those without sense she says,
⁵"Come, eat of my bread
      and drink of the wine I have mixed.
⁶Lay aside immaturity, and live,
      and walk in the way of insight."

The word of the Lord.

RESPONSE: PSALM 19

SEVENTH READING: EZEKIEL 36:24–28
A New Heart and a New Spirit

A reading from Ezekiel:

Thus says the Lord GOD:
24I will take you from the nations,
and gather you from all the countries,
and bring you into your own land.
25I will sprinkle clean water upon you,
and you shall be clean from all your uncleannesses,
and from all your idols I will cleanse you.
26A new heart I will give you,
and a new spirit I will put within you;
and I will remove from your body the heart of stone
and give you a heart of flesh.
27I will put my spirit within you,
and make you follow my statutes and be careful to observe my ordinances.
28Then you shall live in the land that I gave to your ancestors;
and you shall be my people, and I will be your God.

The word of the Lord.

RESPONSE: PSALM 42 and 43

EIGHTH READING: EZEKIEL 37:1–14
The Valley of the Dry Bones

A reading from Ezekiel:

1The hand of the LORD came upon me,
and he brought me out by the spirit of the LORD
and set me down in the middle of a valley;
it was full of bones.
2He led me all around them;
there were very many lying in the valley, and they were very dry.
3He said to me,
"Mortal, can these bones live?"
I answered, "O Lord GOD, you know."

4Then he said to me,
"Prophesy to these bones, and say to them:
O dry bones, hear the word of the LORD.
5Thus says the Lord GOD to these bones:
I will cause breath to enter you, and you shall live.
6I will lay sinews on you,
and will cause flesh to come upon you, and cover you with skin,

and put breath in you, and you shall live;
and you shall know that I am the LORD."

⁷So I prophesied as I had been commanded;
and as I prophesied, suddenly there was a noise, a rattling,
and the bones came together, bone to its bone.
⁸I looked, and there were sinews on them,
and flesh had come upon them, and skin had covered them;
but there was no breath in them.
⁹Then he said to me,
"Prophesy to the breath, prophesy, mortal, and say to the breath:
Thus says the Lord GOD:
Come from the four winds, O breath,
and breathe upon these slain, that they may live."
¹⁰I prophesied as he commanded me,
and the breath came into them,
and they lived, and stood on their feet, a vast multitude.

¹¹Then he said to me,
"Mortal, these bones are the whole house of Israel.
They say, 'Our bones are dried up, and our hope is lost;
we are cut off completely.'
¹²Therefore prophesy, and say to them,
Thus says the Lord GOD:
I am going to open your graves,
and bring you up from your graves, O my people;
and I will bring you back to the land of Israel.
¹³And you shall know that I am the LORD,
when I open your graves,
and bring you up from your graves, O my people.
¹⁴I will put my spirit within you, and you shall live,
and I will place you on your own soil;
then you shall know that I, the LORD, have spoken and will act,"
says the LORD.

The word of the Lord.

RESPONSE: PSALM 143

NINTH READING: ZEPHANIAH 3:14–20
The Gathering of God's People

A reading from Zephaniah:

¹⁴Sing aloud, O daughter Zion;
    shout, O Israel!
Rejoice and exult with all your heart,
    O daughter Jerusalem!
¹⁵The LORD has taken away the judgments against you,
    he has turned away your enemies.
The king of Israel, the LORD, is in your midst;
    you shall fear disaster no more.
¹⁶On that day it shall be said to Jerusalem:
Do not fear, O Zion;
    do not let your hands grow weak.
¹⁷The LORD, your God, is in your midst,
    a warrior who gives victory;
he will rejoice over you with gladness,
    he will renew you in his love;
he will exult over you with loud singing
    ¹⁸as on a day of festival.

I will remove disaster from you,
    so that you will not bear reproach for it.
¹⁹I will deal with all your oppressors
    at that time.
And I will save the lame
    and gather the outcast,
and I will change their shame into praise
    and renown in all the earth.
²⁰At that time I will bring you home,
    at the time when I gather you;
for I will make you renowned and praised
    among all the peoples of the earth,
when I restore your fortunes
    before your eyes, says the LORD.

The word of the Lord.

RESPONSE: PSALM 98

Three additional readings from the Hebrew Scriptures follow on pp. 140–144.
The New Testament and Gospel readings continue on p. 145.

TENTH READING: JONAH 3:1–10
The Call of Jonah

A reading from Jonah.

¹The word of the LORD came to Jonah a second time, saying,
²"Get up, go to Nineveh, that great city,
and proclaim to it the message that I tell you."
³So Jonah set out and went to Nineveh, according to the word of the LORD.

Now Nineveh was an exceedingly large city, a three days' walk across.
⁴Jonah began to go into the city, going a day's walk.
And he cried out,
"Forty days more, and Nineveh shall be overthrown!"
⁵And the people of Nineveh believed God;
they proclaimed a fast,
and everyone, great and small, put on sackcloth.

⁶When the news reached the king of Nineveh,
he rose from his throne, removed his robe,
covered himself with sackcloth, and sat in ashes.
⁷Then he had a proclamation made in Nineveh:
"By the decree of the king and his nobles:
No human being or animal, no herd or flock, shall taste anything.
They shall not feed, nor shall they drink water.
⁸Human beings and animals shall be covered with sackcloth,
and they shall cry mightily to God.
All shall turn from their evil ways
and from the violence that is in their hands.
⁹Who knows? God may relent and change his mind;
he may turn from his fierce anger, so that we do not perish."
¹⁰When God saw what they did,
how they turned from their evil ways,
God changed his mind about the calamity
that he had said he would bring upon them;
and he did not do it.

The word of the Lord.

RESPONSE: JONAH 2:1–3 [4–6] 7–9

ELEVENTH READING: Deuteronomy 31:19–30
The Song of Moses

A reading from Deuteronomy.

[19] Now therefore write this song,
and teach it to the Israelites;
put it in their mouths,
in order that this song may be a witness for me against the Israelites.

[20] For when I have brought them into the land flowing with milk and honey,
which I promised on oath to their ancestors,
and they have eaten their fill and grown fat,
they will turn to other gods and serve them,
despising me and breaking my covenant.
[21] And when many terrible troubles come upon them,
this song will confront them as a witness,
because it will not be lost from the mouths of their descendants.
For I know what they are inclined to do even now,
before I have brought them into the land that I promised them on oath."
[22] That very day Moses wrote this song and taught it to the Israelites.

[23] Then the LORD commissioned Joshua son of Nun and said,
"Be strong and bold,
for you shall bring the Israelites into the land that I promised them;
I will be with you."

[24] When Moses had finished writing down in a book
the words of this law to the very end,
[25] Moses commanded the Levites who carried the ark of the covenant of the
LORD, saying,
[26] "Take this book of the law
and put it beside the ark of the covenant of the LORD your God;
let it remain there as a witness against you.
[27] For I know well how rebellious and stubborn you are.
If you already have been so rebellious toward the LORD
while I am still alive among you,
how much more after my death!
[28] Assemble to me all the elders of your tribes and your officials,
so that I may recite these words in their hearing
and call heaven and earth to witness against them.
[29] For I know that after my death you will surely act corruptly,
turning aside from the way that I have commanded you.
In time to come trouble will befall you,
because you will do what is evil in the sight of the LORD,
provoking him to anger through the work of your hands."

[superscript]30[/superscript]Then Moses recited the words of this song, to the very end,
in the hearing of the whole assembly of Israel.

The word of the Lord.

RESPONSE: Deuteronomy 32:1–4, 7, 36a, 43a

TWELFTH READING: Daniel 3:1–29

A reading from Daniel.

[superscript]1[/superscript]King Nebuchadnezzar made a golden statue whose height was sixty cubits
and whose width was six cubits;
he set it up on the plain of Dura in the province of Babylon.
[superscript]2[/superscript]Then King Nebuchadnezzar sent for the satraps, the prefects,
        and the governors,
the counselors, the treasurers, the justices, the magistrates,
and all the officials of the provinces,
to assemble and come to the dedication of the statue
that King Nebuchadnezzar had set up.

[superscript]3[/superscript]So the satraps, the prefects, and the governors,
the counselors, the treasurers, the justices, the magistrates,
and all the officials of the provinces,
assembled for the dedication of the statue
that King Nebuchadnezzar had set up.
When they were standing before the statue that Nebuchadnezzar had set up,
[superscript]4[/superscript]the herald proclaimed aloud,
"You are commanded, O peoples, nations, and languages,
[superscript]5[/superscript]that when you hear the sound of the horn, pipe, lyre,
trigon, harp, drum, and entire musical ensemble,
you are to fall down and worship the golden statue
that King Nebuchadnezzar has set up.
[superscript]6[/superscript]Whoever does not fall down and worship
shall immediately be thrown into a furnace of blazing fire."
[superscript]7[/superscript]Therefore, as soon as all the peoples heard the sound of the horn, pipe, lyre,
trigon, harp, drum, and entire musical ensemble,
all the peoples, nations, and languages fell down
and worshiped the golden statue that King Nebuchadnezzar had set up.

[superscript]8[/superscript]Accordingly, at this time
certain Chaldeans came forward and denounced the Jews.
[superscript]9[/superscript]They said to King Nebuchadnezzar,
"O king, live forever!
[superscript]10[/superscript]You, O king, have made a decree,
that everyone who hears the sound of the horn, pipe, lyre,
trigon, harp, drum, and entire musical ensemble,
shall fall down and worship the golden statue,

¹¹and whoever does not fall down and worship
shall be thrown into a furnace of blazing fire.
¹²There are certain Jews
whom you have appointed over the affairs of the province of Babylon:
Shadrach, Meshach, and Abednego.
These pay no heed to you, O king.
They do not serve your gods
and they do not worship the golden statue that you have set up."

¹³Then Nebuchadnezzar in furious rage
commanded that Shadrach, Meshach, and Abednego be brought in;
so they brought those men before the king.
¹⁴Nebuchadnezzar said to them,
"Is it true, O Shadrach, Meshach, and Abednego,
that you do not serve my gods
and you do not worship the golden statue that I have set up?
¹⁵Now if you are ready when you hear the sound of the horn, pipe, lyre,
trigon, harp, drum, and entire musical ensemble
to fall down and worship the statue that I have made,
well and good.
But if you do not worship,
you shall immediately be thrown into a furnace of blazing fire,
and who is the god that will deliver you out of my hands?"

¹⁶Shadrach, Meshach, and Abednego answered the king,
"O Nebuchadnezzar,
we have no need to present a defense to you in this matter.
¹⁷If our God whom we serve is able to deliver us
from the furnace of blazing fire and out of your hand, O king,
let him deliver us.
¹⁸But if not, be it known to you, O king,
that we will not serve your gods
and we will not worship the golden statue that you have set up."

¹⁹Then Nebuchadnezzar was so filled with rage
against Shadrach, Meshach, and Abednego
that his face was distorted.
He ordered the furnace heated up seven times more than was customary,
²⁰and ordered some of the strongest guards in his army
to bind Shadrach, Meshach, and Abednego
and to throw them into the furnace of blazing fire.
²¹So the men were bound, still wearing their tunics,
their trousers, their hats, and their other garments,
and they were thrown into the furnace of blazing fire.
²²Because the king's command was urgent and the furnace was so overheated,
the raging flames killed the men who lifted Shadrach, Meshach, and
          Abednego.

²³But the three men, Shadrach, Meshach, and Abednego, fell down, bound, into the furnace of blazing fire.

²⁴Then King Nebuchadnezzar was astonished and rose up quickly.
He said to his counselors,
"Was it not three men that we threw bound into the fire?"
They answered the king, "True, O king."
²⁵He replied, "But I see four men unbound,
walking in the middle of the fire,
and they are not hurt;
and the fourth has the appearance of a god."

²⁶Nebuchadnezzar then approached the door of the furnace of blazing fire
        and said,
"Shadrach, Meshach, and Abednego,
servants of the Most High God,
come out! Come here!"
So Shadrach, Meshach, and Abednego came out from the fire.
²⁷And the satraps, the prefects, the governors,
and the king's counselors gathered together
and saw that the fire had not had any power over the bodies of those men;
the hair of their heads was not singed,
their tunics were not harmed,
and not even the smell of fire came from them.

²⁸Nebuchadnezzar said,
"Blessed be the God of Shadrach, Meshach, and Abednego,
who has sent his angel and delivered his servants who trusted in him.
They disobeyed the king's command and yielded up their bodies
rather than serve and worship any god except their own God.
²⁹Therefore I make a decree:
Any people, nation, or language that utters blasphemy
against the God of Shadrach, Meshach, and Abednego
shall be torn limb from limb,
and their houses laid in ruins;
for there is no other god who is able to deliver in this way."

The word of the Lord.

RESPONSE: SONG OF THE THREE YOUNG MEN 35–65

NEW TESTAMENT READING: ROMANS 6:3–11

A reading from Romans:

[3]Do you not know that all of us who have been baptized into Christ Jesus were baptized into his death?
[4]Therefore we have been buried with him by baptism into death,
so that, just as Christ was raised from the dead by the glory of the Father,
so we too might walk in newness of life.

[5]For if we have been united with him in a death like his,
we will certainly be united with him in a resurrection like his.
[6]We know that our old self was crucified with him
so that the body of sin might be destroyed,
and we might no longer be enslaved to sin.
[7]For whoever has died is freed from sin.
[8]But if we have died with Christ,
we believe that we will also live with him.
[9]We know that Christ, being raised from the dead, will never die again;
death no longer has dominion over him.
[10]The death he died, he died to sin, once for all;
but the life he lives, he lives to God.

[11]So you also must consider yourselves dead to sin
and alive to God in Christ Jesus.

The word of the Lord.

RESPONSE: PSALM 114

GOSPEL: MARK 16:1–8

The Holy Gospel according to Mark, the 16th chapter.

¹When the sabbath was over,
Mary Magdalene, and Mary the mother of James, and Salome bought spices,
so that they might go and anoint him.
²And very early on the first day of the week, when the sun had risen,
they went to the tomb.
³They had been saying to one another,
"Who will roll away the stone for us from the entrance to the tomb?"
⁴When they looked up, they saw that the stone, which was very large,
had already been rolled back.
⁵As they entered the tomb,
they saw a young man, dressed in a white robe,
sitting on the right side;
and they were alarmed.
⁶But he said to them, "Do not be alarmed;
you are looking for Jesus of Nazareth, who was crucified.
He has been raised; he is not here.
Look, there is the place they laid him.
⁷But go, tell his disciples and Peter that he is going ahead of you to Galilee;
there you will see him, just as he told you."

⁸So they went out and fled from the tomb,
for terror and amazement had seized them;
and they said nothing to anyone, for they were afraid.

The Gospel of the Lord.

SEASON OF EASTER

The Resurrection of Our Lord
Easter Day

MARCH 30, 1997   APRIL 23, 2000   APRIL 20, 2003

FIRST READING: Acts 10:34–43
Or Isaiah 25:6–9, following

A reading from Acts:

[34]Peter began to speak to the people:
"I truly understand that God shows no partiality,
[35]but in every nation anyone who fears him and does what is right
is acceptable to him.
[36]You know the message he sent to the people of Israel,
preaching peace by Jesus Christ—
he is Lord of all.
[37]That message spread throughout Judea,
beginning in Galilee after the baptism that John announced:
[38]how God anointed Jesus of Nazareth with the Holy Spirit and with power;
how he went about doing good and healing all who were oppressed by the
devil,
for God was with him.
[39]We are witnesses to all that he did both in Judea and in Jerusalem.
They put him to death by hanging him on a tree;
[40]but God raised him on the third day
and allowed him to appear, [41]not to all the people
but to us who were chosen by God as witnesses,
and who ate and drank with him after he rose from the dead.

[42]"He commanded us to preach to the people
and to testify that he is the one ordained by God
as judge of the living and the dead.
[43]All the prophets testify about him that everyone who believes in him
receives forgiveness of sins through his name."

The word of the Lord.

A reading from Isaiah:

⁶On this mountain the LORD of hosts will make for all peoples
    a feast of rich food, a feast of well-aged wines,
    of rich food filled with marrow, of well-aged wines strained clear.
⁷And he will destroy on this mountain
    the shroud that is cast over all peoples,
    the sheet that is spread over all nations;
    he will swallow up death forever.
⁸Then the Lord GOD will wipe away the tears from all faces,
    and the disgrace of his people he will take away from all the earth,
    for the LORD has spoken.
⁹It will be said on that day,
    Lo, this is our God; we have waited for him, so that he might save us.
    This is the LORD for whom we have waited;
    let us be glad and rejoice in his salvation.

The word of the Lord.

PSALMODY: PSALM 118:1–2, 14–24

SECOND READING: 1 CORINTHIANS 15:1–11
Or Acts 10:34–43, following

A reading from First Corinthians:

¹Now I would remind you, brothers and sisters,
of the good news that I proclaimed to you,
which you in turn received, in which also you stand,
²through which also you are being saved,
if you hold firmly to the message that I proclaimed to you—
unless you have come to believe in vain.

³For I handed on to you as of first importance what I in turn had received:
that Christ died for our sins in accordance with the scriptures,
⁴and that he was buried,
and that he was raised on the third day in accordance with the scriptures,
⁵and that he appeared to Cephas, then to the twelve.
⁶Then he appeared to more than five hundred brothers and sisters at one time,
most of whom are still alive, though some have died.
⁷Then he appeared to James, then to all the apostles.
⁸Last of all, as to one untimely born, he appeared also to me.
⁹For I am the least of the apostles, unfit to be called an apostle,
because I persecuted the church of God.
¹⁰But by the grace of God I am what I am,

and his grace toward me has not been in vain.
On the contrary, I worked harder than any of them—
though it was not I,
but the grace of God that is with me.
[11]Whether then it was I or they,
so we proclaim and so you have come to believe.

The word of the Lord.

OR: Acts 10:34–43

A reading from Acts:

[34]Peter began to speak to the people:
"I truly understand that God shows no partiality,
[35]but in every nation anyone who fears him and does what is right
is acceptable to him.
[36]You know the message he sent to the people of Israel,
preaching peace by Jesus Christ—
he is Lord of all.
[37]That message spread throughout Judea,
beginning in Galilee after the baptism that John announced:
[38]how God anointed Jesus of Nazareth with the Holy Spirit and with power;
how he went about doing good and healing all who were oppressed by the
        devil,
for God was with him.
[39]We are witnesses to all that he did both in Judea and in Jerusalem.
They put him to death by hanging him on a tree;
[40]but God raised him on the third day
and allowed him to appear, [41]not to all the people
but to us who were chosen by God as witnesses,
and who ate and drank with him after he rose from the dead.

[42]"He commanded us to preach to the people
and to testify that he is the one ordained by God
as judge of the living and the dead.
[43]All the prophets testify about him that everyone who believes in him
receives forgiveness of sins through his name."

The word of the Lord.

GOSPEL: JOHN 20:1–18

Or Mark 16:1–8, following

The Holy Gospel according to John, the 20th chapter.

¹Early on the first day of the week, while it was still dark,
Mary Magdalene came to the tomb
and saw that the stone had been removed from the tomb.
²So she ran and went to Simon Peter and the other disciple,
the one whom Jesus loved, and said to them,
"They have taken the Lord out of the tomb,
and we do not know where they have laid him."

³Then Peter and the other disciple set out and went toward the tomb.
⁴The two were running together,
but the other disciple outran Peter and reached the tomb first.
⁵He bent down to look in and saw the linen wrappings lying there,
but he did not go in.
⁶Then Simon Peter came, following him, and went into the tomb.
He saw the linen wrappings lying there,
⁷and the cloth that had been on Jesus' head,
not lying with the linen wrappings but rolled up in a place by itself.
⁸Then the other disciple, who reached the tomb first,
also went in, and he saw and believed;
⁹for as yet they did not understand the scripture,
that he must rise from the dead.
¹⁰Then the disciples returned to their homes.

¹¹But Mary stood weeping outside the tomb.
As she wept, she bent over to look into the tomb;
¹²and she saw two angels in white,
sitting where the body of Jesus had been lying,
one at the head and the other at the feet.
¹³They said to her, "Woman, why are you weeping?"
She said to them,
"They have taken away my Lord,
and I do not know where they have laid him."
¹⁴When she had said this, she turned around and saw Jesus standing there,
but she did not know that it was Jesus.
¹⁵Jesus said to her,
"Woman, why are you weeping? Whom are you looking for?"
Supposing him to be the gardener, she said to him,
"Sir, if you have carried him away,
tell me where you have laid him, and I will take him away."
¹⁶Jesus said to her, "Mary!"
She turned and said to him in Hebrew,
"Rabbouni!" (which means Teacher).
¹⁷Jesus said to her,

"Do not hold on to me, because I have not yet ascended to the Father.
But go to my brothers and say to them,
'I am ascending to my Father and your Father,
to my God and your God.' "

[18]Mary Magdalene went and announced to the disciples,
"I have seen the Lord";
and she told them that he had said these things to her.

The Gospel of the Lord.

OR: MARK 16:1–8

The Holy Gospel according to Mark, the 16th chapter.

[1]When the sabbath was over,
Mary Magdalene, and Mary the mother of James, and Salome bought spices,
so that they might go and anoint him.
[2]And very early on the first day of the week, when the sun had risen,
they went to the tomb.
[3]They had been saying to one another,
"Who will roll away the stone for us from the entrance to the tomb?"
[4]When they looked up, they saw that the stone, which was very large,
had already been rolled back.
[5]As they entered the tomb,
they saw a young man, dressed in a white robe, sitting on the right side;
and they were alarmed.
[6]But he said to them, "Do not be alarmed;
you are looking for Jesus of Nazareth, who was crucified.
He has been raised; he is not here.
Look, there is the place they laid him.
[7]But go, tell his disciples and Peter that he is going ahead of you to Galilee;
there you will see him, just as he told you."

[8]So they went out and fled from the tomb,
for terror and amazement had seized them;
and they said nothing to anyone, for they were afraid.

The Gospel of the Lord.

THE RESURRECTION OF OUR LORD
EASTER EVENING

MARCH 30, 1997   APRIL 23, 2000   APRIL 20, 2003

FIRST READING: ISAIAH 25:6–9

A reading from Isaiah:

⁶On this mountain the LORD of hosts will make for all peoples
 a feast of rich food, a feast of well-aged wines,
 of rich food filled with marrow, of well-aged wines strained clear.
⁷And he will destroy on this mountain
 the shroud that is cast over all peoples,
 the sheet that is spread over all nations;
 he will swallow up death forever.
⁸Then the Lord GOD will wipe away the tears from all faces,
 and the disgrace of his people he will take away from all the earth,
 for the LORD has spoken.

⁹It will be said on that day,
 Lo, this is our God; we have waited for him, so that he might save us.
 This is the LORD for whom we have waited;
 let us be glad and rejoice in his salvation.

The word of the Lord.

PSALMODY: PSALM 114

SECOND READING: 1 CORINTHIANS 5:6b–8

A reading from First Corinthians:

⁶ᵇDo you not know that a little yeast leavens the whole batch of dough?
⁷Clean out the old yeast so that you may be a new batch,
as you really are unleavened.
For our paschal lamb, Christ, has been sacrificed.
⁸Therefore, let us celebrate the festival,
not with the old yeast, the yeast of malice and evil,
but with the unleavened bread of sincerity and truth.

The word of the Lord.

The Holy Gospel according to Luke, the 24th chapter.

¹³Now on that same day when Jesus had appeared to Mary Magdalene,
two of them were going to a village called Emmaus,
about seven miles from Jerusalem,
¹⁴and talking with each other about all these things that had happened.
¹⁵While they were talking and discussing,
Jesus himself came near and went with them,
¹⁶but their eyes were kept from recognizing him.
¹⁷And he said to them,
"What are you discussing with each other while you walk along?"
They stood still, looking sad.
¹⁸Then one of them, whose name was Cleopas, answered him,
"Are you the only stranger in Jerusalem
who does not know the things that have taken place there in these days?"
¹⁹He asked them, "What things?"
They replied, "The things about Jesus of Nazareth,
who was a prophet mighty in deed and word before God and all the people,
²⁰and how our chief priests and leaders
handed him over to be condemned to death and crucified him.
²¹But we had hoped that he was the one to redeem Israel.
Yes, and besides all this,
it is now the third day since these things took place.
²²Moreover, some women of our group astounded us.
They were at the tomb early this morning,
²³and when they did not find his body there, they came back
and told us that they had indeed seen a vision of angels
who said that he was alive.
²⁴Some of those who were with us went to the tomb
and found it just as the women had said;
but they did not see him."

²⁵Then he said to them,
"Oh, how foolish you are,
and how slow of heart to believe all that the prophets have declared!
²⁶Was it not necessary that the Messiah should suffer these things
and then enter into his glory?"
²⁷Then beginning with Moses and all the prophets,
he interpreted to them the things about himself in all the scriptures.

²⁸As they came near the village to which they were going,
he walked ahead as if he were going on.
²⁹But they urged him strongly, saying,
"Stay with us,
because it is almost evening and the day is now nearly over."
So he went in to stay with them.

³⁰When he was at the table with them,
he took bread, blessed and broke it, and gave it to them.
³¹Then their eyes were opened, and they recognized him;
and he vanished from their sight.
³²They said to each other,
"Were not our hearts burning within us
while he was talking to us on the road,
while he was opening the scriptures to us?"

³³That same hour they got up and returned to Jerusalem;
and they found the eleven and their companions gathered together.
³⁴They were saying,
"The Lord has risen indeed, and he has appeared to Simon!"
³⁵Then they told what had happened on the road,
and how he had been made known to them in the breaking of the bread.

³⁶While they were talking about this,
Jesus himself stood among them and said to them,
"Peace be with you."
³⁷They were startled and terrified,
and thought that they were seeing a ghost.
³⁸He said to them,
"Why are you frightened, and why do doubts arise in your hearts?
³⁹Look at my hands and my feet; see that it is I myself.
Touch me and see;
for a ghost does not have flesh and bones as you see that I have."
⁴⁰And when he had said this, he showed them his hands and his feet.
⁴¹While in their joy they were disbelieving and still wondering,
he said to them,
"Have you anything here to eat?"
⁴²They gave him a piece of broiled fish,
⁴³and he took it and ate in their presence.

⁴⁴Then he said to them,
"These are my words that I spoke to you while I was still with you—
that everything written about me
in the law of Moses, the prophets, and the psalms must be fulfilled."
⁴⁵Then he opened their minds to understand the scriptures,
⁴⁶and he said to them,
"Thus it is written,
that the Messiah is to suffer and to rise from the dead on the third day,
⁴⁷and that repentance and forgiveness of sins
is to be proclaimed in his name to all nations, beginning from Jerusalem.
⁴⁸You are witnesses of these things.
⁴⁹And see, I am sending upon you what my Father promised;
so stay here in the city until you have been clothed with power from on high."

The Gospel of the Lord.

SECOND SUNDAY OF EASTER

APRIL 6, 1997   APRIL 30, 2000   APRIL 27, 2003

FIRST READING: ACTS 4:32–35

A reading from Acts:

[32]Now the whole group of those who believed were of one heart and soul,
and no one claimed private ownership of any possessions,
but everything they owned was held in common.
[33]With great power the apostles gave their testimony to the resurrection of the
     Lord Jesus,
and great grace was upon them all.
[34]There was not a needy person among them,
for as many as owned lands or houses sold them
and brought the proceeds of what was sold.
[35]They laid it at the apostles' feet,
and it was distributed to each as any had need.

The word of the Lord.

PSALMODY: PSALM 133

SECOND READING: 1 JOHN 1:1—2:2

A reading from First John:

¹We declare to you what was from the beginning,
what we have heard,
what we have seen with our eyes,
what we have looked at and touched with our hands,
concerning the word of life—
²this life was revealed,
and we have seen it and testify to it,
and declare to you the eternal life that was with the Father and was revealed
       to us—
³we declare to you what we have seen and heard
so that you also may have fellowship with us;
and truly our fellowship is with the Father and with his Son Jesus Christ.
⁴We are writing these things so that our joy may be complete.

⁵This is the message we have heard from him and proclaim to you,
that God is light and in him there is no darkness at all.
⁶If we say that we have fellowship with him while we are walking in darkness,
we lie and do not do what is true;
⁷but if we walk in the light as he himself is in the light,
we have fellowship with one another,
and the blood of Jesus his Son cleanses us from all sin.
⁸If we say that we have no sin, we deceive ourselves,
and the truth is not in us.
⁹If we confess our sins,
he who is faithful and just will forgive us our sins
and cleanse us from all unrighteousness.
¹⁰If we say that we have not sinned, we make him a liar,
and his word is not in us.

²:¹My little children,
I am writing these things to you so that you may not sin.
But if anyone does sin, we have an advocate with the Father,
Jesus Christ the righteous;
²and he is the atoning sacrifice for our sins,
and not for ours only but also for the sins of the whole world.

The word of the Lord.

The Holy Gospel according to John, the 20th chapter.

¹⁹When it was evening on that day, the first day of the week,
and the doors of the house where the disciples had met
were locked for fear of the Jews,
Jesus came and stood among them and said,
"Peace be with you."
²⁰After he said this, he showed them his hands and his side.
Then the disciples rejoiced when they saw the Lord.
²¹Jesus said to them again,
"Peace be with you.
As the Father has sent me, so I send you."
²²When he had said this, he breathed on them and said to them,
"Receive the Holy Spirit.
²³If you forgive the sins of any, they are forgiven them;
if you retain the sins of any, they are retained."

²⁴But Thomas (who was called the Twin), one of the twelve,
was not with them when Jesus came.
²⁵So the other disciples told him, "We have seen the Lord."
But he said to them,
"Unless I see the mark of the nails in his hands,
and put my finger in the mark of the nails and my hand in his side,
I will not believe."

²⁶A week later his disciples were again in the house,
and Thomas was with them.
Although the doors were shut,
Jesus came and stood among them and said,
"Peace be with you."
²⁷Then he said to Thomas,
"Put your finger here and see my hands.
Reach out your hand and put it in my side.
Do not doubt but believe."
²⁸Thomas answered him,
"My Lord and my God!"
²⁹Jesus said to him, "Have you believed because you have seen me?
Blessed are those who have not seen and yet have come to believe."

³⁰Now Jesus did many other signs in the presence of his disciples,
which are not written in this book.
³¹But these are written so that you may come to believe that Jesus is the
        Messiah, the Son of God,
and that through believing you may have life in his name.

The Gospel of the Lord.

Third Sunday of Easter

APRIL 13, 1997   MAY 7, 2000   MAY 4, 2003

FIRST READING: Acts 3:12–19

A reading from Acts:

[12]Peter addressed the people,
"You Israelites, why do you wonder at this,
or why do you stare at us,
as though by our own power or piety we had made this man walk?
[13]The God of Abraham, the God of Isaac, and the God of Jacob,
the God of our ancestors has glorified his servant Jesus,
whom you handed over and rejected in the presence of Pilate,
though he had decided to release him.
[14]But you rejected the Holy and Righteous One
and asked to have a murderer given to you,
[15]and you killed the Author of life,
whom God raised from the dead.
To this we are witnesses.
[16]And by faith in his name, his name itself has made this man strong,
whom you see and know;
and the faith that is through Jesus
has given him this perfect health in the presence of all of you.

[17]"And now, friends, I know that you acted in ignorance, as did also your
rulers.
[18]In this way God fulfilled what he had foretold through all the prophets,
that his Messiah would suffer.
[19]Repent therefore, and turn to God
so that your sins may be wiped out."

The word of the Lord.

PSALMODY: Psalm 4

SECOND READING: 1 JOHN 3:1–7

A reading from First John:

[1]See what love the Father has given us,
that we should be called children of God;
and that is what we are.
The reason the world does not know us is that it did not know him.
[2]Beloved, we are God's children now;
what we will be has not yet been revealed.
What we do know is this:
when he is revealed, we will be like him,
for we will see him as he is.
[3]And all who have this hope in him purify themselves,
just as he is pure.

[4]Everyone who commits sin is guilty of lawlessness;
sin is lawlessness.
[5]You know that he was revealed to take away sins,
and in him there is no sin.
[6]No one who abides in him sins;
no one who sins has either seen him or known him.
[7]Little children, let no one deceive you.
Everyone who does what is right is righteous, just as he is righteous.

The word of the Lord.

The Holy Gospel according to Luke, the 24th chapter.

[36b]Jesus himself stood among them and said to them,
"Peace be with you."
[37]They were startled and terrified,
and thought that they were seeing a ghost.
[38]He said to them,
"Why are you frightened, and why do doubts arise in your hearts?
[39]Look at my hands and my feet; see that it is I myself.
Touch me and see;
for a ghost does not have flesh and bones as you see that I have."
[40]And when he had said this, he showed them his hands and his feet.
[41]While in their joy they were disbelieving and still wondering,
he said to them, "Have you anything here to eat?"
[42]They gave him a piece of broiled fish,
[43]and he took it and ate in their presence.

[44]Then he said to them,
"These are my words that I spoke to you while I was still with you—
that everything written about me
in the law of Moses, the prophets, and the psalms must be fulfilled."
[45]Then he opened their minds to understand the scriptures,
[46]and he said to them,
"Thus it is written, that the Messiah is to suffer
and to rise from the dead on the third day,
[47]and that repentance and forgiveness of sins
is to be proclaimed in his name to all nations,
beginning from Jerusalem.
[48]You are witnesses of these things."

The Gospel of the Lord.

FOURTH SUNDAY OF EASTER

APRIL 20, 1997   MAY 14, 2000   MAY 11, 2003

FIRST READING: ACTS 4:5–12

A reading from Acts:

[5]The next day their rulers, elders, and scribes assembled in Jerusalem,
[6]with Annas the high priest, Caiaphas, John, and Alexander,
and all who were of the high-priestly family.
[7]When they had made the prisoners Peter and John stand in their midst,
     they inquired,
"By what power or by what name did you do this?"
[8]Then Peter, filled with the Holy Spirit, said to them,
"Rulers of the people and elders,
[9]if we are questioned today because of a good deed done to someone who was
     sick
and are asked how this man has been healed,
[10]let it be known to all of you, and to all the people of Israel,
that this man is standing before you in good health
by the name of Jesus Christ of Nazareth,
whom you crucified, whom God raised from the dead.
[11]This Jesus is
    'the stone that was rejected by you, the builders;
      it has become the cornerstone.'
[12]There is salvation in no one else,
for there is no other name under heaven given among mortals
by which we must be saved."

The word of the Lord.

PSALMODY: PSALM 23

SECOND READING: 1 JOHN 3:16–24

A reading from First John:

[16]We know love by this,
that Jesus Christ laid down his life for us—
and we ought to lay down our lives for one another.
[17]How does God's love abide in anyone who has the world's goods
and sees a brother or sister in need and yet refuses help?

[18]Little children, let us love, not in word or speech,
but in truth and action.
[19]And by this we will know that we are from the truth
and will reassure our hearts before him [20]whenever our hearts condemn us;
for God is greater than our hearts, and he knows everything.
[21]Beloved, if our hearts do not condemn us,
we have boldness before God;
[22]and we receive from him whatever we ask,
because we obey his commandments and do what pleases him.

[23]And this is his commandment,
that we should believe in the name of his Son Jesus Christ
and love one another, just as he has commanded us.
[24]All who obey his commandments abide in him,
and he abides in them.
And by this we know that he abides in us,
by the Spirit that he has given us.

The word of the Lord.

GOSPEL: John 10:11–18

The Holy Gospel according to John, the tenth chapter.

Jesus said:
[11]"I am the good shepherd.
The good shepherd lays down his life for the sheep.
[12]The hired hand, who is not the shepherd and does not own the sheep,
sees the wolf coming and leaves the sheep and runs away—
and the wolf snatches them and scatters them.
[13]The hired hand runs away because a hired hand does not care for the sheep.
[14]I am the good shepherd.
I know my own and my own know me,
[15]just as the Father knows me and I know the Father.
And I lay down my life for the sheep.
[16]I have other sheep that do not belong to this fold.
I must bring them also, and they will listen to my voice.
So there will be one flock, one shepherd.
[17]For this reason the Father loves me,
because I lay down my life in order to take it up again.
[18]No one takes it from me, but I lay it down of my own accord.
I have power to lay it down, and I have power to take it up again.
I have received this command from my Father."

The Gospel of the Lord.

FIFTH SUNDAY OF EASTER

APRIL 27, 1997   MAY 21, 2000   MAY 18, 2003

FIRST READING: ACTS 8:26–40

A reading from Acts:

26An angel of the Lord said to Philip,
"Get up and go toward the south
to the road that goes down from Jerusalem to Gaza."
(This is a wilderness road.)
27So he got up and went.
Now there was an Ethiopian eunuch,
a court official of the Candace, queen of the Ethiopians,
in charge of her entire treasury.
He had come to Jerusalem to worship 28and was returning home;
seated in his chariot, he was reading the prophet Isaiah.
29Then the Spirit said to Philip, "Go over to this chariot and join it."
30So Philip ran up to it and heard him reading the prophet Isaiah.
He asked, "Do you understand what you are reading?"
31He replied, "How can I, unless someone guides me?"
And he invited Philip to get in and sit beside him.
32Now the passage of the scripture that he was reading was this:
   "Like a sheep he was led to the slaughter,
     and like a lamb silent before its shearer,
      so he does not open his mouth.
   33In his humiliation justice was denied him.
     Who can describe his generation?
      For his life is taken away from the earth."
34The eunuch asked Philip,
"About whom, may I ask you, does the prophet say this,
about himself or about someone else?"
35Then Philip began to speak,
and starting with this scripture,
he proclaimed to him the good news about Jesus.

36As they were going along the road, they came to some water;
and the eunuch said, "Look, here is water!
What is to prevent me from being baptized?"
38He commanded the chariot to stop,
and both of them, Philip and the eunuch, went down into the water,
and Philip baptized him.

39When they came up out of the water,
the Spirit of the Lord snatched Philip away;
the eunuch saw him no more, and went on his way rejoicing.
40But Philip found himself at Azotus,
and as he was passing through the region,
he proclaimed the good news to all the towns until he came to Caesarea.

The word of the Lord.

PSALMODY: PSALM 22:25–31   *Psalm 22:24–30* LBW/BCP

SECOND READING: 1 JOHN 4:7–21

A reading from First John:

7Beloved, let us love one another, because love is from God;
everyone who loves is born of God and knows God.
8Whoever does not love does not know God, for God is love.
9God's love was revealed among us in this way:
God sent his only Son into the world so that we might live through him.
10In this is love,
not that we loved God but that he loved us
and sent his Son to be the atoning sacrifice for our sins.
11Beloved, since God loved us so much,
we also ought to love one another.
12No one has ever seen God;
if we love one another,
God lives in us, and his love is perfected in us.

13By this we know that we abide in him and he in us,
because he has given us of his Spirit.
14And we have seen and do testify
that the Father has sent his Son as the Savior of the world.
15God abides in those who confess that Jesus is the Son of God,
and they abide in God.
16So we have known and believe the love that God has for us.

God is love, and those who abide in love abide in God,
and God abides in them.
17Love has been perfected among us in this:
that we may have boldness on the day of judgment,
because as he is, so are we in this world.
18There is no fear in love, but perfect love casts out fear;
for fear has to do with punishment,
and whoever fears has not reached perfection in love.
19We love because he first loved us.
20Those who say, "I love God," and hate their brothers or sisters, are liars;

for those who do not love a brother or sister whom they have seen,
cannot love God whom they have not seen.
[21]The commandment we have from him is this:
those who love God must love their brothers and sisters also.

The word of the Lord.

GOSPEL: JOHN 15:1–8

The Holy Gospel according to John, the 15th chapter.

Jesus said:
[1]"I am the true vine, and my Father is the vinegrower.
[2]He removes every branch in me that bears no fruit.
Every branch that bears fruit he prunes to make it bear more fruit.
[3]You have already been cleansed by the word that I have spoken to you.
[4]Abide in me as I abide in you.
Just as the branch cannot bear fruit by itself unless it abides in the vine,
neither can you unless you abide in me.
[5]I am the vine, you are the branches.
Those who abide in me and I in them bear much fruit,
because apart from me you can do nothing.
[6]Whoever does not abide in me is thrown away like a branch and withers;
such branches are gathered, thrown into the fire, and burned.

[7]"If you abide in me, and my words abide in you,
ask for whatever you wish, and it will be done for you.
[8]My Father is glorified by this,
that you bear much fruit and become my disciples."

The Gospel of the Lord.

SIXTH SUNDAY OF EASTER

MAY 4, 1997   MAY 28, 2000   MAY 25, 2003

FIRST READING: ACTS 10:44–48

A reading from Acts:

44While Peter was still speaking,
the Holy Spirit fell upon all who heard the word.
45The circumcised believers who had come with Peter
were astounded that the gift of the Holy Spirit
had been poured out even on the Gentiles,
46for they heard them speaking in tongues and extolling God.
Then Peter said,
47"Can anyone withhold the water for baptizing these people
who have received the Holy Spirit just as we have?"
48So he ordered them to be baptized in the name of Jesus Christ.
Then they invited him to stay for several days.

The word of the Lord.

PSALMODY: PSALM 98

SECOND READING: 1 JOHN 5:1–6

A reading from First John:

1Everyone who believes that Jesus is the Christ has been born of God,
and everyone who loves the parent loves the child.
2By this we know that we love the children of God,
when we love God and obey his commandments.
3For the love of God is this,
that we obey his commandments.
And his commandments are not burdensome,
4for whatever is born of God conquers the world.
And this is the victory that conquers the world, our faith.
5Who is it that conquers the world
but the one who believes that Jesus is the Son of God?

6This is the one who came by water and blood, Jesus Christ,
not with the water only but with the water and the blood.
And the Spirit is the one that testifies,
for the Spirit is the truth.

The word of the Lord.

GOSPEL: JOHN 15:9–17

The Holy Gospel according to John, the 15th chapter.

Jesus said:
9"As the Father has loved me, so I have loved you;
abide in my love.
10If you keep my commandments, you will abide in my love,
just as I have kept my Father's commandments and abide in his love.
11I have said these things to you so that my joy may be in you,
and that your joy may be complete.

12"This is my commandment,
that you love one another as I have loved you.
13No one has greater love than this, to lay down one's life for one's friends.
14You are my friends if you do what I command you.
15I do not call you servants any longer,
because the servant does not know what the master is doing;
but I have called you friends,
because I have made known to you everything that I have heard from my
          Father.
16You did not choose me but I chose you.
And I appointed you to go and bear fruit,
fruit that will last,
so that the Father will give you whatever you ask him in my name.
17I am giving you these commands so that you may love one another."

The Gospel of the Lord.

THE ASCENSION OF OUR LORD

MAY 8, 1997   JUNE 1, 2000   MAY 29, 2003

FIRST READING: ACTS 1:1–11

A reading from Acts:

Luke writes:
[1]In the first book, Theophilus,
I wrote about all that Jesus did and taught from the beginning
[2]until the day when he was taken up to heaven,
after giving instructions through the Holy Spirit
to the apostles whom he had chosen.
[3]After his suffering he presented himself alive to them
by many convincing proofs,
appearing to them during forty days
and speaking about the kingdom of God.
[4]While staying with them, he ordered them not to leave Jerusalem,
but to wait there for the promise of the Father.
"This," he said, "is what you have heard from me;
[5]for John baptized with water,
but you will be baptized with the Holy Spirit not many days from now."

[6]So when they had come together, they asked him,
"Lord, is this the time when you will restore the kingdom to Israel?"
[7]He replied, "It is not for you to know the times or periods
that the Father has set by his own authority.
[8]But you will receive power when the Holy Spirit has come upon you;
and you will be my witnesses
in Jerusalem, in all Judea and Samaria, and to the ends of the earth."
[9]When he had said this, as they were watching,
he was lifted up, and a cloud took him out of their sight.

[10]While he was going and they were gazing up toward heaven,
suddenly two men in white robes stood by them.
[11]They said, "Men of Galilee,
why do you stand looking up toward heaven?
This Jesus, who has been taken up from you into heaven,
will come in the same way as you saw him go into heaven."

The word of the Lord.

PSALMODY: PSALM 47 or PSALM 93

SECOND READING: Ephesians 1:15–23

A reading from Ephesians:

^{15}I have heard of your faith in the Lord Jesus
and your love toward all the saints,
and for this reason ^{16}I do not cease to give thanks for you
as I remember you in my prayers.
^{17}I pray that the God of our Lord Jesus Christ, the Father of glory,
may give you a spirit of wisdom and revelation as you come to know him,
^{18}so that, with the eyes of your heart enlightened,
you may know what is the hope to which he has called you,
what are the riches of his glorious inheritance among the saints,
^{19}and what is the immeasurable greatness of his power for us who believe,
according to the working of his great power.

^{20}God put this power to work in Christ when he raised him from the dead
and seated him at his right hand in the heavenly places,
^{21}far above all rule and authority and power and dominion,
and above every name that is named,
not only in this age but also in the age to come.
^{22}And he has put all things under his feet
and has made him the head over all things for the church,
^{23}which is his body, the fullness of him who fills all in all.

The word of the Lord.

GOSPEL: LUKE 24:44–53

The Holy Gospel according to Luke, the 24th chapter.

[44]Jesus said to the eleven and those with them,
"These are my words that I spoke to you while I was still with you—
that everything written about me
in the law of Moses, the prophets, and the psalms must be fulfilled."
[45]Then he opened their minds to understand the scriptures,
[46]and he said to them,
"Thus it is written, that the Messiah is to suffer
and to rise from the dead on the third day,
[47]and that repentance and forgiveness of sins
is to be proclaimed in his name to all nations,
beginning from Jerusalem.
[48]You are witnesses of these things.
[49]And see, I am sending upon you what my Father promised;
so stay here in the city until you have been clothed with power from on high."

[50]Then he led them out as far as Bethany,
and, lifting up his hands, he blessed them.
[51]While he was blessing them, he withdrew from them
and was carried up into heaven.
[52]And they worshiped him, and returned to Jerusalem with great joy;
[53]and they were continually in the temple blessing God.

The Gospel of the Lord.

Seventh Sunday of Easter

FIRST READING: Acts 1:15–17, 21–26

A reading from Acts:

[15]In those days Peter stood up among the believers
(together the crowd numbered about one hundred twenty persons)
and said, [16]"Friends, the scripture had to be fulfilled,
which the Holy Spirit through David foretold concerning Judas,
who became a guide for those who arrested Jesus—
[17]for he was numbered among us and was allotted his share in this ministry.

[21]"So one of the men who have accompanied us
during all the time that the Lord Jesus went in and out among us,
[22]beginning from the baptism of John
until the day when he was taken up from us—
one of these must become a witness with us to his resurrection."
[23]So they proposed two,
Joseph called Barsabbas, who was also known as Justus,
and Matthias.
[24]Then they prayed and said,
"Lord, you know everyone's heart.
Show us which one of these two you have chosen
[25]to take the place in this ministry and apostleship
from which Judas turned aside to go to his own place."
[26]And they cast lots for them, and the lot fell on Matthias;
and he was added to the eleven apostles.

The word of the Lord.

PSALMODY: Psalm 1

SECOND READING: 1 John 5:9–13

A reading from First John:

⁹If we receive human testimony, the testimony of God is greater;
for this is the testimony of God that he has testified to his Son.
¹⁰Those who believe in the Son of God have the testimony in their hearts.
Those who do not believe in God have made him a liar
by not believing in the testimony that God has given concerning his Son.
¹¹And this is the testimony:
God gave us eternal life, and this life is in his Son.
¹²Whoever has the Son has life;
whoever does not have the Son of God does not have life.

¹³I write these things to you who believe in the name of the Son of God,
so that you may know that you have eternal life.

The word of the Lord.

The Holy Gospel according to John, the 17th chapter.

Jesus prayed:
⁶"I have made your name known to those whom you gave me from the world.
They were yours, and you gave them to me,
and they have kept your word.
⁷Now they know that everything you have given me is from you;
⁸for the words that you gave to me I have given to them,
and they have received them and know in truth that I came from you;
and they have believed that you sent me.
⁹I am asking on their behalf;
I am not asking on behalf of the world,
but on behalf of those whom you gave me, because they are yours.
¹⁰All mine are yours, and yours are mine;
and I have been glorified in them.
¹¹And now I am no longer in the world, but they are in the world,
and I am coming to you.

"Holy Father, protect them in your name that you have given me,
so that they may be one, as we are one.
¹²While I was with them,
I protected them in your name that you have given me.
I guarded them, and not one of them was lost except the one destined to be
        lost,
so that the scripture might be fulfilled.
¹³But now I am coming to you, and I speak these things in the world
so that they may have my joy made complete in themselves.
¹⁴I have given them your word,
and the world has hated them because they do not belong to the world,
just as I do not belong to the world.
¹⁵I am not asking you to take them out of the world,
but I ask you to protect them from the evil one.
¹⁶They do not belong to the world, just as I do not belong to the world.
¹⁷Sanctify them in the truth; your word is truth.
¹⁸As you have sent me into the world,
so I have sent them into the world.
¹⁹And for their sakes I sanctify myself,
so that they also may be sanctified in truth."

The Gospel of the Lord.

VIGIL OF PENTECOST

FIRST READING: EXODUS 19:1–9
Or Acts 2:1–11, following

A reading from Exodus:

[1]On the third new moon after the Israelites had gone out of the land of Egypt,
on that very day, they came into the wilderness of Sinai.
[2]They had journeyed from Rephidim,
entered the wilderness of Sinai, and camped in the wilderness;
Israel camped there in front of the mountain.

[3]Then Moses went up to God;
the LORD called to him from the mountain, saying,
"Thus you shall say to the house of Jacob, and tell the Israelites:
[4]You have seen what I did to the Egyptians,
and how I bore you on eagles' wings and brought you to myself.
[5]Now therefore, if you obey my voice and keep my covenant,
you shall be my treasured possession out of all the peoples.
Indeed, the whole earth is mine,
[6]but you shall be for me a priestly kingdom and a holy nation.
These are the words that you shall speak to the Israelites."

[7]So Moses came, summoned the elders of the people,
and set before them all these words that the LORD had commanded him.
[8]The people all answered as one:
"Everything that the LORD has spoken we will do."
Moses reported the words of the people to the LORD.
[9]Then the LORD said to Moses,
"I am going to come to you in a dense cloud,
in order that the people may hear when I speak with you
and so trust you ever after."

The word of the Lord.

OR: ACTS 2:1–11

A reading from Acts:

¹When the day of Pentecost had come, they were all together in one place.
²And suddenly from heaven there came a sound like the rush of a violent wind,
and it filled the entire house where they were sitting.
³Divided tongues, as of fire, appeared among them,
and a tongue rested on each of them.
⁴All of them were filled with the Holy Spirit
and began to speak in other languages, as the Spirit gave them ability.

⁵Now there were devout Jews from every nation under heaven
        living in Jerusalem.
⁶And at this sound the crowd gathered and was bewildered,
because each one heard them speaking in the native language of each.
⁷Amazed and astonished, they asked,
"Are not all these who are speaking Galileans?
⁸And how is it that we hear, each of us, in our own native language?
⁹Parthians, Medes, Elamites,
and residents of Mesopotamia, Judea and Cappadocia, Pontus and Asia,
¹⁰Phrygia and Pamphylia, Egypt and the parts of Libya belonging to Cyrene,
and visitors from Rome, both Jews and proselytes, ¹¹Cretans and Arabs—
in our own languages we hear them speaking about God's deeds of power."

The word of the Lord.

PSALMODY: PSALM 33:12–22 or PSALM 130

SECOND READING: ROMANS 8:14–17, 22–27

A reading from Romans:

¹⁴All who are led by the Spirit of God are children of God.
¹⁵For you did not receive a spirit of slavery to fall back into fear,
but you have received a spirit of adoption.
When we cry, "Abba! Father!"
¹⁶it is that very Spirit bearing witness with our spirit
that we are children of God,
¹⁷and if children, then heirs,
heirs of God and joint heirs with Christ—
if, in fact, we suffer with him
so that we may also be glorified with him.

²²We know that the whole creation has been groaning in labor pains until now;
²³and not only the creation,
but we ourselves, who have the first fruits of the Spirit,
groan inwardly while we wait for adoption, the redemption of our bodies.
²⁴For in hope we were saved.
Now hope that is seen is not hope.
For who hopes for what is seen?
²⁵But if we hope for what we do not see, we wait for it with patience.

²⁶Likewise the Spirit helps us in our weakness;
for we do not know how to pray as we ought,
but that very Spirit intercedes with sighs too deep for words.
²⁷And God, who searches the heart,
knows what is the mind of the Spirit,
because the Spirit intercedes for the saints according to the will of God.

The word of the Lord.

GOSPEL: JOHN 7:37–39

The Holy Gospel according to John, the seventh chapter.

³⁷On the last day of the festival of Booths, the great day,
while Jesus was standing in the temple, he cried out,
"Let anyone who is thirsty come to me,
³⁸and let the one who believes in me drink.
As the scripture has said,
'Out of the believer's heart shall flow rivers of living water.' "
³⁹Now he said this about the Spirit,
which believers in him were to receive;
for as yet there was no Spirit,
because Jesus was not yet glorified.

The Gospel of the Lord.

THE DAY OF PENTECOST

MAY 18, 1997   JUNE 11, 2000   JUNE 8, 2003

FIRST READING: ACTS 2:1–21
Or Ezekiel 37:1–14, following

A reading from Acts:

¹When the day of Pentecost had come, they were all together in one place.
²And suddenly from heaven there came a sound like the rush of a violent
    wind,
and it filled the entire house where they were sitting.
³Divided tongues, as of fire, appeared among them,
and a tongue rested on each of them.
⁴All of them were filled with the Holy Spirit
and began to speak in other languages, as the Spirit gave them ability.

⁵Now there were devout Jews from every nation under heaven living
    in Jerusalem.
⁶And at this sound the crowd gathered and was bewildered,
because each one heard them speaking in the native language of each.
⁷Amazed and astonished, they asked,
"Are not all these who are speaking Galileans?
⁸And how is it that we hear, each of us, in our own native language?
⁹Parthians, Medes, Elamites,
and residents of Mesopotamia, Judea and Cappadocia, Pontus and Asia,
¹⁰Phrygia and Pamphylia, Egypt and the parts of Libya belonging to Cyrene,
and visitors from Rome, both Jews and proselytes, ¹¹Cretans and Arabs—
in our own languages we hear them speaking about God's deeds of power."

¹²All were amazed and perplexed, saying to one another,
"What does this mean?"
¹³But others sneered and said, "They are filled with new wine."

¹⁴But Peter, standing with the eleven, raised his voice and addressed them,
"Men of Judea and all who live in Jerusalem,
let this be known to you, and listen to what I say.
¹⁵Indeed, these are not drunk, as you suppose,
for it is only nine o'clock in the morning.
¹⁶No, this is what was spoken through the prophet Joel:
    ¹⁷'In the last days it will be, God declares,
    that I will pour out my Spirit upon all flesh,

and your sons and your daughters shall prophesy,
and your young men shall see visions,
    and your old men shall dream dreams.
18Even upon my slaves, both men and women,
    in those days I will pour out my Spirit;
        and they shall prophesy.
19And I will show portents in the heaven above
    and signs on the earth below,
        blood, and fire, and smoky mist.
20The sun shall be turned to darkness
    and the moon to blood,
        before the coming of the Lord's great and glorious day.
21Then everyone who calls on the name of the Lord shall be saved.' "

The word of the Lord.

OR: Ezekiel 37:1–14

A reading from Ezekiel:

1The hand of the LORD came upon me,
and he brought me out by the spirit of the LORD
and set me down in the middle of a valley;
it was full of bones.
2He led me all around them;
there were very many lying in the valley, and they were very dry.
3He said to me, "Mortal, can these bones live?"
I answered, "O Lord GOD, you know."

4Then he said to me, "Prophesy to these bones, and say to them:
O dry bones, hear the word of the LORD.
5Thus says the Lord GOD to these bones:
I will cause breath to enter you, and you shall live.
6I will lay sinews on you,
and will cause flesh to come upon you, and cover you with skin,
and put breath in you, and you shall live;
and you shall know that I am the LORD."

7So I prophesied as I had been commanded;
and as I prophesied, suddenly there was a noise, a rattling,
and the bones came together, bone to its bone.
8I looked, and there were sinews on them,
and flesh had come upon them, and skin had covered them;
but there was no breath in them.
9Then he said to me,
"Prophesy to the breath, prophesy, mortal, and say to the breath:
Thus says the Lord GOD:
Come from the four winds, O breath,

and breathe upon these slain, that they may live."
¹⁰I prophesied as he commanded me,
and the breath came into them,
and they lived, and stood on their feet, a vast multitude.

¹¹Then he said to me,
"Mortal, these bones are the whole house of Israel.
They say, 'Our bones are dried up, and our hope is lost;
we are cut off completely.'
¹²Therefore prophesy, and say to them,
Thus says the Lord GOD:
I am going to open your graves,
and bring you up from your graves, O my people;
and I will bring you back to the land of Israel.
¹³And you shall know that I am the LORD,
when I open your graves,
and bring you up from your graves, O my people.
¹⁴I will put my spirit within you, and you shall live,
and I will place you on your own soil;
then you shall know that I, the LORD, have spoken and will act,
says the LORD."

The word of the Lord.

PSALMODY: PSALM 104:24–34, 35b   *Psalm 104:25–35, 37* LBW/BCP

SECOND READING: ROMANS 8:22–27
Or Acts 2:1–21, following

A reading from Romans:

²²We know that the whole creation has been groaning in labor pains until now;
²³and not only the creation,
but we ourselves, who have the first fruits of the Spirit,
groan inwardly while we wait for adoption, the redemption of our bodies.
²⁴For in hope we were saved.
Now hope that is seen is not hope.
For who hopes for what is seen?
²⁵But if we hope for what we do not see, we wait for it with patience.

²⁶Likewise the Spirit helps us in our weakness;
for we do not know how to pray as we ought,
but that very Spirit intercedes with sighs too deep for words.
²⁷And God, who searches the heart,
knows what is the mind of the Spirit,
because the Spirit intercedes for the saints according to the will of God.

The word of the Lord.

A reading from Acts:

¹When the day of Pentecost had come, they were all together in one place.
²And suddenly from heaven there came a sound like the rush of a violent
       wind,
and it filled the entire house where they were sitting.
³Divided tongues, as of fire, appeared among them,
and a tongue rested on each of them.
⁴All of them were filled with the Holy Spirit
and began to speak in other languages, as the Spirit gave them ability.

⁵Now there were devout Jews from every nation under heaven living
       in Jerusalem.
⁶And at this sound the crowd gathered and was bewildered,
because each one heard them speaking in the native language of each.
⁷Amazed and astonished, they asked,
"Are not all these who are speaking Galileans?
⁸And how is it that we hear, each of us, in our own native language?
⁹Parthians, Medes, Elamites,
and residents of Mesopotamia, Judea and Cappadocia, Pontus and Asia,
¹⁰Phrygia and Pamphylia, Egypt and the parts of Libya belonging to Cyrene,
and visitors from Rome, both Jews and proselytes, ¹¹Cretans and Arabs—
in our own languages we hear them speaking about God's deeds of power."

¹²All were amazed and perplexed, saying to one another,
"What does this mean?"
¹³But others sneered and said, "They are filled with new wine."

¹⁴But Peter, standing with the eleven, raised his voice and addressed them,
"Men of Judea and all who live in Jerusalem,
let this be known to you, and listen to what I say.
¹⁵Indeed, these are not drunk, as you suppose,
for it is only nine o'clock in the morning.
¹⁶No, this is what was spoken through the prophet Joel:
    ¹⁷'In the last days it will be, God declares,
    that I will pour out my Spirit upon all flesh,
        and your sons and your daughters shall prophesy,
    and your young men shall see visions,
        and your old men shall dream dreams.
    ¹⁸Even upon my slaves, both men and women,
        in those days I will pour out my Spirit;
           and they shall prophesy.
    ¹⁹And I will show portents in the heaven above
        and signs on the earth below,
           blood, and fire, and smoky mist.
    ²⁰The sun shall be turned to darkness

and the moon to blood,
before the coming of the Lord's great and glorious day.
[21]Then everyone who calls on the name of the Lord shall be saved.' "

The word of the Lord.

GOSPEL: JOHN 15:26–27; 16:4b–15

The Holy Gospel according to John, the 15th and 16th chapters.

Jesus said,
[26]"When the Advocate comes, whom I will send to you from the Father,
the Spirit of truth who comes from the Father,
he will testify on my behalf.
[27]You also are to testify because you have been with me from the beginning.

[16:4b]"I did not say these things to you from the beginning,
because I was with you.
[5]But now I am going to him who sent me;
yet none of you asks me, 'Where are you going?'
[6]But because I have said these things to you,
sorrow has filled your hearts.
[7]Nevertheless I tell you the truth:
it is to your advantage that I go away,
for if I do not go away, the Advocate will not come to you;
but if I go, I will send him to you.
[8]And when he comes,
he will prove the world wrong about sin and righteousness and judgment:
[9]about sin, because they do not believe in me;
[10]about righteousness, because I am going to the Father
and you will see me no longer;
[11]about judgment, because the ruler of this world has been condemned.

[12]"I still have many things to say to you,
but you cannot bear them now.
[13]When the Spirit of truth comes,
he will guide you into all the truth;
for he will not speak on his own, but will speak whatever he hears,
and he will declare to you the things that are to come.
[14]He will glorify me,
because he will take what is mine and declare it to you.
[15]All that the Father has is mine.
For this reason I said that he will take what is mine and declare it to you."

The Gospel of the Lord.

SEASON AFTER PENTECOST

THE HOLY TRINITY
First Sunday after Pentecost

MAY 25, 1997   JUNE 18, 2000   JUNE 15, 2003

FIRST READING: Isaiah 6:1–8

A reading from Isaiah:

¹In the year that King Uzziah died,
I saw the Lord sitting on a throne, high and lofty;
and the hem of his robe filled the temple.
²Seraphs were in attendance above him;
each had six wings:
with two they covered their faces,
and with two they covered their feet,
and with two they flew.
³And one called to another and said:
    "Holy, holy, holy is the Lord of hosts;
    the whole earth is full of his glory."
⁴The pivots on the thresholds shook at the voices of those who called,
and the house filled with smoke.
⁵And I said: "Woe is me!
I am lost, for I am a man of unclean lips,
and I live among a people of unclean lips;
yet my eyes have seen the King, the Lord of hosts!"

⁶Then one of the seraphs flew to me,
holding a live coal that had been taken from the altar with a pair of tongs.
⁷The seraph touched my mouth with it and said:
"Now that this has touched your lips,
your guilt has departed and your sin is blotted out."
⁸Then I heard the voice of the Lord saying,
"Whom shall I send, and who will go for us?"
And I said, "Here am I; send me!"

The word of the Lord.

PSALMODY: Psalm 29

A reading from Romans:

^{12}Brothers and sisters,
we are debtors, not to the flesh, to live according to the flesh—
^{13}for if you live according to the flesh, you will die;
but if by the Spirit you put to death the deeds of the body,
you will live.
^{14}For all who are led by the Spirit of God are children of God.
^{15}For you did not receive a spirit of slavery to fall back into fear,
but you have received a spirit of adoption.
When we cry, "Abba! Father!"
^{16}it is that very Spirit bearing witness with our spirit that we are children
of God,
^{17}and if children, then heirs,
heirs of God and joint heirs with Christ—
if, in fact, we suffer with him so that we may also be glorified with him.

The word of the Lord.

GOSPEL: JOHN 3:1–17

The Holy Gospel according to John, the third chapter.

^{1}Now there was a Pharisee named Nicodemus, a leader of the Jews.
^{2}He came to Jesus by night and said to him,
"Rabbi, we know that you are a teacher who has come from God;
for no one can do these signs that you do apart from the presence of God."
^{3}Jesus answered him,
"Very truly, I tell you,
no one can see the kingdom of God without being born from above."

^{4}Nicodemus said to him,
"How can anyone be born after having grown old?
Can one enter a second time into the mother's womb and be born?"
^{5}Jesus answered,
"Very truly, I tell you,
no one can enter the kingdom of God without being born of water and Spirit.
^{6}What is born of the flesh is flesh,
and what is born of the Spirit is spirit.
^{7}Do not be astonished that I said to you,
'You must be born from above.'
^{8}The wind blows where it chooses, and you hear the sound of it,
but you do not know where it comes from or where it goes.
So it is with everyone who is born of the Spirit."

^{9}Nicodemus said to him,

"How can these things be?"
[10]Jesus answered him,
"Are you a teacher of Israel, and yet you do not understand these things?
[11]Very truly, I tell you,
we speak of what we know and testify to what we have seen;
yet you do not receive our testimony.
[12]If I have told you about earthly things and you do not believe,
how can you believe if I tell you about heavenly things?

[13]"No one has ascended into heaven
except the one who descended from heaven, the Son of Man.
[14]And just as Moses lifted up the serpent in the wilderness,
so must the Son of Man be lifted up,
[15]that whoever believes in him may have eternal life.

[16]"For God so loved the world that he gave his only Son,
so that everyone who believes in him may not perish
but may have eternal life.
[17]Indeed, God did not send the Son into the world to condemn the world,
but in order that the world might be saved through him."

The Gospel of the Lord.

SUNDAY BETWEEN
MAY 24 AND 28 INCLUSIVE
(if after Trinity Sunday)
PROPER 3

FIRST READING: HOSEA 2:14–20

A reading from Hosea:

> [14]I will now allure her, says the LORD,
>   and bring her into the wilderness,
>   and speak tenderly to her.
> [15]From there I will give her her vineyards,
>   and make the Valley of Achor a door of hope.
> There she shall respond as in the days of her youth,
>   as at the time when she came out of the land of Egypt.

> [16]On that day, says the LORD, you will call me, "My husband,"
> and no longer will you call me, "My Baal."
> [17]For I will remove the names of the Baals from her mouth,
> and they shall be mentioned by name no more.
> [18]I will make for you a covenant on that day with the wild animals,
>   the birds of the air, and the creeping things of the ground;
> and I will abolish the bow, the sword, and war from the land;
> and I will make you lie down in safety.
> [19]And I will take you for my wife forever;
> I will take you for my wife in righteousness and in justice,
> in steadfast love, and in mercy.
> [20]I will take you for my wife in faithfulness;
> and you shall know the LORD.

The word of the Lord.

PSALMODY: PSALM 103:1–13, 22

SECOND READING: 2 CORINTHIANS 3:1–6

A reading from Second Corinthians:

[1]Are we beginning to commend ourselves again?
Surely we do not need, as some do,
letters of recommendation to you or from you, do we?
[2]You yourselves are our letter,
written on our hearts, to be known and read by all;
[3]and you show that you are a letter of Christ,
prepared by us, written not with ink but with the Spirit of the living God,
not on tablets of stone but on tablets of human hearts.
[4]Such is the confidence that we have through Christ toward God.
[5]Not that we are competent of ourselves to claim anything as coming from us;
our competence is from God,
[6]who has made us competent to be ministers of a new covenant,
not of letter but of spirit;
for the letter kills, but the Spirit gives life.

The word of the Lord.

The Holy Gospel according to Mark, the second chapter.

[13]Jesus went out again beside the sea;
the whole crowd gathered around him, and he taught them.
[14]As he was walking along,
he saw Levi son of Alphaeus sitting at the tax booth,
and he said to him, "Follow me."
And he got up and followed him.

[15]And as he sat at dinner in Levi's house,
many tax collectors and sinners were also sitting with Jesus and his
        disciples—
for there were many who followed him.
[16]When the scribes of the Pharisees saw that he was eating with sinners and
        tax collectors,
they said to his disciples,
"Why does he eat with tax collectors and sinners?"
[17]When Jesus heard this, he said to them,
"Those who are well have no need of a physician, but those who are sick;
I have come to call not the righteous but sinners."

[18]Now John's disciples and the Pharisees were fasting;
and people came and said to him,
"Why do John's disciples and the disciples of the Pharisees fast,
but your disciples do not fast?"
[19]Jesus said to them,
"The wedding guests cannot fast while the bridegroom is with them, can they?
As long as they have the bridegroom with them, they cannot fast.
[20]The days will come when the bridegroom is taken away from them,
and then they will fast on that day.

[21]"No one sews a piece of unshrunk cloth on an old cloak;
otherwise, the patch pulls away from it, the new from the old, and a worse tear
        is made.
[22]And no one puts new wine into old wineskins;
otherwise, the wine will burst the skins,
and the wine is lost, and so are the skins;
but one puts new wine into fresh wineskins."

The Gospel of the Lord.

SUNDAY BETWEEN
MAY 29 AND JUNE 4 INCLUSIVE
(if after Trinity Sunday)

PROPER 4

JUNE 1, 1997

FIRST READING: DEUTERONOMY 5:12–15

A reading from Deuteronomy:

¹²Observe the sabbath day and keep it holy,
as the LORD your God commanded you.
¹³Six days you shall labor and do all your work.
¹⁴But the seventh day is a sabbath to the LORD your God;
you shall not do any work—
you, or your son or your daughter, or your male or female slave,
or your ox or your donkey, or any of your livestock,
or the resident alien in your towns,
so that your male and female slave may rest as well as you.
¹⁵Remember that you were a slave in the land of Egypt,
and the LORD your God brought you out from there
with a mighty hand and an outstretched arm;
therefore the LORD your God commanded you to keep the sabbath day.

The word of the Lord.

PSALMODY: PSALM 81:1–10

A reading from Second Corinthians:

[5]We do not proclaim ourselves;
we proclaim Jesus Christ as Lord
and ourselves as your slaves for Jesus' sake.
[6]For it is the God who said, "Let light shine out of darkness,"
who has shone in our hearts
to give the light of the knowledge of the glory of God
in the face of Jesus Christ.

[7]But we have this treasure in clay jars,
so that it may be made clear
that this extraordinary power belongs to God
and does not come from us.
[8]We are afflicted in every way, but not crushed;
perplexed, but not driven to despair;
[9]persecuted, but not forsaken;
struck down, but not destroyed;
[10]always carrying in the body the death of Jesus,
so that the life of Jesus may also be made visible in our bodies.
[11]For while we live,
we are always being given up to death for Jesus' sake,
so that the life of Jesus may be made visible in our mortal flesh.
[12]So death is at work in us, but life in you.

The word of the Lord.

The Holy Gospel according to Mark, the second and third chapters.

²³One sabbath Jesus was going through the grainfields;
and as they made their way his disciples began to pluck heads of grain.
²⁴The Pharisees said to him,
"Look, why are they doing what is not lawful on the sabbath?"
²⁵And he said to them,
"Have you never read what David did
when he and his companions were hungry and in need of food?
²⁶He entered the house of God, when Abiathar was high priest,
and ate the bread of the Presence,
which it is not lawful for any but the priests to eat,
and he gave some to his companions."

²⁷Then he said to them,
"The sabbath was made for humankind,
and not humankind for the sabbath;
²⁸so the Son of Man is lord even of the sabbath."

³:¹Again he entered the synagogue,
and a man was there who had a withered hand.
²They watched him to see whether he would cure him on the sabbath,
so that they might accuse him.
³And he said to the man who had the withered hand,
"Come forward."
⁴Then he said to them,
"Is it lawful to do good or to do harm on the sabbath,
to save life or to kill?"
But they were silent.
⁵He looked around at them with anger;
he was grieved at their hardness of heart and said to the man,
"Stretch out your hand."
He stretched it out, and his hand was restored.
⁶The Pharisees went out
and immediately conspired with the Herodians against him,
how to destroy him.

The Gospel of the Lord.

SUNDAY BETWEEN
JUNE 5 AND 11 INCLUSIVE
(if after Trinity Sunday)

PROPER 5

JUNE 8, 1997

FIRST READING: GENESIS 3:8–15

A reading from Genesis:

[8]Adam and Eve heard the sound of the LORD God walking in the garden
at the time of the evening breeze,
and the man and his wife hid themselves
from the presence of the LORD God among the trees of the garden.
[9]But the LORD God called to the man,
and said to him, "Where are you?"
[10]He said,
"I heard the sound of you in the garden,
and I was afraid, because I was naked; and I hid myself."
[11]He said, "Who told you that you were naked?
Have you eaten from the tree of which I commanded you not to eat?"
[12]The man said, "The woman whom you gave to be with me,
she gave me fruit from the tree, and I ate."
[13]Then the LORD God said to the woman,
"What is this that you have done?"
The woman said, "The serpent tricked me, and I ate."

[14]The LORD God said to the serpent,
   "Because you have done this,
      cursed are you among all animals
      and among all wild creatures;
   upon your belly you shall go,
      and dust you shall eat
      all the days of your life.
[15]I will put enmity between you and the woman,
      and between your offspring and hers;
   he will strike your head,
      and you will strike his heel."

The word of the Lord.

PSALMODY: PSALM 130

SECOND READING: 2 CORINTHIANS 4:13—5:1

A reading from Second Corinthians:

¹³Just as we have the same spirit of faith that is in accordance with scripture—
"I believed, and so I spoke"—
we also believe, and so we speak,
¹⁴because we know that the one who raised the Lord Jesus
will raise us also with Jesus,
and will bring us with you into his presence.
¹⁵Yes, everything is for your sake,
so that grace, as it extends to more and more people,
may increase thanksgiving, to the glory of God.

¹⁶So we do not lose heart.
Even though our outer nature is wasting away,
our inner nature is being renewed day by day.
¹⁷For this slight momentary affliction
is preparing us for an eternal weight of glory beyond all measure,
¹⁸because we look not at what can be seen
but at what cannot be seen;
for what can be seen is temporary,
but what cannot be seen is eternal.
⁵:¹For we know that if the earthly tent we live in is destroyed,
we have a building from God,
a house not made with hands, eternal in the heavens.

The word of the Lord.

GOSPEL: MARK 3:20–35

The Holy Gospel according to Mark, the third chapter.

Jesus went home;
[20]and the crowd came together again,
so that Jesus and the disciples could not even eat.
[21]When his family heard it, they went out to restrain him,
for people were saying, "He has gone out of his mind."
[22]And the scribes who came down from Jerusalem said,
"He has Beelzebul,
and by the ruler of the demons he casts out demons."

[23]And he called them to him, and spoke to them in parables,
"How can Satan cast out Satan?
[24]If a kingdom is divided against itself, that kingdom cannot stand.
[25]And if a house is divided against itself,
that house will not be able to stand.
[26]And if Satan has risen up against himself and is divided,
he cannot stand, but his end has come.
[27]But no one can enter a strong man's house
and plunder his property without first tying up the strong man;
then indeed the house can be plundered.
[28]Truly I tell you, people will be forgiven for their sins
and whatever blasphemies they utter;
[29]but whoever blasphemes against the Holy Spirit can never have forgiveness,
but is guilty of an eternal sin"—
[30]for they had said, "He has an unclean spirit."

[31]Then his mother and his brothers came;
and standing outside, they sent to him and called him.
[32]A crowd was sitting around him; and they said to him,
"Your mother and your brothers and sisters are outside, asking for you."
[33]And he replied,
"Who are my mother and my brothers?"
[34]And looking at those who sat around him, he said,
"Here are my mother and my brothers!
[35]Whoever does the will of God is my brother and sister and mother."

The Gospel of the Lord.

SUNDAY BETWEEN
JUNE 12 AND 18 INCLUSIVE
(if after Trinity Sunday)

PROPER 6

JUNE 15, 1997

FIRST READING: EZEKIEL 17:22–24

A reading from Ezekiel:

²²Thus says the Lord GOD:
I myself will take a sprig
    from the lofty top of a cedar;
    I will set it out.
I will break off a tender one
    from the topmost of its young twigs;
I myself will plant it
    on a high and lofty mountain.
²³On the mountain height of Israel
    I will plant it,
in order that it may produce boughs and bear fruit,
    and become a noble cedar.
Under it every kind of bird will live;
    in the shade of its branches will nest
    winged creatures of every kind.
²⁴All the trees of the field shall know
    that I am the LORD.
I bring low the high tree,
    I make high the low tree;
I dry up the green tree
    and make the dry tree flourish.
I the LORD have spoken;
    I will accomplish it.

The word of the Lord.

PSALMODY: PSALM 92:1–4, 12–15
                                         Psalm 92:1–4, 11–14 LBW/BCP

SECOND READING: 2 Corinthians 5:6–10 [11–13] 14–17

A reading from Second Corinthians:

⁶So we are always confident;
even though we know that while we are at home in the body
we are away from the Lord—
⁷for we walk by faith, not by sight.
⁸Yes, we do have confidence,
and we would rather be away from the body and at home with the Lord.
⁹So whether we are at home or away,
we make it our aim to please him.
¹⁰For all of us must appear before the judgment seat of Christ,
so that each may receive recompense for what has been done in the body,
whether good or evil.

[¹¹Therefore, knowing the fear of the Lord,
we try to persuade others;
but we ourselves are well known to God,
and I hope that we are also well known to your consciences.
¹²We are not commending ourselves to you again,
but giving you an opportunity to boast about us,
so that you may be able to answer those who boast in outward appearance
and not in the heart.
¹³For if we are beside ourselves, it is for God;
if we are in our right mind, it is for you.]

¹⁴For the love of Christ urges us on,
because we are convinced that one has died for all;
therefore all have died.
¹⁵And he died for all,
so that those who live might live no longer for themselves,
but for him who died and was raised for them.

¹⁶From now on, therefore,
we regard no one from a human point of view;
even though we once knew Christ from a human point of view,
we know him no longer in that way.
¹⁷So if anyone is in Christ, there is a new creation:
everything old has passed away;
see, everything has become new!

The word of the Lord.

GOSPEL: MARK 4:26–34

The Holy Gospel according to Mark, the fourth chapter.

[26]Jesus said,
"The kingdom of God is as if someone would scatter seed on the ground,
[27]and would sleep and rise night and day,
and the seed would sprout and grow,
he does not know how.
[28]The earth produces of itself, first the stalk,
then the head, then the full grain in the head.
[29]But when the grain is ripe, at once he goes in with his sickle,
because the harvest has come."

[30]He also said, "With what can we compare the kingdom of God,
or what parable will we use for it?
[31]It is like a mustard seed, which, when sown upon the ground,
is the smallest of all the seeds on earth;
[32]yet when it is sown it grows up and becomes the greatest of all shrubs,
and puts forth large branches,
so that the birds of the air can make nests in its shade."

[33]With many such parables he spoke the word to them,
as they were able to hear it;
[34]he did not speak to them except in parables,
but he explained everything in private to his disciples.

The Gospel of the Lord.

SUNDAY BETWEEN
JUNE 19 AND 25 INCLUSIVE
(if after Trinity Sunday)

PROPER 7

JUNE 22, 1997   JUNE 25, 2000   JUNE 22, 2003

FIRST READING: JOB 38:1–11

A reading from Job:

¹The LORD answered Job out of the whirlwind:
²"Who is this that darkens counsel by words without knowledge?
³Gird up your loins like a man,
    I will question you, and you shall declare to me.

⁴"Where were you when I laid the foundation of the earth?
    Tell me, if you have understanding.
⁵Who determined its measurements—surely you know!
    Or who stretched the line upon it?
⁶On what were its bases sunk,
    or who laid its cornerstone
⁷when the morning stars sang together
    and all the heavenly beings shouted for joy?

⁸"Or who shut in the sea with doors
    when it burst out from the womb?—
⁹when I made the clouds its garment,
    and thick darkness its swaddling band,
¹⁰and prescribed bounds for it,
    and set bars and doors,
¹¹and said, 'Thus far shall you come, and no farther,
    and here shall your proud waves be stopped'?"

The word of the Lord.

PSALMODY: PSALM 107:1–3, 23–32

SECOND READING: 2 Corinthians 6:1–13

A reading from Second Corinthians:

[1]As we work together with him,
we urge you also not to accept the grace of God in vain.
[2]For he says,
"At an acceptable time I have listened to you,
and on a day of salvation I have helped you."
See, now is the acceptable time;
see, now is the day of salvation!
[3]We are putting no obstacle in anyone's way,
so that no fault may be found with our ministry,
[4]but as servants of God we have commended ourselves in every way:
through great endurance,
in afflictions, hardships, calamities, [5]beatings, imprisonments,
riots, labors, sleepless nights, hunger;
[6]by purity, knowledge, patience, kindness, holiness of spirit,
genuine love, [7]truthful speech, and the power of God;
with the weapons of righteousness for the right hand and for the left;
[8]in honor and dishonor,
in ill repute and good repute.
We are treated as impostors, and yet are true;
[9]as unknown, and yet are well known;
as dying, and see—we are alive;
as punished, and yet not killed;
[10]as sorrowful, yet always rejoicing;
as poor, yet making many rich;
as having nothing, and yet possessing everything.

[11]We have spoken frankly to you Corinthians;
our heart is wide open to you.
[12]There is no restriction in our affections, but only in yours.
[13]In return—I speak as to children—
open wide your hearts also.

The word of the Lord.

GOSPEL: MARK 4:35–41

The Holy Gospel according to Mark, the fourth chapter.

[35]When evening had come, Jesus said to the disciples,
"Let us go across to the other side."
[36]And leaving the crowd behind,
they took him with them in the boat, just as he was.
Other boats were with him.

[37]A great windstorm arose,
and the waves beat into the boat,
so that the boat was already being swamped.
[38]But he was in the stern, asleep on the cushion;
and they woke him up and said to him,
"Teacher, do you not care that we are perishing?"
[39]He woke up and rebuked the wind,
and said to the sea, "Peace! Be still!"
Then the wind ceased, and there was a dead calm.
[40]He said to them, "Why are you afraid?
Have you still no faith?"

[41]And they were filled with great awe and said to one another,
"Who then is this, that even the wind and the sea obey him?"

The Gospel of the Lord.

SUNDAY BETWEEN JUNE 26 AND JULY 2 INCLUSIVE

PROPER 8

JUNE 29, 1997   JULY 2, 2000   JUNE 29, 2003

FIRST READING: LAMENTATIONS 3:22–33

Alternate Reading: Wisdom of Solomon 1:13–15; 2:23–24 (p. 406)

A reading from Lamentations:

²²The steadfast love of the LORD never ceases,
 his mercies never come to an end;
²³they are new every morning;
 great is your faithfulness.
²⁴"The LORD is my portion," says my soul,
 "therefore I will hope in him."

²⁵The LORD is good to those who wait for him,
 to the soul that seeks him.
²⁶It is good that one should wait quietly
 for the salvation of the LORD.
²⁷It is good for one to bear
 the yoke in youth,
²⁸to sit alone in silence
 when the Lord has imposed it,
²⁹to put one's mouth to the dust
 (there may yet be hope),
³⁰to give one's cheek to the smiter,
 and be filled with insults.

³¹For the Lord will not
 reject forever.
³²Although he causes grief, he will have compassion
 according to the abundance of his steadfast love;
³³for he does not willingly afflict
 or grieve anyone.

The word of the Lord.

PSALMODY: PSALM 30

SECOND READING: 2 Corinthians 8:7–15

A reading from Second Corinthians:

[7]Now as you excel in everything—
in faith, in speech, in knowledge, in utmost eagerness,
and in our love for you—
so we want you to excel also in this generous undertaking.

[8]I do not say this as a command,
but I am testing the genuineness of your love against the earnestness
        of others.
[9]For you know the generous act of our Lord Jesus Christ,
that though he was rich,
yet for your sakes he became poor,
so that by his poverty you might become rich.
[10]And in this matter I am giving my advice:
it is appropriate for you who began last year not only to do something
but even to desire to do something—
[11]now finish doing it,
so that your eagerness may be matched by completing it according to your
        means.
[12]For if the eagerness is there,
the gift is acceptable according to what one has—
not according to what one does not have.
[13]I do not mean that there should be relief for others and pressure on you,
but it is a question of a fair balance between [14]your present abundance and
        their need,
so that their abundance may be for your need,
in order that there may be a fair balance.
[15]As it is written,
        "The one who had much did not have too much,
            and the one who had little did not have too little."

The word of the Lord.

The Holy Gospel according to Mark, the fifth chapter.

[21]When Jesus had crossed again in the boat to the other side,
a great crowd gathered around him; and he was by the sea.
[22]Then one of the leaders of the synagogue named Jairus came
and, when he saw him,
fell at his feet [23]and begged him repeatedly,
"My little daughter is at the point of death.
Come and lay your hands on her,
so that she may be made well, and live."
[24]So he went with him.

And a large crowd followed him and pressed in on him.
[25]Now there was a woman who had been suffering from hemorrhages
for twelve years.
[26]She had endured much under many physicians,
and had spent all that she had;
and she was no better, but rather grew worse.
[27]She had heard about Jesus,
and came up behind him in the crowd and touched his cloak,
[28]for she said, "If I but touch his clothes, I will be made well."
[29]Immediately her hemorrhage stopped;
and she felt in her body that she was healed of her disease.
[30]Immediately aware that power had gone forth from him,
Jesus turned about in the crowd and said,
"Who touched my clothes?"
[31]And his disciples said to him,
"You see the crowd pressing in on you;
how can you say, 'Who touched me?' "
[32]He looked all around to see who had done it.
[33]But the woman, knowing what had happened to her,
came in fear and trembling, fell down before him,
and told him the whole truth.
[34]He said to her, "Daughter, your faith has made you well;
go in peace, and be healed of your disease."

[35]While he was still speaking,
some people came from the leader's house to say,
"Your daughter is dead.
Why trouble the teacher any further?"
[36]But overhearing what they said,
Jesus said to the leader of the synagogue,
"Do not fear, only believe."
[37]He allowed no one to follow him
except Peter, James, and John, the brother of James.

[38]When they came to the house of the leader of the synagogue,
he saw a commotion, people weeping and wailing loudly.
[39]When he had entered, he said to them,
"Why do you make a commotion and weep?
The child is not dead but sleeping."
[40]And they laughed at him.
Then he put them all outside,
and took the child's father and mother and those who were with him,
and went in where the child was.
[41]He took her by the hand and said to her,
"Talitha cum," which means, "Little girl, get up!"
[42]And immediately the girl got up and began to walk about
(she was twelve years of age).
At this they were overcome with amazement.
[43]He strictly ordered them that no one should know this,
and told them to give her something to eat.

The Gospel of the Lord.

SUNDAY BETWEEN
JULY 3 AND 9 INCLUSIVE

PROPER 9

JULY 6, 1997   JULY 9, 2000   JULY 6, 2003

FIRST READING: EZEKIEL 2:1–5

A reading from Ezekiel:

[1]A voice said to me:
O mortal, stand up on your feet, and I will speak with you.
[2]And when he spoke to me,
a spirit entered into me and set me on my feet;
and I heard him speaking to me.
[3]He said to me,
Mortal, I am sending you to the people of Israel,
to a nation of rebels who have rebelled against me;
they and their ancestors have transgressed against me to this very day.
[4]The descendants are impudent and stubborn.
I am sending you to them, and you shall say to them,
"Thus says the Lord GOD."
[5]Whether they hear or refuse to hear
(for they are a rebellious house),
they shall know that there has been a prophet among them.

The word of the Lord.

PSALMODY: PSALM 123

SECOND READING: 2 Corinthians 12:2–10

A reading from Second Corinthians:

[2]I know a person in Christ who fourteen years ago was caught up to the third
        heaven—
whether in the body or out of the body I do not know; God knows.
[3]And I know that such a person—
whether in the body or out of the body I do not know; God knows—
[4]was caught up into Paradise and heard things that are not to be told,
that no mortal is permitted to repeat.
[5]On behalf of such a one I will boast,
but on my own behalf I will not boast, except of my weaknesses.
[6]But if I wish to boast, I will not be a fool,
for I will be speaking the truth.
But I refrain from it,
so that no one may think better of me than what is seen in me or heard
        from me,
[7]even considering the exceptional character of the revelations.

Therefore, to keep me from being too elated,
a thorn was given me in the flesh,
a messenger of Satan to torment me, to keep me from being too elated.
[8]Three times I appealed to the Lord about this,
that it would leave me,
[9]but he said to me,
"My grace is sufficient for you,
for power is made perfect in weakness."
So, I will boast all the more gladly of my weaknesses,
so that the power of Christ may dwell in me.
[10]Therefore I am content with weaknesses, insults, hardships,
persecutions, and calamities for the sake of Christ;
for whenever I am weak,
then I am strong.

The word of the Lord.

GOSPEL: MARK 6:1–13

The Holy Gospel according to Mark, the sixth chapter.

¹Jesus came to his hometown,
and his disciples followed him.
²On the sabbath he began to teach in the synagogue,
and many who heard him were astounded.
They said, "Where did this man get all this?
What is this wisdom that has been given to him?
What deeds of power are being done by his hands!
³Is not this the carpenter, the son of Mary
and brother of James and Joses and Judas and Simon,
and are not his sisters here with us?"
And they took offense at him.

⁴Then Jesus said to them,
"Prophets are not without honor, except in their hometown,
and among their own kin, and in their own house."
⁵And he could do no deed of power there,
except that he laid his hands on a few sick people and cured them.
⁶And he was amazed at their unbelief.

Then he went about among the villages teaching.
⁷He called the twelve and began to send them out two by two,
and gave them authority over the unclean spirits.
⁸He ordered them to take nothing for their journey except a staff;
no bread, no bag, no money in their belts;
⁹but to wear sandals and not to put on two tunics.
¹⁰He said to them,
"Wherever you enter a house, stay there until you leave the place.
¹¹If any place will not welcome you and they refuse to hear you,
as you leave, shake off the dust that is on your feet as a testimony against
        them."
¹²So they went out and proclaimed that all should repent.
¹³They cast out many demons,
and anointed with oil many who were sick and cured them.

The Gospel of the Lord.

PROPER 10

JULY 13, 1997   JULY 16, 2000   JULY 13, 2003

FIRST READING: AMOS 7:7–15

A reading from Amos:

⁷This is what the Lord GOD showed me:
the Lord was standing beside a wall built with a plumb line,
with a plumb line in his hand.
⁸And the LORD said to me,
"Amos, what do you see?"
And I said, "A plumb line."
Then the Lord said,
 "See, I am setting a plumb line
  in the midst of my people Israel;
  I will never again pass them by;
 ⁹the high places of Isaac shall be made desolate,
  and the sanctuaries of Israel shall be laid waste,
  and I will rise against the house of Jeroboam with the sword."

¹⁰Then Amaziah, the priest of Bethel,
sent to King Jeroboam of Israel, saying,
"Amos has conspired against you in the very center of the house of Israel;
the land is not able to bear all his words.
¹¹For thus Amos has said,
 'Jeroboam shall die by the sword,
  and Israel must go into exile
  away from his land.' "
¹²And Amaziah said to Amos,
"O seer, go, flee away to the land of Judah,
earn your bread there, and prophesy there;
¹³but never again prophesy at Bethel,
for it is the king's sanctuary, and it is a temple of the kingdom."

¹⁴Then Amos answered Amaziah,
"I am no prophet, nor a prophet's son;
but I am a herdsman, and a dresser of sycamore trees,

[15]and the L{ORD} took me from following the flock,
and the L{ORD} said to me,
'Go, prophesy to my people Israel.' "

The word of the Lord.

PSALMODY: PSALM **85:8–13**

SECOND READING: EPHESIANS 1:3–14

A reading from Ephesians:

[3]Blessed be the God and Father of our Lord Jesus Christ,
who has blessed us in Christ
with every spiritual blessing in the heavenly places,
[4]just as he chose us in Christ before the foundation of the world
to be holy and blameless before him in love.
[5]He destined us for adoption as his children through Jesus Christ,
according to the good pleasure of his will,
[6]to the praise of his glorious grace
that he freely bestowed on us in the Beloved.

[7]In him we have redemption through his blood,
the forgiveness of our trespasses,
according to the riches of his grace [8]that he lavished on us.

With all wisdom and insight
[9]he has made known to us the mystery of his will,
according to his good pleasure that he set forth in Christ,
[10]as a plan for the fullness of time,
to gather up all things in him,
things in heaven and things on earth.
[11]In Christ we have also obtained an inheritance,
having been destined according to the purpose of him
who accomplishes all things according to his counsel and will,
[12]so that we, who were the first to set our hope on Christ,
might live for the praise of his glory.
[13]In him you also, when you had heard the word of truth,
the gospel of your salvation, and had believed in him,
were marked with the seal of the promised Holy Spirit;
[14]this is the pledge of our inheritance
toward redemption as God's own people,
to the praise of his glory.

The word of the Lord.

GOSPEL: MARK 6:14–29

The Holy Gospel according to Mark, the sixth chapter.

[14]King Herod heard of the disciples' preaching,
for Jesus' name had become known.
Some were saying,
"John the baptizer has been raised from the dead;
and for this reason these powers are at work in him."

¹⁵But others said, "It is Elijah."

And others said, "It is a prophet, like one of the prophets of old."

¹⁶But when Herod heard of it, he said,

"John, whom I beheaded, has been raised."

¹⁷For Herod himself had sent men who arrested John,

bound him, and put him in prison on account of Herodias,

his brother Philip's wife, because Herod had married her.

¹⁸For John had been telling Herod,

"It is not lawful for you to have your brother's wife."

¹⁹And Herodias had a grudge against him, and wanted to kill him.

But she could not, ²⁰for Herod feared John,

knowing that he was a righteous and holy man,

and he protected him.

When he heard him, he was greatly perplexed;

and yet he liked to listen to him.

²¹But an opportunity came when Herod on his birthday

gave a banquet for his courtiers and officers and for the leaders of Galilee.

²²When his daughter Herodias came in and danced,

she pleased Herod and his guests;

and the king said to the girl,

"Ask me for whatever you wish, and I will give it."

²³And he solemnly swore to her,

"Whatever you ask me, I will give you, even half of my kingdom."

²⁴She went out and said to her mother, "What should I ask for?"

She replied, "The head of John the baptizer."

²⁵Immediately she rushed back to the king and requested,

"I want you to give me at once the head of John the Baptist on a platter."

²⁶The king was deeply grieved;

yet out of regard for his oaths and for the guests,

he did not want to refuse her.

²⁷Immediately the king sent a soldier of the guard with orders to bring John's
    head.

He went and beheaded him in the prison,

²⁸brought his head on a platter, and gave it to the girl.

Then the girl gave it to her mother.

²⁹When his disciples heard about it,

they came and took his body, and laid it in a tomb.

The Gospel of the Lord.

S U N D A Y   B E T W E E N
J U L Y   17   A N D   23   I N C L U S I V E

PROPER 11

JULY 20, 1997   JULY 23, 2000   JULY 20, 2003

FIRST READING: JEREMIAH 23:1–6

A reading from Jeremiah:

¹Woe to the shepherds who destroy and scatter the sheep of my pasture!
says the LORD.
²Therefore thus says the LORD, the God of Israel,
concerning the shepherds who shepherd my people:
It is you who have scattered my flock,
and have driven them away,
and you have not attended to them.
So I will attend to you for your evil doings, says the LORD.

³Then I myself will gather the remnant of my flock
out of all the lands where I have driven them,
and I will bring them back to their fold,
and they shall be fruitful and multiply.
⁴I will raise up shepherds over them who will shepherd them,
and they shall not fear any longer, or be dismayed,
nor shall any be missing, says the LORD.

⁵The days are surely coming, says the LORD,
when I will raise up for David a righteous Branch,
and he shall reign as king and deal wisely,
and shall execute justice and righteousness in the land.
⁶In his days Judah will be saved and Israel will live in safety.
And this is the name by which he will be called:
"The LORD is our righteousness."

The word of the Lord.

PSALMODY: PSALM 23

SECOND READING: EPHESIANS 2:11–22

A reading from Ephesians:

[11]Remember that at one time you Gentiles by birth,
called "the uncircumcision" by those who are called "the circumcision"—
a physical circumcision made in the flesh by human hands—
[12]remember that you were at that time without Christ,
being aliens from the commonwealth of Israel,
and strangers to the covenants of promise,
having no hope and without God in the world.

[13]But now in Christ Jesus you who once were far off
have been brought near by the blood of Christ.
[14]For he is our peace;
in his flesh he has made both groups into one
and has broken down the dividing wall,
that is, the hostility between us.
[15]He has abolished the law with its commandments and ordinances,
that he might create in himself one new humanity in place of the two,
thus making peace,
[16]and might reconcile both groups to God in one body through the cross,
thus putting to death that hostility through it.
[17]So he came and proclaimed peace to you who were far off
and peace to those who were near;
[18]for through him both of us have access in one Spirit to the Father.

[19]So then you are no longer strangers and aliens,
but you are citizens with the saints
and also members of the household of God,
[20]built upon the foundation of the apostles and prophets,
with Christ Jesus himself as the cornerstone.
[21]In him the whole structure is joined together
and grows into a holy temple in the Lord;
[22]in whom you also are built together spiritually into a dwelling place for God.

The word of the Lord.

The Holy Gospel according to Mark, the sixth chapter.

[30]The apostles gathered around Jesus,
and told him all that they had done and taught.
[31]He said to them,
"Come away to a deserted place all by yourselves and rest a while."
For many were coming and going,
and they had no leisure even to eat.
[32]And they went away in the boat to a deserted place by themselves.
[33]Now many saw them going and recognized them,
and they hurried there on foot from all the towns and arrived ahead of them.

[34]As he went ashore, he saw a great crowd;
and he had compassion for them,
because they were like sheep without a shepherd;
and he began to teach them many things.

[53]When they had crossed over,
they came to land at Gennesaret and moored the boat.
[54]When they got out of the boat, people at once recognized him,
[55]and rushed about that whole region
and began to bring the sick on mats to wherever they heard he was.
[56]And wherever he went, into villages or cities or farms,
they laid the sick in the marketplaces,
and begged him that they might touch even the fringe of his cloak;
and all who touched it were healed.

The Gospel of the Lord.

SUNDAY BETWEEN
JULY 24 AND 30 INCLUSIVE

PROPER 12

JULY 27, 1997   JULY 30, 2000   JULY 27, 2003

FIRST READING: 2 KINGS 4:42–44

A reading from Second Kings:

[42]A man came from Baal-shalishah,
bringing food from the first fruits to Elisha, the man of God:
twenty loaves of barley and fresh ears of grain in his sack.
Elisha said, "Give it to the people and let them eat."
[43]But his servant said,
"How can I set this before a hundred people?"
So he repeated,
"Give it to the people and let them eat, for thus says the LORD,
'They shall eat and have some left.' "
[44]He set it before them,
they ate, and had some left,
according to the word of the LORD.

The word of the Lord.

PSALMODY: PSALM 145:10–18   *Psalm 145:10–19* LBW/BCP

SECOND READING: Ephesians 3:14–21

A reading from Ephesians:

^{14}For this reason I bow my knees before the Father,
^{15}from whom every family in heaven and on earth takes its name.
^{16}I pray that, according to the riches of his glory,
he may grant that you may be strengthened in your inner being
with power through his Spirit,
^{17}and that Christ may dwell in your hearts through faith,
as you are being rooted and grounded in love.
^{18}I pray that you may have the power to comprehend, with all the saints,
what is the breadth and length and height and depth,
^{19}and to know the love of Christ that surpasses knowledge,
so that you may be filled with all the fullness of God.

^{20}Now to him who by the power at work within us
is able to accomplish abundantly far more than all we can ask or imagine,
^{21}to him be glory in the church and in Christ Jesus
to all generations, forever and ever. Amen.

The word of the Lord.

GOSPEL: John 6:1–21

The Holy Gospel according to John, the sixth chapter.

^{1}Jesus went to the other side of the Sea of Galilee,
also called the Sea of Tiberias.
^{2}A large crowd kept following him,
because they saw the signs that he was doing for the sick.
^{3}Jesus went up the mountain and sat down there with his disciples.
^{4}Now the Passover, the festival of the Jews, was near.
^{5}When he looked up and saw a large crowd coming toward him,
Jesus said to Philip,
"Where are we to buy bread for these people to eat?"
^{6}He said this to test him,
for he himself knew what he was going to do.
^{7}Philip answered him,
"Six months' wages would not buy enough bread for each of them to get
       a little."
^{8}One of his disciples, Andrew, Simon Peter's brother, said to him,
^{9}"There is a boy here who has five barley loaves and two fish.
But what are they among so many people?"

^{10}Jesus said, "Make the people sit down."
Now there was a great deal of grass in the place;
so they sat down, about five thousand in all.

¹¹Then Jesus took the loaves, and when he had given thanks,
he distributed them to those who were seated;
so also the fish, as much as they wanted.
¹²When they were satisfied, he told his disciples,
"Gather up the fragments left over,
so that nothing may be lost."
¹³So they gathered them up,
and from the fragments of the five barley loaves, left by those who had eaten,
they filled twelve baskets.
¹⁴When the people saw the sign that he had done, they began to say,
"This is indeed the prophet who is to come into the world."

¹⁵When Jesus realized that they were about to come
and take him by force to make him king,
he withdrew again to the mountain by himself.

¹⁶When evening came, his disciples went down to the sea,
¹⁷got into a boat, and started across the sea to Capernaum.
It was now dark, and Jesus had not yet come to them.
¹⁸The sea became rough because a strong wind was blowing.
¹⁹When they had rowed about three or four miles,
they saw Jesus walking on the sea and coming near the boat,
and they were terrified.
²⁰But he said to them,
"It is I; do not be afraid."
²¹Then they wanted to take him into the boat,
and immediately the boat reached the land toward which they were going.

The Gospel of the Lord.

SUNDAY BETWEEN
JULY 31 AND AUGUST 6 INCLUSIVE

PROPER 13

AUGUST 3, 1997   AUGUST 6, 2000   AUGUST 3, 2003

FIRST READING: EXODUS 16:2–4, 9–15

A reading from Exodus:

²The whole congregation of the Israelites
complained against Moses and Aaron in the wilderness.
³The Israelites said to them,
"If only we had died by the hand of the LORD in the land of Egypt,
when we sat by the fleshpots and ate our fill of bread;
for you have brought us out into this wilderness
to kill this whole assembly with hunger."

⁴Then the LORD said to Moses,
"I am going to rain bread from heaven for you,
and each day the people shall go out and gather enough for that day.
In that way I will test them,
whether they will follow my instruction or not."

⁹Then Moses said to Aaron,
"Say to the whole congregation of the Israelites,
'Draw near to the LORD, for he has heard your complaining.' "
¹⁰And as Aaron spoke to the whole congregation of the Israelites,
they looked toward the wilderness,
and the glory of the LORD appeared in the cloud.
¹¹The LORD spoke to Moses and said,
¹²"I have heard the complaining of the Israelites; say to them,
'At twilight you shall eat meat,
and in the morning you shall have your fill of bread;
then you shall know that I am the LORD your God.' "

¹³In the evening quails came up and covered the camp;
and in the morning there was a layer of dew around the camp.
¹⁴When the layer of dew lifted,
there on the surface of the wilderness was a fine flaky substance,
as fine as frost on the ground.

[15]When the Israelites saw it, they said to one another,
"What is it?" For they did not know what it was.
Moses said to them,
"It is the bread that the LORD has given you to eat."

The word of the Lord.

PSALMODY: PSALM 78:23–29

SECOND READING: EPHESIANS 4:1–16

A reading from Ephesians:

¹I therefore, the prisoner in the Lord,
beg you to lead a life worthy of the calling to which you have been called,
²with all humility and gentleness,
with patience, bearing with one another in love,
³making every effort to maintain the unity of the Spirit in the bond of peace.
⁴There is one body and one Spirit,
just as you were called to the one hope of your calling,
⁵one Lord, one faith, one baptism,
⁶one God and Father of all,
who is above all and through all and in all.

⁷But each of us was given grace according to the measure of Christ's gift.
⁸Therefore it is said,
"When he ascended on high he made captivity itself a captive;
he gave gifts to his people."
⁹(When it says, "He ascended," what does it mean
but that he had also descended into the lower parts of the earth?
¹⁰He who descended is the same one who ascended far above all the heavens,
so that he might fill all things.)
¹¹The gifts he gave were that some would be apostles, some prophets,
some evangelists, some pastors and teachers,
¹²to equip the saints for the work of ministry,
for building up the body of Christ,
¹³until all of us come to the unity of the faith
and of the knowledge of the Son of God,
to maturity, to the measure of the full stature of Christ.

¹⁴We must no longer be children,
tossed to and fro and blown about by every wind of doctrine,
by people's trickery, by their craftiness in deceitful scheming.
¹⁵But speaking the truth in love,
we must grow up in every way into him who is the head, into Christ,
¹⁶from whom the whole body,
joined and knit together by every ligament with which it is equipped,
as each part is working properly,
promotes the body's growth in building itself up in love.

The word of the Lord.

GOSPEL: JOHN 6:24–35

The Holy Gospel according to John, the sixth chapter.

24When the crowd saw that neither Jesus nor his disciples were beside the sea,
they themselves got into the boats and went to Capernaum looking for Jesus.
25When they found him on the other side of the sea,
they said to him, "Rabbi, when did you come here?"
26Jesus answered them, "Very truly, I tell you,
you are looking for me, not because you saw signs,
but because you ate your fill of the loaves.
27Do not work for the food that perishes,
but for the food that endures for eternal life,
which the Son of Man will give you.
For it is on him that God the Father has set his seal."

28Then they said to him,
"What must we do to perform the works of God?"
29Jesus answered them, "This is the work of God,
that you believe in him whom he has sent."
30So they said to him,
"What sign are you going to give us then,
so that we may see it and believe you?
What work are you performing?
31Our ancestors ate the manna in the wilderness;
as it is written, 'He gave them bread from heaven to eat.' "
32Then Jesus said to them,
"Very truly, I tell you, it was not Moses who gave you the bread from heaven,
but it is my Father who gives you the true bread from heaven.
33For the bread of God is that which comes down from heaven
and gives life to the world."
34They said to him, "Sir, give us this bread always."

35Jesus said to them,
"I am the bread of life.
Whoever comes to me will never be hungry,
and whoever believes in me will never be thirsty."

The Gospel of the Lord.

SUNDAY BETWEEN
AUGUST 7 AND 13 INCLUSIVE

PROPER 14

AUGUST 10, 1997   *AUGUST 13, 2000*   *AUGUST 10, 2003*

FIRST READING: 1 KINGS 19:4–8

A reading from First Kings:

⁴Elijah went a day's journey into the wilderness,
and came and sat down under a solitary broom tree.
He asked that he might die:
"It is enough;
now, O LORD, take away my life,
for I am no better than my ancestors."

⁵Then he lay down under the broom tree and fell asleep.
Suddenly an angel touched him and said to him,
"Get up and eat."
⁶He looked,
and there at his head was a cake baked on hot stones, and a jar of water.
He ate and drank, and lay down again.

⁷The angel of the LORD came a second time,
touched him, and said, "Get up and eat,
otherwise the journey will be too much for you."
⁸He got up, and ate and drank;
then he went in the strength of that food
forty days and forty nights to Horeb the mount of God.

The word of the Lord.

PSALMODY: PSALM 34:1–8

SECOND READING: Ephesians 4:25—5:2

A reading from Ephesians:

25So then, putting away falsehood,
let all of us speak the truth to our neighbors,
for we are members of one another.
26Be angry but do not sin;
do not let the sun go down on your anger,
27and do not make room for the devil.
28Thieves must give up stealing;
rather let them labor and work honestly with their own hands,
so as to have something to share with the needy.
29Let no evil talk come out of your mouths,
but only what is useful for building up, as there is need,
so that your words may give grace to those who hear.
30And do not grieve the Holy Spirit of God,
with which you were marked with a seal for the day of redemption.
31Put away from you all bitterness and wrath
and anger and wrangling and slander, together with all malice,
32and be kind to one another,
tenderhearted, forgiving one another,
as God in Christ has forgiven you.

5:1Therefore be imitators of God, as beloved children,
2and live in love, as Christ loved us and gave himself up for us,
a fragrant offering and sacrifice to God.

The word of the Lord.

GOSPEL: JOHN 6:35, 41–51

The Holy Gospel according to John, the sixth chapter.

³⁵Jesus said to them,
"I am the bread of life.
Whoever comes to me will never be hungry,
and whoever believes in me will never be thirsty."

⁴¹Then the Jews began to complain about him because he said,
"I am the bread that came down from heaven."
⁴²They were saying,
"Is not this Jesus, the son of Joseph, whose father and mother we know?
How can he now say, 'I have come down from heaven'?"
⁴³Jesus answered them,
"Do not complain among yourselves.
⁴⁴No one can come to me unless drawn by the Father who sent me;
and I will raise that person up on the last day.
⁴⁵It is written in the prophets,
'And they shall all be taught by God.'
Everyone who has heard and learned from the Father comes to me.
⁴⁶Not that anyone has seen the Father except the one who is from God;
he has seen the Father.

⁴⁷"Very truly, I tell you,
whoever believes has eternal life.
⁴⁸I am the bread of life.
⁴⁹Your ancestors ate the manna in the wilderness, and they died.
⁵⁰This is the bread that comes down from heaven,
so that one may eat of it and not die.
⁵¹I am the living bread that came down from heaven.
Whoever eats of this bread will live forever;
and the bread that I will give for the life of the world is my flesh."

The Gospel of the Lord.

SUNDAY BETWEEN
AUGUST 14 AND 20 INCLUSIVE

PROPER 15

AUGUST 17, 1997   AUGUST 20, 2000   AUGUST 17, 2003

FIRST READING: PROVERBS 9:1–6

A reading from Proverbs:

¹Wisdom has built her house,
     she has hewn her seven pillars.
²She has slaughtered her animals, she has mixed her wine,
     she has also set her table.
³She has sent out her servant girls, she calls
     from the highest places in the town,
⁴"You that are simple, turn in here!"
     To those without sense she says,
⁵"Come, eat of my bread
     and drink of the wine I have mixed.
⁶Lay aside immaturity, and live,
     and walk in the way of insight."

The word of the Lord.

PSALMODY: PSALM 34:9–14

SECOND READING: Ephesians 5:15–20

A reading from Ephesians:

[15]Be careful then how you live,
not as unwise people but as wise,
[16]making the most of the time, because the days are evil.
[17]So do not be foolish,
but understand what the will of the Lord is.
[18]Do not get drunk with wine, for that is debauchery;
but be filled with the Spirit,
[19]as you sing psalms and hymns and spiritual songs among yourselves,
singing and making melody to the Lord in your hearts,
[20]giving thanks to God the Father
at all times and for everything
in the name of our Lord Jesus Christ.

The word of the Lord.

GOSPEL: JOHN 6:51–58

The Holy Gospel according to John, the sixth chapter.

Jesus said,
51"I am the living bread that came down from heaven.
Whoever eats of this bread will live forever;
and the bread that I will give for the life of the world is my flesh."

52The Jews then disputed among themselves, saying,
"How can this man give us his flesh to eat?"
53So Jesus said to them,
"Very truly, I tell you,
unless you eat the flesh of the Son of Man and drink his blood,
you have no life in you.
54Those who eat my flesh and drink my blood have eternal life,
and I will raise them up on the last day;
55for my flesh is true food and my blood is true drink.
56Those who eat my flesh and drink my blood abide in me,
and I in them.
57Just as the living Father sent me, and I live because of the Father,
so whoever eats me will live because of me.
58This is the bread that came down from heaven,
not like that which your ancestors ate, and they died.
But the one who eats this bread will live forever."

The Gospel of the Lord.

S U N D A Y   B E T W E E N
A U G U S T   **21**   A N D   **27**   I N C L U S I V E

PROPER 16

AUGUST 24, 1997   AUGUST 27, 2000   AUGUST 24, 2003

FIRST READING: JOSHUA 24:1–2a, 14–18

A reading from Joshua:

¹Joshua gathered all the tribes of Israel to Shechem,
and summoned the elders, the heads, the judges, and the officers of Israel;
and they presented themselves before God.
²And Joshua said to all the people,
¹⁴"Now therefore revere the LORD,
and serve him in sincerity and in faithfulness;
put away the gods that your ancestors served beyond the River and in Egypt,
and serve the LORD.
¹⁵Now if you are unwilling to serve the LORD,
choose this day whom you will serve,
whether the gods your ancestors served in the region beyond the River
or the gods of the Amorites in whose land you are living;
but as for me and my household, we will serve the LORD."

¹⁶Then the people answered,
"Far be it from us that we should forsake the LORD to serve other gods;
¹⁷for it is the LORD our God who brought us and our ancestors up from the
    land of Egypt,
out of the house of slavery,
and who did those great signs in our sight.
He protected us along all the way that we went,
and among all the peoples through whom we passed;
¹⁸and the LORD drove out before us all the peoples,
the Amorites who lived in the land.
Therefore we also will serve the LORD,
for he is our God."

The word of the Lord.

PSALMODY: PSALM 34:15–22

SECOND READING: EPHESIANS 6:10–20

A reading from Ephesians:

¹⁰Be strong in the Lord and in the strength of his power.
¹¹Put on the whole armor of God,
so that you may be able to stand against the wiles of the devil.
¹²For our struggle is not against enemies of blood and flesh,
but against the rulers, against the authorities,
against the cosmic powers of this present darkness,
against the spiritual forces of evil in the heavenly places.

¹³Therefore take up the whole armor of God,
so that you may be able to withstand on that evil day,
and having done everything, to stand firm.
¹⁴Stand therefore, and fasten the belt of truth around your waist,
and put on the breastplate of righteousness.
¹⁵As shoes for your feet
put on whatever will make you ready to proclaim the gospel of peace.
¹⁶With all of these, take the shield of faith,
with which you will be able to quench all the flaming arrows of the evil one.
¹⁷Take the helmet of salvation,
and the sword of the Spirit, which is the word of God.

¹⁸Pray in the Spirit at all times in every prayer and supplication.
To that end keep alert
and always persevere in supplication for all the saints.
¹⁹Pray also for me,
so that when I speak,
a message may be given to me
to make known with boldness the mystery of the gospel,
²⁰for which I am an ambassador in chains.
Pray that I may declare it boldly, as I must speak.

The word of the Lord.

The Holy Gospel according to John, the sixth chapter.

Jesus said,
[56]"Those who eat my flesh and drink my blood abide in me,
and I in them.
[57]Just as the living Father sent me,
and I live because of the Father,
so whoever eats me will live because of me.
[58]This is the bread that came down from heaven,
not like that which your ancestors ate, and they died.
But the one who eats this bread will live forever."
[59]He said these things while he was teaching in the synagogue at Capernaum.

[60]When many of his disciples heard it, they said,
"This teaching is difficult; who can accept it?"
[61]But Jesus, being aware that his disciples were complaining about it,
said to them, "Does this offend you?
[62]Then what if you were to see the Son of Man ascending to where he was
    before?
[63]It is the spirit that gives life; the flesh is useless.
The words that I have spoken to you are spirit and life.
[64]But among you there are some who do not believe."
For Jesus knew from the first who were the ones that did not believe,
and who was the one that would betray him.
[65]And he said,
"For this reason I have told you
that no one can come to me unless it is granted by the Father."

[66]Because of this many of his disciples turned back
and no longer went about with him.
[67]So Jesus asked the twelve,
"Do you also wish to go away?"
[68]Simon Peter answered him, "Lord, to whom can we go?
You have the words of eternal life.
[69]We have come to believe and know that you are the Holy One of God."

The Gospel of the Lord.

FIRST READING: DEUTERONOMY 4:1–2, 6–9

A reading from Deuteronomy:

¹So now, Israel,
give heed to the statutes and ordinances that I am teaching you to observe,
so that you may live to enter and occupy the land that the LORD,
the God of your ancestors, is giving you.
²You must neither add anything to what I command you
nor take away anything from it,
but keep the commandments of the LORD your God
with which I am charging you.
⁶You must observe them diligently,
for this will show your wisdom and discernment to the peoples,
who, when they hear all these statutes, will say,
"Surely this great nation is a wise and discerning people!"
⁷For what other great nation has a god so near to it
as the LORD our God is whenever we call to him?
⁸And what other great nation has statutes and ordinances
as just as this entire law that I am setting before you today?

⁹But take care and watch yourselves closely,
so as neither to forget the things that your eyes have seen
nor to let them slip from your mind all the days of your life;
make them known to your children and your children's children.

The word of the Lord.

PSALMODY: PSALM 15

SECOND READING: JAMES 1:17–27

A reading from James:

[17]Every generous act of giving, with every perfect gift,
is from above, coming down from the Father of lights,
with whom there is no variation or shadow due to change.
[18]In fulfillment of his own purpose
he gave us birth by the word of truth,
so that we would become a kind of first fruits of his creatures.

[19]You must understand this, my beloved:
let everyone be quick to listen, slow to speak, slow to anger;
[20]for your anger does not produce God's righteousness.
[21]Therefore rid yourselves of all sordidness and rank growth of wickedness,
and welcome with meekness the implanted word
that has the power to save your souls.

[22]But be doers of the word,
and not merely hearers who deceive themselves.
[23]For if any are hearers of the word and not doers,
they are like those who look at themselves in a mirror;
[24]for they look at themselves and, on going away,
immediately forget what they were like.
[25]But those who look into the perfect law, the law of liberty,
and persevere, being not hearers who forget but doers who act—
they will be blessed in their doing.

[26]If any think they are religious,
and do not bridle their tongues but deceive their hearts,
their religion is worthless.
[27]Religion that is pure and undefiled before God, the Father, is this:
to care for orphans and widows in their distress,
and to keep oneself unstained by the world.

The word of the Lord.

GOSPEL: MARK 7:1–8, 14–15, 21–23

The Holy Gospel according to Mark, the seventh chapter.

[1]Now when the Pharisees and some of the scribes
who had come from Jerusalem gathered around Jesus,
[2]they noticed that some of his disciples were eating with defiled hands,
that is, without washing them.
[3](For the Pharisees, and all the Jews,
do not eat unless they thoroughly wash their hands,
thus observing the tradition of the elders;

[4]and they do not eat anything from the market unless they wash it;
and there are also many other traditions that they observe,
the washing of cups, pots, and bronze kettles.)
[5]So the Pharisees and the scribes asked him,
"Why do your disciples not live according to the tradition of the elders,
but eat with defiled hands?"
[6]He said to them,
"Isaiah prophesied rightly about you hypocrites, as it is written,
'This people honors me with their lips,
but their hearts are far from me;
[7]in vain do they worship me,
teaching human precepts as doctrines.'
[8]You abandon the commandment of God and hold to human tradition."

[14]Then he called the crowd again and said to them,
"Listen to me, all of you, and understand:
[15]there is nothing outside a person that by going in can defile,
but the things that come out are what defile."
[21]For it is from within, from the human heart,
that evil intentions come:
fornication, theft, murder, [22]adultery,
avarice, wickedness, deceit, licentiousness,
envy, slander, pride, folly.
[23]All these evil things come from within,
and they defile a person."

The Gospel of the Lord.

Sunday between September 4 and 10 inclusive

PROPER 18

SEPTEMBER 7, 1997   SEPTEMBER 10, 2000   SEPTEMBER 7, 2003

FIRST READING: Isaiah 35:4–7a

A reading from Isaiah:

4Say to those who are of a fearful heart,
    "Be strong, do not fear!
Here is your God.
    He will come with vengeance,
with terrible recompense.
    He will come and save you."

5Then the eyes of the blind shall be opened,
    and the ears of the deaf unstopped;
6then the lame shall leap like a deer,
    and the tongue of the speechless sing for joy.
For waters shall break forth in the wilderness,
    and streams in the desert;
7the burning sand shall become a pool,
    and the thirsty ground springs of water.

The word of the Lord.

PSALMODY: Psalm 146

SECOND READING: JAMES 2:1–10 [11–13] 14–17

A reading from James:

[1]My brothers and sisters,
do you with your acts of favoritism
really believe in our glorious Lord Jesus Christ?
[2]For if a person with gold rings and in fine clothes comes into your assembly,
and if a poor person in dirty clothes also comes in,
[3]and if you take notice of the one wearing the fine clothes and say,
"Have a seat here, please,"
while to the one who is poor you say,
"Stand there," or, "Sit at my feet,"
[4]have you not made distinctions among yourselves,
and become judges with evil thoughts?
[5]Listen, my beloved brothers and sisters.
Has not God chosen the poor in the world to be rich in faith
and to be heirs of the kingdom that he has promised to those who love him?
[6]But you have dishonored the poor.
Is it not the rich who oppress you?
Is it not they who drag you into court?
[7]Is it not they who blaspheme the excellent name that was invoked over you?

[8]You do well if you really fulfill the royal law according to the scripture,
"You shall love your neighbor as yourself."
[9]But if you show partiality,
you commit sin and are convicted by the law as transgressors.
[10]For whoever keeps the whole law but fails in one point
has become accountable for all of it.

[[11]For the one who said, "You shall not commit adultery,"
also said, "You shall not murder."
Now if you do not commit adultery but if you murder,
you have become a transgressor of the law.
[12]So speak and so act as those who are to be judged by the law of liberty.
[13]For judgment will be without mercy to anyone who has shown no mercy;
mercy triumphs over judgment.]

[14]What good is it, my brothers and sisters,
if you say you have faith but do not have works?
Can faith save you?
[15]If a brother or sister is naked and lacks daily food,
[16]and one of you says to them,
"Go in peace; keep warm and eat your fill,"
and yet you do not supply their bodily needs,
what is the good of that?
[17]So faith by itself, if it has no works, is dead.

The word of the Lord.

The Holy Gospel according to Mark, the seventh chapter.

[24]Jesus set out and went away to the region of Tyre.
He entered a house and did not want anyone to know he was there.
Yet he could not escape notice,
[25]but a woman whose little daughter had an unclean spirit
immediately heard about him,
and she came and bowed down at his feet.
[26]Now the woman was a Gentile, of Syrophoenician origin.
She begged him to cast the demon out of her daughter.
[27]He said to her, "Let the children be fed first,
for it is not fair to take the children's food and throw it to the dogs."
[28]But she answered him,
"Sir, even the dogs under the table eat the children's crumbs."
[29]Then he said to her,
"For saying that, you may go—
the demon has left your daughter."
[30]So she went home, found the child lying on the bed, and the demon gone.

[31]Then he returned from the region of Tyre,
and went by way of Sidon towards the Sea of Galilee,
in the region of the Decapolis.
[32]They brought to him a deaf man who had an impediment in his speech;
and they begged him to lay his hand on him.
[33]He took him aside in private, away from the crowd,
and put his fingers into his ears,
and he spat and touched his tongue.
[34]Then looking up to heaven, he sighed and said to him,
"Ephphatha," that is, "Be opened."
[35]And immediately his ears were opened,
his tongue was released, and he spoke plainly.
[36]Then Jesus ordered them to tell no one;
but the more he ordered them,
the more zealously they proclaimed it.
[37]They were astounded beyond measure, saying,
"He has done everything well;
he even makes the deaf to hear and the mute to speak."

The Gospel of the Lord.

SUNDAY BETWEEN
SEPTEMBER 11 AND 17 INCLUSIVE

PROPER 19

SEPTEMBER 14, 1997   SEPTEMBER 17, 2000   SEPTEMBER 14, 2003

FIRST READING: ISAIAH 50:4–9a

A reading from Isaiah:

⁴The Lord GOD has given me
    the tongue of a teacher,
that I may know how to sustain
    the weary with a word.
Morning by morning he wakens—
    wakens my ear
    to listen as those who are taught.
⁵The Lord GOD has opened my ear,
    and I was not rebellious,
    I did not turn backward.
⁶I gave my back to those who struck me,
    and my cheeks to those who pulled out the beard;
I did not hide my face
    from insult and spitting.

⁷The Lord GOD helps me;
    therefore I have not been disgraced;
therefore I have set my face like flint,
    and I know that I shall not be put to shame;
    ⁸he who vindicates me is near.
Who will contend with me?
    Let us stand up together.
Who are my adversaries?
    Let them confront me.
⁹It is the Lord GOD who helps me;
    who will declare me guilty?

The word of the Lord.

PSALMODY: PSALM 116:1–9

Psalm 116:1–8 LBW/BCP

SECOND READING: James 3:1–12

A reading from James:

¹Not many of you should become teachers, my brothers and sisters,
for you know that we who teach will be judged with greater strictness.
²For all of us make many mistakes.
Anyone who makes no mistakes in speaking is perfect,
able to keep the whole body in check with a bridle.
³If we put bits into the mouths of horses to make them obey us,
we guide their whole bodies.
⁴Or look at ships:
though they are so large that it takes strong winds to drive them,
yet they are guided by a very small rudder
wherever the will of the pilot directs.

⁵So also the tongue is a small member,
yet it boasts of great exploits.
How great a forest is set ablaze by a small fire!
⁶And the tongue is a fire.
The tongue is placed among our members as a world of iniquity;
it stains the whole body,
sets on fire the cycle of nature,
and is itself set on fire by hell.
⁷For every species of beast and bird, of reptile and sea creature,
can be tamed and has been tamed by the human species,
⁸but no one can tame the tongue—
a restless evil, full of deadly poison.
⁹With it we bless the Lord and Father,
and with it we curse those who are made in the likeness of God.
¹⁰From the same mouth come blessing and cursing.
My brothers and sisters, this ought not to be so.
¹¹Does a spring pour forth from the same opening both fresh and brackish
        water?
¹²Can a fig tree, my brothers and sisters, yield olives, or a grapevine figs?
No more can salt water yield fresh.

The word of the Lord.

GOSPEL: MARK 8:27–38

The Holy Gospel according to Mark, the eighth chapter.

27Jesus went on with his disciples to the villages of Caesarea Philippi;
and on the way he asked his disciples,
"Who do people say that I am?"
28And they answered him,
"John the Baptist; and others, Elijah;
and still others, one of the prophets."
29He asked them, "But who do you say that I am?"
Peter answered him, "You are the Messiah."
30And he sternly ordered them not to tell anyone about him.

31Then he began to teach them that the Son of Man must undergo great
    suffering,
and be rejected by the elders, the chief priests, and the scribes,
and be killed, and after three days rise again.
32He said all this quite openly.
And Peter took him aside and began to rebuke him.
33But turning and looking at his disciples,
he rebuked Peter and said,
"Get behind me, Satan!
For you are setting your mind not on divine things but on human things."

34He called the crowd with his disciples, and said to them,
"If any want to become my followers,
let them deny themselves and take up their cross and follow me.
35For those who want to save their life will lose it,
and those who lose their life for my sake,
and for the sake of the gospel, will save it.
36For what will it profit them to gain the whole world and forfeit their life?
37Indeed, what can they give in return for their life?
38Those who are ashamed of me and of my words
in this adulterous and sinful generation,
of them the Son of Man will also be ashamed
when he comes in the glory of his Father with the holy angels."

The Gospel of the Lord.

SUNDAY BETWEEN
SEPTEMBER 18 AND 24 INCLUSIVE

PROPER 20

SEPTEMBER 21, 1997   *SEPTEMBER 24, 2000*   *SEPTEMBER 21, 2003*

FIRST READING: JEREMIAH 11:18–20

Alternate Reading: Wisdom of Solomon 1:16—2:1, 12–22 (p. 407)

A reading from Jeremiah:

¹⁸It was the LORD who made it known to me, and I knew;
    then you showed me their evil deeds.
¹⁹But I was like a gentle lamb
    led to the slaughter.
And I did not know it was against me
    that they devised schemes, saying,
"Let us destroy the tree with its fruit,
    let us cut him off from the land of the living,
    so that his name will no longer be remembered!"

²⁰But you, O LORD of hosts, who judge righteously,
    who try the heart and the mind,
let me see your retribution upon them,
    for to you I have committed my cause.

The word of the Lord.

PSALMODY: PSALM 54

SECOND READING: JAMES 3:13—4:3, 7–8a

A reading from James:

[13]Who is wise and understanding among you?
Show by your good life that your works are done with gentleness born
      of wisdom.
[14]But if you have bitter envy and selfish ambition in your hearts,
do not be boastful and false to the truth.
[15]Such wisdom does not come down from above,
but is earthly, unspiritual, devilish.
[16]For where there is envy and selfish ambition,
there will also be disorder and wickedness of every kind.
[17]But the wisdom from above is first pure,
then peaceable, gentle, willing to yield,
full of mercy and good fruits,
without a trace of partiality or hypocrisy.
[18]And a harvest of righteousness is sown in peace for those who make peace.

[4:1]Those conflicts and disputes among you, where do they come from?
Do they not come from your cravings that are at war within you?
[2]You want something and do not have it;
so you commit murder.
And you covet something and cannot obtain it;
so you engage in disputes and conflicts.
You do not have, because you do not ask.
[3]You ask and do not receive, because you ask wrongly,
in order to spend what you get on your pleasures.

[7]Submit yourselves therefore to God.
Resist the devil, and he will flee from you.
[8]Draw near to God, and he will draw near to you.

The word of the Lord.

GOSPEL: MARK 9:30–37

The Holy Gospel according to Mark, the ninth chapter.

[30]Jesus and the disciples went on and passed through Galilee.
He did not want anyone to know it;
[31]for he was teaching his disciples, saying to them,
"The Son of Man is to be betrayed into human hands,
and they will kill him,
and three days after being killed, he will rise again."
[32]But they did not understand what he was saying and were afraid to ask him.

[33]Then they came to Capernaum;
and when he was in the house he asked them,
"What were you arguing about on the way?"
[34]But they were silent,
for on the way they had argued with one another who was the greatest.
[35]He sat down, called the twelve, and said to them,
"Whoever wants to be first must be last of all and servant of all."
[36]Then he took a little child and put it among them;
and taking it in his arms, he said to them,
[37]"Whoever welcomes one such child in my name welcomes me,
and whoever welcomes me welcomes not me but the one who sent me."

The Gospel of the Lord.

SUNDAY BETWEEN
SEPTEMBER 25 AND OCTOBER 1
INCLUSIVE

PROPER 21

SEPTEMBER 28, 1997   OCTOBER 1, 2000   SEPTEMBER 28, 2003

FIRST READING: NUMBERS 11:4–6, 10–16, 24–29

A reading from Numbers:

⁴The rabble among them had a strong craving;
and the Israelites also wept again, and said,
"If only we had meat to eat!
⁵We remember the fish we used to eat in Egypt for nothing,
the cucumbers, the melons, the leeks, the onions, and the garlic;
⁶but now our strength is dried up,
and there is nothing at all but this manna to look at."

¹⁰Moses heard the people weeping throughout their families,
all at the entrances of their tents.
Then the LORD became very angry, and Moses was displeased.
¹¹So Moses said to the LORD,
"Why have you treated your servant so badly?
Why have I not found favor in your sight,
that you lay the burden of all this people on me?
¹²Did I conceive all this people?
Did I give birth to them, that you should say to me,
'Carry them in your bosom, as a nurse carries a sucking child,'
to the land that you promised on oath to their ancestors?
¹³Where am I to get meat to give to all this people?
For they come weeping to me and say, 'Give us meat to eat!'
¹⁴I am not able to carry all this people alone,
for they are too heavy for me.
¹⁵If this is the way you are going to treat me,
put me to death at once—
if I have found favor in your sight—
and do not let me see my misery."

¹⁶So the LORD said to Moses,
"Gather for me seventy of the elders of Israel,
whom you know to be the elders of the people and officers over them;
bring them to the tent of meeting,
and have them take their place there with you."

²⁴So Moses went out and told the people the words of the LORD;
and he gathered seventy elders of the people,
and placed them all around the tent.
²⁵Then the LORD came down in the cloud and spoke to him,
and took some of the spirit that was on him
and put it on the seventy elders;
and when the spirit rested upon them, they prophesied.
But they did not do so again.

²⁶Two men remained in the camp, one named Eldad,
and the other named Medad,
and the spirit rested on them;
they were among those registered,
but they had not gone out to the tent,
and so they prophesied in the camp.
²⁷And a young man ran and told Moses,
"Eldad and Medad are prophesying in the camp."
²⁸And Joshua son of Nun, the assistant of Moses, one of his chosen men, said,
"My lord Moses, stop them!"
²⁹But Moses said to him,
"Are you jealous for my sake?
Would that all the LORD's people were prophets,
and that the LORD would put his spirit on them!"

The word of the Lord.

PSALMODY: PSALM 19:7–14

SECOND READING: James 5:13–20

A reading from James:

¹³Are any among you suffering?
They should pray.
Are any cheerful?
They should sing songs of praise.
¹⁴Are any among you sick?
They should call for the elders of the church and have them pray over them,
anointing them with oil in the name of the Lord.
¹⁵The prayer of faith will save the sick,
and the Lord will raise them up;
and anyone who has committed sins will be forgiven.
¹⁶Therefore confess your sins to one another,
and pray for one another, so that you may be healed.
The prayer of the righteous is powerful and effective.

¹⁷Elijah was a human being like us,
and he prayed fervently that it might not rain,
and for three years and six months it did not rain on the earth.
¹⁸Then he prayed again,
and the heaven gave rain and the earth yielded its harvest.

¹⁹My brothers and sisters,
if anyone among you wanders from the truth and is brought back by another,
²⁰you should know that whoever brings back a sinner from wandering
will save the sinner's soul from death
and will cover a multitude of sins.

The word of the Lord.

The Holy Gospel according to Mark, the ninth chapter.

[38]John said to Jesus,
"Teacher, we saw someone casting out demons in your name,
and we tried to stop him, because he was not following us."
[39]But Jesus said, "Do not stop him;
for no one who does a deed of power in my name
will be able soon afterward to speak evil of me.
[40]Whoever is not against us is for us.
[41]For truly I tell you,
whoever gives you a cup of water to drink
because you bear the name of Christ
will by no means lose the reward.

[42]"If any of you put a stumbling block
before one of these little ones who believe in me,
it would be better for you if a great millstone were hung around your neck
and you were thrown into the sea.
[43]If your hand causes you to stumble, cut it off;
it is better for you to enter life maimed
than to have two hands and to go to hell, to the unquenchable fire.
[45]And if your foot causes you to stumble, cut it off;
it is better for you to enter life lame
than to have two feet and to be thrown into hell.
[47]And if your eye causes you to stumble, tear it out;
it is better for you to enter the kingdom of God with one eye
than to have two eyes and to be thrown into hell,
[48]where their worm never dies, and the fire is never quenched.

[49]"For everyone will be salted with fire.
[50]Salt is good;
but if salt has lost its saltiness, how can you season it?
Have salt in yourselves,
and be at peace with one another."

The Gospel of the Lord.

SUNDAY BETWEEN
OCTOBER 2 AND 8 INCLUSIVE

PROPER 22

OCTOBER 5, 1997   OCTOBER 8, 2000   OCTOBER 5, 2003

FIRST READING: GENESIS 2:18–24

A reading from Genesis:

18The LORD God said,
"It is not good that the man should be alone;
I will make him a helper as his partner."
19So out of the ground the LORD God formed every animal of the field
and every bird of the air,
and brought them to the man to see what he would call them;
and whatever the man called every living creature, that was its name.
20The man gave names to all cattle, and to the birds of the air,
and to every animal of the field;
but for the man there was not found a helper as his partner.

21So the LORD God caused a deep sleep to fall upon the man, and he slept;
then he took one of his ribs and closed up its place with flesh.
22And the rib that the LORD God had taken from the man he made into
        a woman
and brought her to the man.
23Then the man said,
    "This at last is bone of my bones
        and flesh of my flesh;
    this one shall be called Woman,
        for out of Man this one was taken."
24Therefore a man leaves his father and his mother and clings to his wife,
and they become one flesh.

The word of the Lord.

PSALMODY: PSALM 8

SECOND READING: HEBREWS 1:1–4; 2:5–12

A reading from Hebrews:

[1]Long ago God spoke to our ancestors in many and various ways by the
    prophets,
[2]but in these last days he has spoken to us by a Son,
whom he appointed heir of all things,
through whom he also created the worlds.
[3]He is the reflection of God's glory
and the exact imprint of God's very being,
and he sustains all things by his powerful word.
When he had made purification for sins,
he sat down at the right hand of the Majesty on high,
[4]having become as much superior to angels
as the name he has inherited is more excellent than theirs.

[2:5]Now God did not subject the coming world,
about which we are speaking, to angels.
[6]But someone has testified somewhere,
    "What are human beings that you are mindful of them,
        or mortals, that you care for them?
    [7]You have made them for a little while lower than the angels;
        you have crowned them with glory and honor,
        [8]subjecting all things under their feet."
Now in subjecting all things to them,
God left nothing outside their control.
As it is, we do not yet see everything in subjection to them,
[9]but we do see Jesus,
who for a little while was made lower than the angels,
now crowned with glory and honor because of the suffering of death,
so that by the grace of God he might taste death for everyone.

[10]It was fitting that God,
for whom and through whom all things exist,
in bringing many children to glory,
should make the pioneer of their salvation perfect through sufferings.
[11]For the one who sanctifies and those who are sanctified all have one Father.
For this reason Jesus is not ashamed to call them brothers and sisters,
[12]saying,
    "I will proclaim your name to my brothers and sisters,
        in the midst of the congregation I will praise you."

The word of the Lord.

GOSPEL: MARK 10:2–16

The Holy Gospel according to Mark, the tenth chapter.

[2]Some Pharisees came, and to test Jesus they asked,
"Is it lawful for a man to divorce his wife?"
[3]He answered them, "What did Moses command you?"
[4]They said,
"Moses allowed a man to write a certificate of dismissal and to divorce her."
[5]But Jesus said to them,
"Because of your hardness of heart he wrote this commandment for you.
[6]But from the beginning of creation, 'God made them male and female.'
[7]'For this reason a man shall leave his father and mother
and be joined to his wife,
[8]and the two shall become one flesh.'
So they are no longer two, but one flesh.
[9]Therefore what God has joined together, let no one separate."
[10]Then in the house the disciples asked him again about this matter.
[11]He said to them,
"Whoever divorces his wife and marries another commits adultery against
        her;
[12]and if she divorces her husband and marries another, she commits adultery."

[13]People were bringing little children to him in order that he might touch
        them;
and the disciples spoke sternly to them.
[14]But when Jesus saw this, he was indignant and said to them,
"Let the little children come to me; do not stop them;
for it is to such as these that the kingdom of God belongs.
[15]Truly I tell you,
whoever does not receive the kingdom of God as a little child
will never enter it."
[16]And he took them up in his arms, laid his hands on them, and blessed them.

The Gospel of the Lord.

SUNDAY BETWEEN
OCTOBER 9 AND 15 INCLUSIVE

PROPER 23

OCTOBER 12, 1997   *OCTOBER 15, 2000*   *OCTOBER 12, 2003*

FIRST READING: AMOS 5:6–7, 10–15

A reading from Amos:

⁶Seek the LORD and live,
    or he will break out against the house of Joseph like fire,
    and it will devour Bethel, with no one to quench it.
⁷Ah, you that turn justice to wormwood,
    and bring righteousness to the ground!

¹⁰They hate the one who reproves in the gate,
    and they abhor the one who speaks the truth.
¹¹Therefore because you trample on the poor
    and take from them levies of grain,
you have built houses of hewn stone,
    but you shall not live in them;
you have planted pleasant vineyards,
    but you shall not drink their wine.
¹²For I know how many are your transgressions,
    and how great are your sins—
you who afflict the righteous, who take a bribe,
    and push aside the needy in the gate.
¹³Therefore the prudent will keep silent in such a time;
    for it is an evil time.

¹⁴Seek good and not evil,
    that you may live;
and so the LORD, the God of hosts, will be with you,
    just as you have said.
¹⁵Hate evil and love good,
    and establish justice in the gate;
it may be that the LORD, the God of hosts,
    will be gracious to the remnant of Joseph.

The word of the Lord.

PSALMODY: PSALM 90:12–17

SECOND READING: HEBREWS 4:12–16

A reading from Hebrews:

[12]Indeed, the word of God is living and active,
sharper than any two-edged sword,
piercing until it divides soul from spirit, joints from marrow;
it is able to judge the thoughts and intentions of the heart.
[13]And before him no creature is hidden,
but all are naked and laid bare
to the eyes of the one to whom we must render an account.

[14]Since, then, we have a great high priest who has passed through the
heavens,
Jesus, the Son of God,
let us hold fast to our confession.
[15]For we do not have a high priest who is unable to sympathize with our
weaknesses,
but we have one who in every respect has been tested as we are,
yet without sin.
[16]Let us therefore approach the throne of grace with boldness,
so that we may receive mercy and find grace to help in time of need.

The word of the Lord.

GOSPEL: MARK 10:17–31

The Holy Gospel according to Mark, the tenth chapter.

[17]As Jesus was setting out on a journey,
a man ran up and knelt before him, and asked him,
"Good Teacher, what must I do to inherit eternal life?"
[18]Jesus said to him,
"Why do you call me good? No one is good but God alone.
[19]You know the commandments:
'You shall not murder; You shall not commit adultery;
You shall not steal; You shall not bear false witness;
You shall not defraud; Honor your father and mother.'"
[20]He said to him,
"Teacher, I have kept all these since my youth."
[21]Jesus, looking at him, loved him and said,
"You lack one thing;
go, sell what you own, and give the money to the poor,
and you will have treasure in heaven;
then come, follow me."
[22]When he heard this, he was shocked and went away grieving,
for he had many possessions.

[23]Then Jesus looked around and said to his disciples,
"How hard it will be for those who have wealth to enter the kingdom of God!"
[24]And the disciples were perplexed at these words.
But Jesus said to them again,
"Children, how hard it is to enter the kingdom of God!
[25]It is easier for a camel to go through the eye of a needle
than for someone who is rich to enter the kingdom of God."
[26]They were greatly astounded and said to one another,
"Then who can be saved?"
[27]Jesus looked at them and said,
"For mortals it is impossible, but not for God;
for God all things are possible."

[28]Peter began to say to him,
"Look, we have left everything and followed you."
[29]Jesus said, "Truly I tell you,
there is no one who has left house or brothers or sisters
or mother or father or children or fields,
for my sake and for the sake of the good news,
[30]who will not receive a hundredfold now in this age—
houses, brothers and sisters,
mothers and children, and fields, with persecutions—
and in the age to come eternal life.
[31]But many who are first will be last,
and the last will be first."

The Gospel of the Lord.

SUNDAY BETWEEN
OCTOBER 16 AND 22 INCLUSIVE

PROPER 24

OCTOBER 19, 1997   OCTOBER 22, 2000   OCTOBER 19, 2003

FIRST READING: ISAIAH 53:4–12

A reading from Isaiah:

⁴Surely he has borne our infirmities
    and carried our diseases;
yet we accounted him stricken,
    struck down by God, and afflicted.
⁵But he was wounded for our transgressions,
    crushed for our iniquities;
upon him was the punishment that made us whole,
    and by his bruises we are healed.
⁶All we like sheep have gone astray;
    we have all turned to our own way,
and the LORD has laid on him
    the iniquity of us all.

⁷He was oppressed, and he was afflicted,
    yet he did not open his mouth;
like a lamb that is led to the slaughter,
    and like a sheep that before its shearers is silent,
    so he did not open his mouth.
⁸By a perversion of justice he was taken away.
    Who could have imagined his future?
For he was cut off from the land of the living,
    stricken for the transgression of my people.
⁹They made his grave with the wicked
    and his tomb with the rich,
although he had done no violence,
    and there was no deceit in his mouth.

¹⁰Yet it was the will of the LORD to crush him with pain.
When you make his life an offering for sin,
    he shall see his offspring, and shall prolong his days;
through him the will of the LORD shall prosper.
    ¹¹Out of his anguish he shall see light;
he shall find satisfaction through his knowledge.

The righteous one, my servant, shall make many righteous,
  and he shall bear their iniquities.
¹²Therefore I will allot him a portion with the great,
  and he shall divide the spoil with the strong;
because he poured out himself to death,
  and was numbered with the transgressors;
yet he bore the sin of many,
  and made intercession for the transgressors.

The word of the Lord.

PSALMODY: PSALM 91:9–16

SECOND READING: HEBREWS 5:1–10

A reading from Hebrews:

¹Every high priest chosen from among mortals
is put in charge of things pertaining to God on their behalf,
to offer gifts and sacrifices for sins.
²He is able to deal gently with the ignorant and wayward,
since he himself is subject to weakness;
³and because of this he must offer sacrifice for his own sins
as well as for those of the people.
⁴And one does not presume to take this honor,
but takes it only when called by God, just as Aaron was.

⁵So also Christ did not glorify himself in becoming a high priest,
but was appointed by the one who said to him,
    "You are my Son,
        today I have begotten you";
⁶as he says also in another place,
    "You are a priest forever,
        according to the order of Melchizedek."

⁷In the days of his flesh, Jesus offered up prayers and supplications,
with loud cries and tears,
to the one who was able to save him from death,
and he was heard because of his reverent submission.
⁸Although he was a Son, he learned obedience through what he suffered;
⁹and having been made perfect,
he became the source of eternal salvation for all who obey him,
¹⁰having been designated by God a high priest according to the order
        of Melchizedek.

The word of the Lord.

The Holy Gospel according to Mark, the tenth chapter.

[35]James and John, the sons of Zebedee, came forward to Jesus and said
     to him,
"Teacher, we want you to do for us whatever we ask of you."
[36]And he said to them, "What is it you want me to do for you?"
[37]And they said to him,
"Grant us to sit, one at your right hand and one at your left, in your glory."
[38]But Jesus said to them,
"You do not know what you are asking.
Are you able to drink the cup that I drink,
or be baptized with the baptism that I am baptized with?"
[39]They replied, "We are able."
Then Jesus said to them,
"The cup that I drink you will drink;
and with the baptism with which I am baptized, you will be baptized;
[40]but to sit at my right hand or at my left is not mine to grant,
but it is for those for whom it has been prepared."

[41]When the ten heard this, they began to be angry with James and John.
[42]So Jesus called them and said to them,
"You know that among the Gentiles
those whom they recognize as their rulers lord it over them,
and their great ones are tyrants over them.
[43]But it is not so among you;
but whoever wishes to become great among you must be your servant,
[44]and whoever wishes to be first among you must be slave of all.
[45]For the Son of Man came not to be served but to serve,
and to give his life a ransom for many."

The Gospel of the Lord.

SUNDAY BETWEEN
OCTOBER 23 AND 29 INCLUSIVE

PROPER 25

OCTOBER 26, 1997　　*OCTOBER 29, 2000*　　*OCTOBER 26, 2003*

FIRST READING: JEREMIAH 31:7–9

A reading from Jeremiah:

⁷Thus says the LORD:
Sing aloud with gladness for Jacob,
　　and raise shouts for the chief of the nations;
proclaim, give praise, and say,
　　"Save, O LORD, your people,
　　the remnant of Israel."
⁸See, I am going to bring them from the land of the north,
　　and gather them from the farthest parts of the earth,
among them the blind and the lame,
　　those with child and those in labor, together;
　　a great company, they shall return here.
⁹With weeping they shall come,
　　and with consolations I will lead them back,
I will let them walk by brooks of water,
　　in a straight path in which they shall not stumble;
for I have become a father to Israel,
　　and Ephraim is my firstborn.

The word of the Lord.

PSALMODY: PSALM 126

SECOND READING: HEBREWS 7:23–28

A reading from Hebrews:

²³The former priests were many in number,
because they were prevented by death from continuing in office;
²⁴but he holds his priesthood permanently,
because he continues forever.
²⁵Consequently he is able for all time to save those who approach God through
him,
since he always lives to make intercession for them.

²⁶For it was fitting that we should have such a high priest,
holy, blameless, undefiled, separated from sinners,
and exalted above the heavens.
²⁷Unlike the other high priests,
he has no need to offer sacrifices day after day,
first for his own sins, and then for those of the people;
this he did once for all when he offered himself.
²⁸For the law appoints as high priests those who are subject to weakness,
but the word of the oath, which came later than the law,
appoints a Son who has been made perfect forever.

The word of the Lord.

GOSPEL: MARK 10:46–52

The Holy Gospel according to Mark, the tenth chapter.

⁴⁶As Jesus and his disciples and a large crowd were leaving Jericho,
Bartimaeus son of Timaeus, a blind beggar, was sitting by the roadside.
⁴⁷When he heard that it was Jesus of Nazareth,
he began to shout out and say,
"Jesus, Son of David, have mercy on me!"
⁴⁸Many sternly ordered him to be quiet,
but he cried out even more loudly,
"Son of David, have mercy on me!"
⁴⁹Jesus stood still and said, "Call him here."
And they called the blind man, saying to him,
"Take heart; get up, he is calling you."
⁵⁰So throwing off his cloak, he sprang up and came to Jesus.
⁵¹Then Jesus said to him,
"What do you want me to do for you?"
The blind man said to him, "My teacher, let me see again."
⁵²Jesus said to him,
"Go; your faith has made you well."
Immediately he regained his sight and followed him on the way.

The Gospel of the Lord.

SUNDAY BETWEEN
OCTOBER 30 AND NOVEMBER 5
INCLUSIVE

PROPER 26

NOVEMBER 2, 1997　　*NOVEMBER 5, 2000*　　*NOVEMBER 2, 2003*

FIRST READING: DEUTERONOMY 6:1–9

A reading from Deuteronomy:

Moses said to the people,
¹Now this is the commandment—the statutes and the ordinances—
that the LORD your God charged me to teach you to observe
in the land that you are about to cross into and occupy,
²so that you and your children and your children's children,
may fear the LORD your God all the days of your life,
and keep all his decrees and his commandments that I am commanding you,
so that your days may be long.
³Hear therefore, O Israel, and observe them diligently,
so that it may go well with you,
and so that you may multiply greatly in a land flowing with milk and honey,
as the LORD, the God of your ancestors, has promised you.

⁴Hear, O Israel: The LORD is our God, the LORD alone.
⁵You shall love the LORD your God with all your heart,
and with all your soul, and with all your might.
⁶Keep these words that I am commanding you today in your heart.
⁷Recite them to your children
and talk about them when you are at home and when you are away,
when you lie down and when you rise.
⁸Bind them as a sign on your hand,
fix them as an emblem on your forehead,
⁹and write them on the doorposts of your house and on your gates.

The word of the Lord.

PSALMODY: PSALM 119:1–8

SECOND READING: HEBREWS 9:11–14

A reading from Hebrews:

[11]When Christ came as a high priest of the good things that have come,
then through the greater and perfect tent
(not made with hands, that is, not of this creation),
[12]he entered once for all into the Holy Place,
not with the blood of goats and calves,
but with his own blood, thus obtaining eternal redemption.
[13]For if the blood of goats and bulls,
with the sprinkling of the ashes of a heifer,
sanctifies those who have been defiled so that their flesh is purified,
[14]how much more will the blood of Christ,
who through the eternal Spirit offered himself without blemish to God,
purify our conscience from dead works to worship the living God!

The word of the Lord.

GOSPEL: MARK 12:28–34

The Holy Gospel according to Mark, the twelfth chapter.

[28]One of the scribes came near and heard Jesus and the Sadducees disputing
with one another,
and seeing that Jesus answered them well, he asked him,
"Which commandment is the first of all?"
[29]Jesus answered, "The first is,
'Hear, O Israel: the Lord our God, the Lord is one;
[30]you shall love the Lord your God with all your heart, and with all your soul,
and with all your mind, and with all your strength.'
[31]The second is this,
'You shall love your neighbor as yourself.'
There is no other commandment greater than these."

[32]Then the scribe said to him,
"You are right, Teacher;
you have truly said that 'he is one, and besides him there is no other';
[33]and 'to love him with all the heart, and with all the understanding,
and with all the strength,'
and 'to love one's neighbor as oneself,'—
this is much more important than all whole burnt offerings and sacrifices."
[34]When Jesus saw that he answered wisely, he said to him,
"You are not far from the kingdom of God."
After that no one dared to ask him any question.

The Gospel of the Lord.

SUNDAY BETWEEN
NOVEMBER 6 AND 12 INCLUSIVE

PROPER 27

NOVEMBER 9, 1997   NOVEMBER 12, 2000   NOVEMBER 9, 2003

FIRST READING: 1 KINGS 17:8–16

A reading from First Kings:

⁸The word of the LORD came to Elijah, saying,
⁹"Go now to Zarephath, which belongs to Sidon, and live there;
for I have commanded a widow there to feed you."
¹⁰So he set out and went to Zarephath.
When he came to the gate of the town,
a widow was there gathering sticks;
he called to her and said,
"Bring me a little water in a vessel, so that I may drink."
¹¹As she was going to bring it, he called to her and said,
"Bring me a morsel of bread in your hand."
¹²But she said,
"As the LORD your God lives, I have nothing baked,
only a handful of meal in a jar, and a little oil in a jug;
I am now gathering a couple of sticks,
so that I may go home and prepare it for myself and my son,
that we may eat it, and die."

¹³Elijah said to her, "Do not be afraid; go and do as you have said;
but first make me a little cake of it and bring it to me,
and afterwards make something for yourself and your son.
¹⁴For thus says the LORD the God of Israel:
The jar of meal will not be emptied
and the jug of oil will not fail
until the day that the LORD sends rain on the earth."

¹⁵She went and did as Elijah said,
so that she as well as he and her household ate for many days.
¹⁶The jar of meal was not emptied, neither did the jug of oil fail,
according to the word of the LORD that he spoke by Elijah.

The word of the Lord.

PSALMODY: PSALM 146

A reading from Hebrews:

^{24}Christ did not enter a sanctuary made by human hands,
a mere copy of the true one,
but he entered into heaven itself,
now to appear in the presence of God on our behalf.
^{25}Nor was it to offer himself again and again,
as the high priest enters the Holy Place year after year
with blood that is not his own;
^{26}for then he would have had to suffer again and again
since the foundation of the world.

But as it is,
he has appeared once for all at the end of the age
to remove sin by the sacrifice of himself.
^{27}And just as it is appointed for mortals to die once,
and after that the judgment,
^{28}so Christ, having been offered once to bear the sins of many,
will appear a second time,
not to deal with sin,
but to save those who are eagerly waiting for him.

The word of the Lord.

The Holy Gospel according to Mark, the twelfth chapter.

[38]As Jesus taught, he said,
"Beware of the scribes, who like to walk around in long robes,
and to be greeted with respect in the marketplaces,
[39]and to have the best seats in the synagogues and places of honor
       at banquets!
[40]They devour widows' houses
and for the sake of appearance say long prayers.
They will receive the greater condemnation."

[41]He sat down opposite the treasury,
and watched the crowd putting money into the treasury.
Many rich people put in large sums.
[42]A poor widow came and put in two small copper coins,
which are worth a penny.
[43]Then he called his disciples and said to them,
"Truly I tell you,
this poor widow has put in more than all those who are contributing to the
       treasury.
[44]For all of them have contributed out of their abundance;
but she out of her poverty has put in everything she had,
all she had to live on."

The Gospel of the Lord.

SUNDAY BETWEEN
NOVEMBER 13 AND 19 INCLUSIVE

PROPER 28

NOVEMBER 16, 1997   *NOVEMBER 19, 2000*   *NOVEMBER 16, 2003*

FIRST READING: DANIEL 12:1–3

A reading from Daniel:

[1]"At that time Michael, the great prince, the protector of your people,
shall arise.
There shall be a time of anguish,
such as has never occurred since nations first came into existence.
But at that time your people shall be delivered,
everyone who is found written in the book.
[2]Many of those who sleep in the dust of the earth shall awake,
some to everlasting life,
and some to shame and everlasting contempt.
[3]Those who are wise shall shine like the brightness of the sky,
and those who lead many to righteousness,
like the stars forever and ever."

The word of the Lord.

PSALMODY: PSALM 16

SECOND READING: HEBREWS 10:11–14 [15–18] 19–25

A reading from Hebrews:

[11]Every priest stands day after day at his service,
offering again and again the same sacrifices that can never take away sins.
[12]But when Christ had offered for all time a single sacrifice for sins,
"he sat down at the right hand of God,"
[13]and since then has been waiting
"until his enemies would be made a footstool for his feet."
[14]For by a single offering he has perfected for all time those who are
    sanctified.

[[15]And the Holy Spirit also testifies to us, for after saying,
    [16]"This is the covenant that I will make with them
        after those days, says the Lord:
    I will put my laws in their hearts,
        and I will write them on their minds,"
[17]he also adds,
    "I will remember their sins and their lawless deeds no more."
[18]Where there is forgiveness of these,
there is no longer any offering for sin.]

[19]Therefore, my friends,
since we have confidence to enter the sanctuary by the blood of Jesus,
[20]by the new and living way that he opened for us through the curtain
(that is, through his flesh),
[21]and since we have a great priest over the house of God,
[22]let us approach with a true heart in full assurance of faith,
with our hearts sprinkled clean from an evil conscience
and our bodies washed with pure water.
[23]Let us hold fast to the confession of our hope without wavering,
for he who has promised is faithful.
[24]And let us consider how to provoke one another to love and good deeds,
[25]not neglecting to meet together, as is the habit of some,
but encouraging one another,
and all the more as you see the Day approaching.

The word of the Lord.

GOSPEL: MARK 13:1–8

The Holy Gospel according to Mark, the 13th chapter.

[1]As Jesus came out of the temple, one of his disciples said to him,
"Look, Teacher, what large stones and what large buildings!"
[2]Then Jesus asked him, "Do you see these great buildings?
Not one stone will be left here upon another;
all will be thrown down."

[3]When he was sitting on the Mount of Olives opposite the temple,
Peter, James, John, and Andrew asked him privately,
[4]"Tell us, when will this be,
and what will be the sign that all these things are about to be accomplished?"
[5]Then Jesus began to say to them,
"Beware that no one leads you astray.
[6]Many will come in my name and say, 'I am he!'
and they will lead many astray.
[7]When you hear of wars and rumors of wars, do not be alarmed;
this must take place, but the end is still to come.
[8]For nation will rise against nation,
and kingdom against kingdom;
there will be earthquakes in various places;
there will be famines.
This is but the beginning of the birth pangs."

The Gospel of the Lord.

CHRIST THE KING

Last Sunday after Pentecost[†]

PROPER 29

NOVEMBER 23, 1997   *NOVEMBER 26, 2000*   *NOVEMBER 23, 2003*

FIRST READING: DANIEL 7:9–10, 13–14

A reading from Daniel:

[9]As I watched,
thrones were set in place,
   and an Ancient One took his throne,
his clothing was white as snow,
   and the hair of his head like pure wool;
his throne was fiery flames,
   and its wheels were burning fire.
[10]A stream of fire issued
   and flowed out from his presence.
A thousand thousands served him,
   and ten thousand times ten thousand stood attending him.
The court sat in judgment,
   and the books were opened.

[13]As I watched in the night visions,
I saw one like a human being
   coming with the clouds of heaven.
And he came to the Ancient One
   and was presented before him.
[14]To him was given dominion
   and glory and kingship,
that all peoples, nations, and languages
   should serve him.
His dominion is an everlasting dominion
   that shall not pass away,
and his kingship is one
   that shall never be destroyed.

The word of the Lord.

PSALMODY: PSALM 93

[†]*Sunday between November 20 and 26 inclusive*

SECOND READING: Revelation 1:4b–8

A reading from Revelation:

4bGrace to you and peace from him who is and who was and who is to come,
and from the seven spirits who are before his throne,
5and from Jesus Christ,
the faithful witness, the firstborn of the dead,
and the ruler of the kings of the earth.
To him who loves us and freed us from our sins by his blood,
6and made us to be a kingdom,
priests serving his God and Father,
to him be glory and dominion forever and ever. Amen.
    7Look! He is coming with the clouds;
        every eye will see him,
    even those who pierced him;
        and on his account all the tribes of the earth will wail.
So it is to be. Amen.

8"I am the Alpha and the Omega,"
says the Lord God,
who is and who was and who is to come,
the Almighty.

The word of the Lord.

GOSPEL: John 18:33–37

The Holy Gospel according to John, the 18th chapter.

33Pilate entered the headquarters again,
summoned Jesus, and asked him,
"Are you the King of the Jews?"
34Jesus answered,
"Do you ask this on your own, or did others tell you about me?"
35Pilate replied, "I am not a Jew, am I?
Your own nation and the chief priests have handed you over to me.
What have you done?"
36Jesus answered, "My kingdom is not from this world.
If my kingdom were from this world,
my followers would be fighting to keep me from being handed over to the Jews.
But as it is, my kingdom is not from here."
37Pilate asked him, "So you are a king?"
Jesus answered, "You say that I am a king.
For this I was born, and for this I came into the world,
to testify to the truth.
Everyone who belongs to the truth listens to my voice."

The Gospel of the Lord.

LESSER FESTIVALS
AND OCCASIONS

ST. ANDREW, APOSTLE

NOVEMBER 30

FIRST READING: Ezekiel 3:16–21

A reading from Ezekiel:

¹⁶At the end of seven days, the word of the Lord came to me:
¹⁷Mortal, I have made you a sentinel for the house of Israel;
whenever you hear a word from my mouth,
you shall give them warning from me.
¹⁸If I say to the wicked, "You shall surely die,"
and you give them no warning,
or speak to warn the wicked from their wicked way, in order to save their life,
those wicked persons shall die for their iniquity;
but their blood I will require at your hand.
¹⁹But if you warn the wicked,
and they do not turn from their wickedness, or from their wicked way,
they shall die for their iniquity; but you will have saved your life.

²⁰Again, if the righteous turn from their righteousness and commit iniquity,
and I lay a stumbling block before them, they shall die;
because you have not warned them, they shall die for their sin,
and their righteous deeds that they have done shall not be remembered;
but their blood I will require at your hand.
²¹If, however, you warn the righteous not to sin, and they do not sin,
they shall surely live, because they took warning;
and you will have saved your life.

The word of the Lord.

PSALMODY: Psalm 19:1–6

SECOND READING: Romans 10:10–18

A reading from Romans:

¹⁰One believes with the heart and so is justified,
and one confesses with the mouth and so is saved.
¹¹The scripture says,
"No one who believes in him will be put to shame."

¹²For there is no distinction between Jew and Greek;
the same Lord is Lord of all and is generous to all who call on him.
¹³For, "Everyone who calls on the name of the Lord shall be saved."

¹⁴But how are they to call on one in whom they have not believed?
And how are they to believe in one of whom they have never heard?
And how are they to hear without someone to proclaim him?
¹⁵And how are they to proclaim him unless they are sent?
As it is written,
"How beautiful are the feet of those who bring good news!"
¹⁶But not all have obeyed the good news; for Isaiah says,
"Lord, who has believed our message?"
¹⁷So faith comes from what is heard,
and what is heard comes through the word of Christ.
¹⁸But I ask, have they not heard? Indeed they have; for
    "Their voice has gone out to all the earth,
        and their words to the ends of the world."

The word of the Lord.

GOSPEL: JOHN 1:35–42

The Holy Gospel according to John, the first chapter.

³⁵The next day John again was standing with two of his disciples,
³⁶and as he watched Jesus walk by, he exclaimed,
"Look, here is the Lamb of God!"
³⁷The two disciples heard him say this, and they followed Jesus.
³⁸When Jesus turned and saw them following, he said to them,
"What are you looking for?"
They said to him,
"Rabbi" (which translated means Teacher),
"where are you staying?"
³⁹He said to them, "Come and see."

They came and saw where he was staying,
and they remained with him that day.
It was about four o'clock in the afternoon.
⁴⁰One of the two who heard John speak and followed him
was Andrew, Simon Peter's brother.
⁴¹He first found his brother Simon and said to him,
"We have found the Messiah" (which is translated Anointed).
⁴²He brought Simon to Jesus, who looked at him and said,
"You are Simon son of John.
You are to be called Cephas" (which is translated Peter).

The Gospel of the Lord.

St. Thomas, Apostle

DECEMBER 21

FIRST READING: JUDGES 6:36–40

A reading from Judges:

36Gideon said to God,
"In order to see whether you will deliver Israel by my hand, as you have said,
37I am going to lay a fleece of wool on the threshing floor;
if there is dew on the fleece alone, and it is dry on all the ground,
then I shall know that you will deliver Israel by my hand, as you have said."
38And it was so.
When he rose early next morning and squeezed the fleece,
he wrung enough dew from the fleece to fill a bowl with water.

39Then Gideon said to God, "Do not let your anger burn against me,
let me speak one more time;
let me, please, make trial with the fleece just once more;
let it be dry only on the fleece, and on all the ground let there be dew."
40And God did so that night.
It was dry on the fleece only, and on all the ground there was dew.

The word of the Lord.

PSALMODY: PSALM 136:1–4, 23–26

SECOND READING: EPHESIANS 4:11–16

A reading from Ephesians:

11The gifts he gave were that some would be apostles,
some prophets, some evangelists, some pastors and teachers,
12to equip the saints for the work of ministry,
for building up the body of Christ,
13until all of us come to the unity of the faith
and of the knowledge of the Son of God,
to maturity, to the measure of the full stature of Christ.

14We must no longer be children,
tossed to and fro and blown about by every wind of doctrine,
by people's trickery, by their craftiness in deceitful scheming.

¹⁵But speaking the truth in love,
we must grow up in every way into him who is the head, into Christ,
¹⁶from whom the whole body,
joined and knit together by every ligament with which it is equipped,
as each part is working properly,
promotes the body's growth in building itself up in love.

The word of the Lord.

GOSPEL: JOHN 14:1–7

The Holy Gospel according to John, the 14th chapter.

Jesus said to the disciples:
¹"Do not let your hearts be troubled.
Believe in God, believe also in me.
²In my Father's house there are many dwelling places.
If it were not so, would I have told you that I go to prepare a place for you?
³And if I go and prepare a place for you,
I will come again and will take you to myself,
so that where I am, there you may be also.
⁴And you know the way to the place where I am going."

⁵Thomas said to him, "Lord, we do not know where you are going.
How can we know the way?"
⁶Jesus said to him, "I am the way, and the truth, and the life.
No one comes to the Father except through me.
⁷If you know me, you will know my Father also.
From now on you do know him and have seen him."

The Gospel of the Lord.

ST. STEPHEN, DEACON AND MARTYR

DECEMBER 26

FIRST READING: 2 CHRONICLES 24:17–22

A reading from Second Chronicles:

¹⁷Now after the death of Jehoiada the officials of Judah came
and did obeisance to the king;
then the king listened to them.
¹⁸They abandoned the house of the LORD, the God of their ancestors,
and served the sacred poles and the idols.
And wrath came upon Judah and Jerusalem for this guilt of theirs.
¹⁹Yet he sent prophets among them to bring them back to the LORD;
they testified against them, but they would not listen.

²⁰Then the spirit of God took possession of Zechariah
son of the priest Jehoiada;
he stood above the people and said to them,
"Thus says God:
Why do you transgress the commandments of the LORD,
so that you cannot prosper?
Because you have forsaken the LORD, he has also forsaken you."
²¹But they conspired against him,
and by command of the king
they stoned him to death in the court of the house of the LORD.
²²King Joash did not remember the kindness that Jehoiada,
Zechariah's father, had shown him, but killed his son.
As he was dying, he said, "May the LORD see and avenge!"

The word of the Lord.

PSALMODY: PSALM 17:1–9, 15   *Psalm 17:1–9, 16* LBW/BCP

SECOND READING: ACTS 6:8—7:2a, 51–60

A reading from Acts:

⁸Stephen, full of grace and power,
did great wonders and signs among the people.
⁹Then some of those who belonged to the synagogue of the Freedmen
        (as it was called),

Cyrenians, Alexandrians, and others of those from Cilicia and Asia,
stood up and argued with Stephen.
[10]But they could not withstand the wisdom and the Spirit with which he spoke.
[11]Then they secretly instigated some men to say,
"We have heard him speak blasphemous words against Moses and God."

[12]They stirred up the people as well as the elders and the scribes;
then they suddenly confronted him, seized him,
and brought him before the council.
[13]They set up false witnesses who said,
"This man never stops saying things against this holy place and the law;
[14]for we have heard him say that this Jesus of Nazareth will destroy this place
and will change the customs that Moses handed on to us."
[15]And all who sat in the council looked intently at him,
and they saw that his face was like the face of an angel.
[7:1]Then the high priest asked him,
"Are these things so?"
[2]And Stephen replied: "Brothers and fathers, listen to me.

[51]"You stiff-necked people, uncircumcised in heart and ears,
you are forever opposing the Holy Spirit, just as your ancestors used to do.
[52]Which of the prophets did your ancestors not persecute?
They killed those who foretold the coming of the Righteous One,
and now you have become his betrayers and murderers.
[53]You are the ones that received the law as ordained by angels,
and yet you have not kept it."

[54]When they heard these things, they became enraged
and ground their teeth at Stephen.
[55]But filled with the Holy Spirit,
he gazed into heaven and saw the glory of God
and Jesus standing at the right hand of God.
[56]"Look," he said,
"I see the heavens opened
and the Son of Man standing at the right hand of God!"

[57]But they covered their ears,
and with a loud shout all rushed together against him.
[58]Then they dragged him out of the city and began to stone him;
and the witnesses laid their coats at the feet of a young man named Saul.
[59]While they were stoning Stephen, he prayed,
"Lord Jesus, receive my spirit."
[60]Then he knelt down and cried out in a loud voice,
"Lord, do not hold this sin against them."
When he had said this, he died.

The word of the Lord.

GOSPEL: MATTHEW 23:34–39

The Holy Gospel according to Matthew, the 23rd chapter.

Jesus said:
34"Therefore I send you prophets, sages, and scribes,
some of whom you will kill and crucify,
and some you will flog in your synagogues and pursue from town to town,
35so that upon you may come all the righteous blood shed on earth,
from the blood of righteous Abel to the blood of Zechariah son of Barachiah,
whom you murdered between the sanctuary and the altar.
36Truly I tell you, all this will come upon this generation.

37"Jerusalem, Jerusalem,
the city that kills the prophets and stones those who are sent to it!
How often have I desired to gather your children together
as a hen gathers her brood under her wings,
and you were not willing!
38See, your house is left to you, desolate.
39For I tell you, you will not see me again until you say,
'Blessed is the one who comes in the name of the Lord.' "

The Gospel of the Lord.

St. John, Apostle and Evangelist

DECEMBER 27

FIRST READING: Genesis 1:1–5, 26–31

A reading from Genesis:

¹In the beginning when God created the heavens and the earth,
²the earth was a formless void
and darkness covered the face of the deep,
while a wind from God swept over the face of the waters.
³Then God said, "Let there be light"; and there was light.
⁴And God saw that the light was good;
and God separated the light from the darkness.
⁵God called the light Day, and the darkness he called Night.
And there was evening and there was morning, the first day.

²⁶Then God said,
"Let us make humankind in our image, according to our likeness;
and let them have dominion over the fish of the sea,
and over the birds of the air, and over the cattle,
and over all the wild animals of the earth,
and over every creeping thing that creeps upon the earth."

> ²⁷So God created humankind in his image,
>   in the image of God he created them;
>   male and female he created them.
²⁸God blessed them, and God said to them,
"Be fruitful and multiply, and fill the earth and subdue it;
and have dominion over the fish of the sea
and over the birds of the air
and over every living thing that moves upon the earth."

²⁹God said,
"See, I have given you every plant yielding seed that is upon the face
     of all the earth,
and every tree with seed in its fruit;
you shall have them for food.
³⁰And to every beast of the earth, and to every bird of the air,
and to everything that creeps on the earth,
everything that has the breath of life,
I have given every green plant for food."

And it was so.

³¹God saw everything that he had made,
and indeed, it was very good.
And there was evening and there was morning, the sixth day.

The word of the Lord.

PSALMODY: Psalm 116:12–19

Psalm 116:10–17 LBW/BCP

SECOND READING: 1 John 1:1—2:2

A reading from First John:

¹We declare to you what was from the beginning,
what we have heard, what we have seen with our eyes,
what we have looked at and touched with our hands,
concerning the word of life—
²this life was revealed, and we have seen it and testify to it,
and declare to you the eternal life that was with the Father
and was revealed to us—
³we declare to you what we have seen and heard
so that you also may have fellowship with us;
and truly our fellowship is with the Father and with his Son Jesus Christ.
⁴We are writing these things so that our joy may be complete.

⁵This is the message we have heard from him and proclaim to you,
that God is light and in him there is no darkness at all.
⁶If we say that we have fellowship with him while we are walking in darkness,
we lie and do not do what is true;
⁷but if we walk in the light as he himself is in the light,
we have fellowship with one another,
and the blood of Jesus his Son cleanses us from all sin.
⁸If we say that we have no sin, we deceive ourselves,
and the truth is not in us.
⁹If we confess our sins,
he who is faithful and just will forgive us our sins
and cleanse us from all unrighteousness.
¹⁰If we say that we have not sinned, we make him a liar,
and his word is not in us.

²:¹My little children,
I am writing these things to you so that you may not sin.
But if anyone does sin, we have an advocate with the Father,
Jesus Christ the righteous;
²and he is the atoning sacrifice for our sins,
and not for ours only but also for the sins of the whole world.

The word of the Lord.

GOSPEL: JOHN 21:20–25

The Holy Gospel according to John, the 21st chapter.

²⁰Peter turned and saw the disciple whom Jesus loved following them;
he was the one who had reclined next to Jesus at the supper and had said,
"Lord, who is it that is going to betray you?"
²¹When Peter saw him, he said to Jesus,
"Lord, what about him?"
²²Jesus said to him,
"If it is my will that he remain until I come, what is that to you?
Follow me!"
²³So the rumor spread in the community that this disciple would not die.
Yet Jesus did not say to him that he would not die, but,
"If it is my will that he remain until I come, what is that to you?"

²⁴This is the disciple who is testifying to these things
and has written them, and we know that his testimony is true.
²⁵But there are also many other things that Jesus did;
if every one of them were written down,
I suppose that the world itself could not contain the books that would be
   written.

The Gospel of the Lord.

The Holy Innocents, Martyrs

DECEMBER 28

FIRST READING: JEREMIAH 31:15–17

A reading from Jeremiah:

[15]Thus says the LORD:
A voice is heard in Ramah,
    lamentation and bitter weeping.
Rachel is weeping for her children;
    she refuses to be comforted for her children,
    because they are no more.
[16]Thus says the LORD:
Keep your voice from weeping,
    and your eyes from tears;
for there is a reward for your work,
                    says the LORD:
    they shall come back from the land of the enemy;
[17]there is hope for your future,
                    says the LORD:
    your children shall come back to their own country.

The word of the Lord.

PSALMODY: PSALM 124

SECOND READING: 1 PETER 4:12–19

A reading from First Peter:

[12]Beloved, do not be surprised at the fiery ordeal
that is taking place among you to test you,
as though something strange were happening to you.
[13]But rejoice insofar as you are sharing Christ's sufferings,
so that you may also be glad and shout for joy when his glory is revealed.
[14]If you are reviled for the name of Christ, you are blessed,
because the spirit of glory, which is the Spirit of God, is resting on you.
[15]But let none of you suffer as a murderer, a thief,
a criminal, or even as a mischief maker.

16Yet if any of you suffers as a Christian, do not consider it a disgrace,
but glorify God because you bear this name.
17For the time has come for judgment to begin with the household of God;
if it begins with us,
what will be the end for those who do not obey the gospel of God?
18And

  "If it is hard for the righteous to be saved,
    what will become of the ungodly and the sinners?"
19Therefore, let those suffering in accordance with God's will
entrust themselves to a faithful Creator, while continuing to do good.

The word of the Lord.

GOSPEL: MATTHEW 2:13–18

The Holy Gospel according to Matthew, the second chapter.

13Now after the wise men had left,
an angel of the Lord appeared to Joseph in a dream and said,
"Get up, take the child and his mother, and flee to Egypt,
and remain there until I tell you;
for Herod is about to search for the child, to destroy him."
14Then Joseph got up, took the child and his mother by night,
and went to Egypt,
15and remained there until the death of Herod.
This was to fulfill what had been spoken by the Lord through the prophet,
"Out of Egypt I have called my son."

16When Herod saw that he had been tricked by the wise men,
he was infuriated,
and he sent and killed all the children in and around Bethlehem
who were two years old or under,
according to the time that he had learned from the wise men.
17Then was fulfilled what had been spoken through the prophet Jeremiah:
  18"A voice was heard in Ramah,
    wailing and loud lamentation,
  Rachel weeping for her children;
    she refused to be consoled, because they are no more."

The Gospel of the Lord.

THE NAME OF JESUS

JANUARY 1

FIRST READING: NUMBERS 6:22–27

A reading from Numbers:

22The LORD spoke to Moses, saying:
23Speak to Aaron and his sons, saying,
Thus you shall bless the Israelites:
You shall say to them,
    24The LORD bless you and keep you;
    25the LORD make his face to shine upon you, and be gracious to you;
    26the LORD lift up his countenance upon you, and give you peace.

27So they shall put my name on the Israelites, and I will bless them.

The word of the Lord.

PSALMODY: PSALM 8

SECOND READING: GALATIANS 4:4–7

Or Philippians 2:5–11, following

A reading from Galatians:

4When the fullness of time had come,
God sent his Son, born of a woman, born under the law,
5in order to redeem those who were under the law,
so that we might receive adoption as children.
6And because you are children,
God has sent the Spirit of his Son into our hearts,
crying, "Abba! Father!"
7So you are no longer a slave but a child,
and if a child then also an heir, through God.

The word of the Lord.

A reading from Philippians:

⁵Let the same mind be in you that was in Christ Jesus,
> ⁶who, though he was in the form of God,
>> did not regard equality with God
>> as something to be exploited,
> ⁷but emptied himself,
>> taking the form of a slave,
>> being born in human likeness.
> And being found in human form,
>> ⁸he humbled himself
>> and became obedient to the point of death—
>> even death on a cross.
⁹Therefore God also highly exalted him
and gave him the name that is above every name,
¹⁰so that at the name of Jesus every knee should bend,
in heaven and on earth and under the earth,
¹¹and every tongue should confess that Jesus Christ is Lord,
to the glory of God the Father.

The word of the Lord.

GOSPEL: LUKE 2:15–21

The Holy Gospel according to Luke, the second chapter.

¹⁵When the angels had left them and gone into heaven,
the shepherds said to one another,
"Let us go now to Bethlehem
and see this thing that has taken place,
which the Lord has made known to us."
¹⁶So they went with haste and found Mary and Joseph,
and the child lying in the manger.
¹⁷When they saw this,
they made known what had been told them about this child;
¹⁸and all who heard it were amazed at what the shepherds told them.
¹⁹But Mary treasured all these words and pondered them in her heart.
²⁰The shepherds returned,
glorifying and praising God for all they had heard and seen,
as it had been told them.

²¹After eight days had passed, it was time to circumcise the child;
and he was called Jesus,
the name given by the angel before he was conceived in the womb.

The Gospel of the Lord.

THE CONFESSION OF ST. PETER

JANUARY 18

FIRST READING: ACTS 4:8–13

A reading from Acts:

⁸Peter, filled with the Holy Spirit, said to the authorities,
"Rulers of the people and elders,
⁹if we are questioned today
because of a good deed done to someone who was sick
and are asked how this man has been healed,
¹⁰let it be known to all of you, and to all the people of Israel,
that this man is standing before you in good health
by the name of Jesus Christ of Nazareth,
whom you crucified, whom God raised from the dead.
¹¹This Jesus is
 'the stone that was rejected by you, the builders;
   it has become the cornerstone.'
¹²There is salvation in no one else,
for there is no other name under heaven given among mortals
by which we must be saved."

¹³Now when they saw the boldness of Peter and John
and realized that they were uneducated and ordinary men,
they were amazed and recognized them as companions of Jesus.

The word of the Lord.

PSALMODY: PSALM 18:1–6, 16–19   *Psalm 18:1–7, 17–20* LBW/BCP

SECOND READING: 1 CORINTHIANS 10:1–5

A reading from First Corinthians:

¹I do not want you to be unaware, brothers and sisters,
that our ancestors were all under the cloud,
and all passed through the sea,
²and all were baptized into Moses in the cloud and in the sea,
³and all ate the same spiritual food,
⁴and all drank the same spiritual drink.
For they drank from the spiritual rock that followed them,
and the rock was Christ.
⁵Nevertheless, God was not pleased with most of them,
and they were struck down in the wilderness.

The word of the Lord.

GOSPEL: MATTHEW 16:13–19

The Holy Gospel according to Matthew, the 16th chapter.

¹³Now when Jesus came into the district of Caesarea Philippi,
he asked his disciples, "Who do people say that the Son of Man is?"
¹⁴And they said,
"Some say John the Baptist, but others Elijah,
and still others Jeremiah or one of the prophets."
¹⁵He said to them, "But who do you say that I am?"
¹⁶Simon Peter answered,
"You are the Messiah, the Son of the living God."

¹⁷And Jesus answered him,
"Blessed are you, Simon son of Jonah!
For flesh and blood has not revealed this to you,
but my Father in heaven.
¹⁸And I tell you, you are Peter,
and on this rock I will build my church,
and the gates of Hades will not prevail against it.
¹⁹I will give you the keys of the kingdom of heaven,
and whatever you bind on earth will be bound in heaven,
and whatever you loose on earth will be loosed in heaven."

The Gospel of the Lord.

THE CONVERSION OF ST. PAUL

JANUARY 25

FIRST READING: ACTS 9:1–22

A reading from Acts:

¹Saul, still breathing threats and murder against the disciples of the Lord,
went to the high priest
²and asked him for letters to the synagogues at Damascus,
so that if he found any who belonged to the Way, men or women,
he might bring them bound to Jerusalem.

³Now as he was going along and approaching Damascus,
suddenly a light from heaven flashed around him.
⁴He fell to the ground and heard a voice saying to him,
"Saul, Saul, why do you persecute me?"
⁵He asked, "Who are you, Lord?"
The reply came, "I am Jesus, whom you are persecuting.
⁶But get up and enter the city,
and you will be told what you are to do."
⁷The men who were traveling with him stood speechless
because they heard the voice but saw no one.
⁸Saul got up from the ground,
and though his eyes were open, he could see nothing;
so they led him by the hand and brought him into Damascus.
⁹For three days he was without sight, and neither ate nor drank.

¹⁰Now there was a disciple in Damascus named Ananias.
The Lord said to him in a vision, "Ananias."
He answered, "Here I am, Lord."
¹¹The Lord said to him,
"Get up and go to the street called Straight,
and at the house of Judas look for a man of Tarsus named Saul.
At this moment he is praying,
¹²and he has seen in a vision a man named Ananias come in
and lay his hands on him so that he might regain his sight."
¹³But Ananias answered,
"Lord, I have heard from many about this man,
how much evil he has done to your saints in Jerusalem;
¹⁴and here he has authority from the chief priests
to bind all who invoke your name."

¹⁵But the Lord said to him,
"Go, for he is an instrument whom I have chosen
to bring my name before Gentiles and kings and before the people of Israel;
¹⁶I myself will show him how much he must suffer for the sake of my name."

¹⁷So Ananias went and entered the house.
He laid his hands on Saul and said,
"Brother Saul, the Lord Jesus, who appeared to you on your way here,
has sent me so that you may regain your sight
and be filled with the Holy Spirit."
¹⁸And immediately something like scales fell from his eyes,
and his sight was restored.
Then he got up and was baptized,
¹⁹and after taking some food, he regained his strength.

For several days he was with the disciples in Damascus,
²⁰and immediately he began to proclaim Jesus in the synagogues, saying,
"He is the Son of God."
²¹All who heard him were amazed and said,
"Is not this the man who made havoc in Jerusalem
among those who invoked this name?
And has he not come here
for the purpose of bringing them bound before the chief priests?"
²²Saul became increasingly more powerful
and confounded the Jews who lived in Damascus
by proving that Jesus was the Messiah.

The word of the Lord.

PSALMODY: PSALM 67

SECOND READING: GALATIANS 1:11–24

A reading from Galatians:

¹¹I want you to know, brothers and sisters,
that the gospel that was proclaimed by me is not of human origin;
¹²for I did not receive it from a human source,
nor was I taught it,
but I received it through a revelation of Jesus Christ.

¹³You have heard, no doubt, of my earlier life in Judaism.
I was violently persecuting the church of God and was trying to destroy it.
¹⁴I advanced in Judaism beyond many among my people of the same age,
for I was far more zealous for the traditions of my ancestors.

¹⁵But when God, who had set me apart before I was born
and called me through his grace,

was pleased [16]to reveal his Son to me,
so that I might proclaim him among the Gentiles,
I did not confer with any human being,
[17]nor did I go up to Jerusalem to those who were already apostles before me,
but I went away at once into Arabia,
and afterwards I returned to Damascus.
[18]Then after three years I did go up to Jerusalem to visit Cephas
and stayed with him fifteen days;
[19]but I did not see any other apostle except James the Lord's brother.
[20]In what I am writing to you, before God, I do not lie!
[21]Then I went into the regions of Syria and Cilicia,
[22]and I was still unknown by sight to the churches of Judea that are in Christ;
[23]they only heard it said,
"The one who formerly was persecuting us
is now proclaiming the faith he once tried to destroy."
[24]And they glorified God because of me.

The word of the Lord.

GOSPEL: LUKE 21:10–19

The Holy Gospel according to Luke, the 21st chapter.

[10]Jesus said to the disciples,
"Nation will rise against nation, and kingdom against kingdom;
[11]there will be great earthquakes,
and in various places famines and plagues;
and there will be dreadful portents and great signs from heaven.

[12]"But before all this occurs, they will arrest you and persecute you;
they will hand you over to synagogues and prisons,
and you will be brought before kings and governors because of my name.
[13]This will give you an opportunity to testify.
[14]So make up your minds not to prepare your defense in advance;
[15]for I will give you words and a wisdom
that none of your opponents will be able to withstand or contradict.
[16]You will be betrayed even by parents and brothers,
by relatives and friends;
and they will put some of you to death.
[17]You will be hated by all because of my name.
[18]But not a hair of your head will perish.
[19]By your endurance you will gain your souls."

The Gospel of the Lord.

THE PRESENTATION OF OUR LORD
FEBRUARY 2

FIRST READING: Malachi 3:1–4

A reading from Malachi:

¹See, I am sending my messenger to prepare the way before me,
and the Lord whom you seek will suddenly come to his temple.
The messenger of the covenant in whom you delight—
indeed, he is coming, says the Lord of hosts.
²But who can endure the day of his coming,
and who can stand when he appears?

For he is like a refiner's fire and like fullers' soap;
³he will sit as a refiner and purifier of silver,
and he will purify the descendants of Levi
and refine them like gold and silver,
until they present offerings to the Lord in righteousness.
⁴Then the offering of Judah and Jerusalem will be pleasing to the Lord
as in the days of old and as in former years.

The word of the Lord.

PSALMODY: Psalm 84 or Psalm 24:7–10

SECOND READING: Hebrews 2:14–18

A reading from Hebrews:

¹⁴Since, therefore, the children share flesh and blood,
Jesus himself likewise shared the same things,
so that through death he might destroy the one who has the power of death,
that is, the devil,
¹⁵and free those who all their lives were held in slavery by the fear of death.

[16]For it is clear that he did not come to help angels,
but the descendants of Abraham.
[17]Therefore he had to become like his brothers and sisters in every respect,
so that he might be a merciful and faithful high priest in the service of God,
to make a sacrifice of atonement for the sins of the people.
[18]Because he himself was tested by what he suffered,
he is able to help those who are being tested.

The word of the Lord.

GOSPEL: LUKE 2:22–40

The Holy Gospel according to Luke, the second chapter.

[22]When the time came for their purification according to the law of Moses,
Mary and Joseph brought Jesus up to Jerusalem to present him to the Lord
[23](as it is written in the law of the Lord,
"Every firstborn male shall be designated as holy to the Lord"),
[24]and they offered a sacrifice according to what is stated in the law of the Lord,
"a pair of turtledoves or two young pigeons."

[25]Now there was a man in Jerusalem whose name was Simeon;
this man was righteous and devout,
looking forward to the consolation of Israel,
and the Holy Spirit rested on him.
[26]It had been revealed to him by the Holy Spirit
that he would not see death before he had seen the Lord's Messiah.
[27]Guided by the Spirit, Simeon came into the temple;
and when the parents brought in the child Jesus,
to do for him what was customary under the law,
[28]Simeon took him in his arms and praised God, saying,
> [29]"Master, now you are dismissing your servant in peace,
>   according to your word;
> [30]for my eyes have seen your salvation,
>   [31]which you have prepared in the presence of all peoples,
> [32]a light for revelation to the Gentiles
>   and for glory to your people Israel."
[33]And the child's father and mother were amazed at what was being said
     about him.

[34]Then Simeon blessed them and said to his mother Mary,
"This child is destined for the falling and the rising of many in Israel,
and to be a sign that will be opposed
[35]so that the inner thoughts of many will be revealed—
and a sword will pierce your own soul too."

³⁶There was also a prophet,
Anna the daughter of Phanuel, of the tribe of Asher.
She was of a great age,
having lived with her husband seven years after her marriage,
³⁷then as a widow to the age of eighty-four.
She never left the temple
but worshiped there with fasting and prayer night and day.
³⁸At that moment she came, and began to praise God
and to speak about the child to all who were looking for the redemption of
    Jerusalem.

³⁹When they had finished everything required by the law of the Lord,
they returned to Galilee, to their own town of Nazareth.
⁴⁰The child grew and became strong, filled with wisdom;
and the favor of God was upon him.

The Gospel of the Lord.

ST. MATTHIAS, APOSTLE

FEBRUARY 24

FIRST READING: ISAIAH 66:1–2

A reading from Isaiah:

¹Thus says the LORD:
Heaven is my throne
    and the earth is my footstool;
what is the house that you would build for me,
    and what is my resting place?
²All these things my hand has made,
    and so all these things are mine,
                     says the LORD.
But this is the one to whom I will look,
    to the humble and contrite in spirit,
    who trembles at my word.

The word of the Lord.

PSALMODY: PSALM 56

SECOND READING: ACTS 1:15–26

A reading from Acts:

¹⁵In those days Peter stood up among the believers
(together the crowd numbered about one hundred twenty persons)
and said,
¹⁶"Friends, the scripture had to be fulfilled,
which the Holy Spirit through David foretold concerning Judas,
who became a guide for those who arrested Jesus—
¹⁷for he was numbered among us and was allotted his share in this ministry."
¹⁸(Now this man acquired a field with the reward of his wickedness;
and falling headlong, he burst open in the middle
and all his bowels gushed out.
¹⁹This became known to all the residents of Jerusalem,
so that the field was called in their language Hakeldama,
that is, Field of Blood.)

²⁰"For it is written in the book of Psalms,

> 'Let his homestead become desolate,
>> and let there be no one to live in it';

and

> 'Let another take his position of overseer.'

²¹"So one of the men who have accompanied us
during all the time that the Lord Jesus went in and out among us,
²²beginning from the baptism of John
until the day when he was taken up from us—
one of these must become a witness with us to his resurrection."
²³So they proposed two,
Joseph called Barsabbas, who was also known as Justus, and Matthias.
²⁴Then they prayed and said,
"Lord, you know everyone's heart.
Show us which one of these two you have chosen
²⁵to take the place in this ministry and apostleship
from which Judas turned aside to go to his own place."
²⁶And they cast lots for them, and the lot fell on Matthias;
and he was added to the eleven apostles.

The word of the Lord.

GOSPEL: LUKE 6:12–16

The Holy Gospel according to Luke, the sixth chapter.

¹²During those days Jesus went out to the mountain to pray;
and he spent the night in prayer to God.
¹³And when day came, he called his disciples and chose twelve of them,
whom he also named apostles:
¹⁴Simon, whom he named Peter, and his brother Andrew,
and James, and John, and Philip, and Bartholomew,
¹⁵and Matthew, and Thomas, and James son of Alphaeus,
and Simon, who was called the Zealot,
¹⁶and Judas son of James, and Judas Iscariot, who became a traitor.

The Gospel of the Lord.

The Annunciation of Our Lord

MARCH 25

FIRST READING: Isaiah 7:10–14

A reading from Isaiah:

¹⁰The Lord spoke to Ahaz, saying,
¹¹Ask a sign of the Lord your God;
let it be deep as Sheol or high as heaven.
¹²But Ahaz said, I will not ask,
and I will not put the Lord to the test.
¹³Then Isaiah said:
"Hear then, O house of David!
Is it too little for you to weary mortals, that you weary my God also?
¹⁴Therefore the Lord himself will give you a sign.
Look, the young woman is with child and shall bear a son,
and shall name him Immanuel."

The word of the Lord.

PSALMODY: Psalm 45 or Psalm 40:5–10*   **Psalm 40:5–11* LBW/BCP

SECOND READING: Hebrews 10:4–10

A reading from Hebrews:

⁴It is impossible for the blood of bulls and goats to take away sins.
⁵Consequently, when Christ came into the world, he said,
   "Sacrifices and offerings you have not desired,
      but a body you have prepared for me;
   ⁶in burnt offerings and sin offerings
      you have taken no pleasure.
   ⁷Then I said, 'See, God, I have come to do your will, O God'
      (in the scroll of the book it is written of me)."
⁸When he said above,
"You have neither desired nor taken pleasure in sacrifices
and offerings and burnt offerings and sin offerings"
(these are offered according to the law),
⁹then he added, "See, I have come to do your will."

He abolishes the first in order to establish the second.
[10]And it is by God's will that we have been sanctified
through the offering of the body of Jesus Christ once for all.

The word of the Lord.

GOSPEL: LUKE 1:26–38

The Holy Gospel according to Luke, the first chapter.

[26]In the sixth month the angel Gabriel was sent by God
to a town in Galilee called Nazareth,
[27]to a virgin engaged to a man whose name was Joseph, of the house of David.
The virgin's name was Mary.
[28]And he came to her and said,
"Greetings, favored one! The Lord is with you."
[29]But she was much perplexed by his words
and pondered what sort of greeting this might be.

[30]The angel said to her,
"Do not be afraid, Mary, for you have found favor with God.
[31]And now, you will conceive in your womb and bear a son,
and you will name him Jesus.
[32]He will be great, and will be called the Son of the Most High,
and the Lord God will give to him the throne of his ancestor David.
[33]He will reign over the house of Jacob forever,
and of his kingdom there will be no end."
[34]Mary said to the angel,
"How can this be, since I am a virgin?"
[35]The angel said to her,
"The Holy Spirit will come upon you,
and the power of the Most High will overshadow you;
therefore the child to be born will be holy;
he will be called Son of God.
[36]And now, your relative Elizabeth in her old age has also conceived a son;
and this is the sixth month for her who was said to be barren.
[37]For nothing will be impossible with God."

[38]Then Mary said, "Here am I, the servant of the Lord;
let it be with me according to your word."

Then the angel departed from her.

The Gospel of the Lord.

St. Mark, Evangelist

APRIL 25

FIRST READING: Isaiah 52:7–10

A reading from Isaiah:

⁷How beautiful upon the mountains
    are the feet of the messenger who announces peace,
who brings good news,
    who announces salvation,
    who says to Zion, "Your God reigns."
⁸Listen! Your sentinels lift up their voices,
    together they sing for joy;
for in plain sight they see
    the return of the Lord to Zion.
⁹Break forth together into singing,
    you ruins of Jerusalem;
for the Lord has comforted his people,
    he has redeemed Jerusalem.
¹⁰The Lord has bared his holy arm
    before the eyes of all the nations;
and all the ends of the earth shall see
    the salvation of our God.

The word of the Lord.

PSALMODY: Psalm 57

SECOND READING: 2 Timothy 4:6–11, 18

A reading from Second Timothy:

Paul writes:
⁶As for me, I am already being poured out as a libation,
and the time of my departure has come.
⁷I have fought the good fight,
I have finished the race,
I have kept the faith.
⁸From now on there is reserved for me the crown of righteousness,
which the Lord, the righteous judge, will give me on that day,
and not only to me
but also to all who have longed for his appearing.

⁹Do your best to come to me soon,
¹⁰for Demas, in love with this present world,

has deserted me and gone to Thessalonica;
Crescens has gone to Galatia, Titus to Dalmatia.
[11]Only Luke is with me.
Get Mark and bring him with you, for he is useful in my ministry.

[18]The Lord will rescue me from every evil attack
and save me for his heavenly kingdom.
To him be the glory forever and ever. Amen.

The word of the Lord.

GOSPEL: MARK 1:1–15

The Holy Gospel according to Mark, the first chapter.

[1]The beginning of the good news of Jesus Christ, the Son of God.
[2]As it is written in the prophet Isaiah,
    "See, I am sending my messenger ahead of you,
      who will prepare your way;
   [3]the voice of one crying out in the wilderness:
      'Prepare the way of the Lord,
      make his paths straight,' "
[4]John the baptizer appeared in the wilderness,
proclaiming a baptism of repentance for the forgiveness of sins.
[5]And people from the whole Judean countryside
and all the people of Jerusalem were going out to him,
and were baptized by him in the river Jordan, confessing their sins.
[6]Now John was clothed with camel's hair, with a leather belt around his waist,
and he ate locusts and wild honey.
[7]He proclaimed, "The one who is more powerful than I is coming after me;
I am not worthy to stoop down and untie the thong of his sandals.
[8]I have baptized you with water;
but he will baptize you with the Holy Spirit."

[9]In those days Jesus came from Nazareth of Galilee
and was baptized by John in the Jordan.
[10]And just as he was coming up out of the water,
he saw the heavens torn apart and the Spirit descending like a dove on him.
[11]And a voice came from heaven,
"You are my Son, the Beloved; with you I am well pleased."

[12]And the Spirit immediately drove him out into the wilderness.
[13]He was in the wilderness forty days, tempted by Satan;
and he was with the wild beasts; and the angels waited on him.

[14]Now after John was arrested, Jesus came to Galilee,
proclaiming the good news of God, [15]and saying,
"The time is fulfilled, and the kingdom of God has come near;
repent, and believe in the good news."

The Gospel of the Lord.

St. Philip and St. James, Apostles

MAY 1

FIRST READING: Isaiah 30:18–21

A reading from Isaiah:

> 18The LORD waits to be gracious to you;
>> therefore he will rise up to show mercy to you.
> For the LORD is a God of justice;
>> blessed are all those who wait for him.

> 19Truly, O people in Zion, inhabitants of Jerusalem,
> you shall weep no more.
> He will surely be gracious to you at the sound of your cry;
> when he hears it, he will answer you.
> 20Though the Lord may give you the bread of adversity
> and the water of affliction,
> yet your Teacher will not hide himself any more,
> but your eyes shall see your Teacher.
> 21And when you turn to the right or when you turn to the left,
> your ears shall hear a word behind you, saying,
> "This is the way; walk in it."

The word of the Lord.

PSALMODY: Psalm 44:1–3, 20–26

SECOND READING: 2 Corinthians 4:1–6

A reading from Second Corinthians:

> 1Since it is by God's mercy that we are engaged in this ministry,
> we do not lose heart.
> 2We have renounced the shameful things that one hides;
> we refuse to practice cunning or to falsify God's word;
> but by the open statement of the truth
> we commend ourselves to the conscience of everyone in the sight of God.
> 3And even if our gospel is veiled,
> it is veiled to those who are perishing.
> 4In their case the god of this world has blinded the minds of the unbelievers,

to keep them from seeing the light of the gospel of the glory of Christ,
who is the image of God.

⁵For we do not proclaim ourselves;
we proclaim Jesus Christ as Lord
and ourselves as your slaves for Jesus' sake.
⁶For it is the God who said, "Let light shine out of darkness,"
who has shone in our hearts
to give the light of the knowledge of the glory of God
in the face of Jesus Christ.

The word of the Lord.

GOSPEL: JOHN 14:8–14

The Holy Gospel according to John, the 14th chapter.

⁸Philip said to Jesus,
"Lord, show us the Father, and we will be satisfied."
⁹Jesus said to him,
"Have I been with you all this time, Philip,
and you still do not know me?
Whoever has seen me has seen the Father.
How can you say, 'Show us the Father'?
¹⁰Do you not believe that I am in the Father and the Father is in me?
The words that I say to you I do not speak on my own;
but the Father who dwells in me does his works.
¹¹Believe me that I am in the Father and the Father is in me;
but if you do not, then believe me because of the works themselves.

¹²"Very truly, I tell you,
the one who believes in me will also do the works that I do and,
in fact, will do greater works than these,
because I am going to the Father.
¹³I will do whatever you ask in my name,
so that the Father may be glorified in the Son.
¹⁴If in my name you ask me for anything, I will do it."

The Gospel of the Lord.

THE VISITATION

MAY 31

FIRST READING: 1 SAMUEL 2:1–10

A reading from First Samuel:

¹Hannah prayed and said,

"My heart exults in the LORD;
    my strength is exalted in my God.
My mouth derides my enemies,
    because I rejoice in my victory.

²"There is no Holy One like the LORD,
    no one besides you;
    there is no Rock like our God.
³Talk no more so very proudly,
    let not arrogance come from your mouth;
for the LORD is a God of knowledge,
    and by him actions are weighed.
⁴The bows of the mighty are broken,
    but the feeble gird on strength.
⁵Those who were full have hired themselves out for bread,
    but those who were hungry are fat with spoil.
The barren has borne seven,
    but she who has many children is forlorn.
⁶The LORD kills and brings to life;
    he brings down to Sheol and raises up.
⁷The LORD makes poor and makes rich;
    he brings low, he also exalts.
⁸He raises up the poor from the dust;
    he lifts the needy from the ash heap,
to make them sit with princes
    and inherit a seat of honor.
For the pillars of the earth are the LORD's,
    and on them he has set the world.

⁹"He will guard the feet of his faithful ones,
    but the wicked shall be cut off in darkness;
    for not by might does one prevail.
¹⁰The LORD! His adversaries shall be shattered;

the Most High will thunder in heaven.
The LORD will judge the ends of the earth;
   he will give strength to his king,
   and exalt the power of his anointed."

The word of the Lord.

PSALMODY: PSALM 113

SECOND READING: ROMANS 12:9–16b

A reading from Romans:

9Let love be genuine;
hate what is evil, hold fast to what is good;
10love one another with mutual affection;
outdo one another in showing honor.
11Do not lag in zeal, be ardent in spirit, serve the Lord.
12Rejoice in hope, be patient in suffering, persevere in prayer.
13Contribute to the needs of the saints;
extend hospitality to strangers.

14Bless those who persecute you; bless and do not curse them.
15Rejoice with those who rejoice, weep with those who weep.
16Live in harmony with one another;
do not be haughty, but associate with the lowly.

The word of the Lord.

The Holy Gospel according to Luke, the first chapter.

³⁹In those days Mary set out
and went with haste to a Judean town in the hill country,
⁴⁰where she entered the house of Zechariah and greeted Elizabeth.
⁴¹When Elizabeth heard Mary's greeting, the child leaped in her womb.
And Elizabeth was filled with the Holy Spirit
⁴²and exclaimed with a loud cry,
"Blessed are you among women, and blessed is the fruit of your womb.
⁴³And why has this happened to me,
that the mother of my Lord comes to me?
⁴⁴For as soon as I heard the sound of your greeting,
the child in my womb leaped for joy.
⁴⁵And blessed is she who believed
that there would be a fulfillment of what was spoken to her by the Lord."

⁴⁶And Mary said,
    "My soul magnifies the Lord,
        ⁴⁷and my spirit rejoices in God my Savior,
    ⁴⁸for he has looked with favor on the lowliness of his servant.
        Surely, from now on all generations will call me blessed;
    ⁴⁹for the Mighty One has done great things for me,
        and holy is his name.
    ⁵⁰His mercy is for those who fear him
        from generation to generation.
    ⁵¹He has shown strength with his arm;
        he has scattered the proud in the thoughts of their hearts.
    ⁵²He has brought down the powerful from their thrones,
        and lifted up the lowly;
    ⁵³he has filled the hungry with good things,
        and sent the rich away empty.
    ⁵⁴He has helped his servant Israel,
        in remembrance of his mercy,
    ⁵⁵according to the promise he made to our ancestors,
        to Abraham and to his descendants forever."

⁵⁶And Mary remained with her about three months
and then returned to her home.

⁵⁷Now the time came for Elizabeth to give birth,
and she bore a son.

The Gospel of the Lord.

St. Barnabas, Apostle

JUNE 11

FIRST READING: Isaiah 42:5–12

A reading from Isaiah:

⁵Thus says God, the LORD,
    who created the heavens and stretched them out,
    who spread out the earth and what comes from it,
who gives breath to the people upon it
    and spirit to those who walk in it:
⁶I am the LORD, I have called you in righteousness,
    I have taken you by the hand and kept you;
I have given you as a covenant to the people,
    a light to the nations,
    ⁷to open the eyes that are blind,
to bring out the prisoners from the dungeon,
    from the prison those who sit in darkness.
⁸I am the LORD, that is my name;
    my glory I give to no other,
    nor my praise to idols.
⁹See, the former things have come to pass,
    and new things I now declare;
before they spring forth,
    I tell you of them.

¹⁰Sing to the LORD a new song,
    his praise from the end of the earth!
Let the sea roar and all that fills it,
    the coastlands and their inhabitants.
¹¹Let the desert and its towns lift up their voice,
    the villages that Kedar inhabits;
let the inhabitants of Sela sing for joy,
    let them shout from the tops of the mountains.
¹²Let them give glory to the LORD,
    and declare his praise in the coastlands.

The word of the Lord.

PSALMODY: Psalm 112

A reading from Acts:

^{19}Now those who were scattered because of the persecution
  that took place over Stephen
traveled as far as Phoenicia, Cyprus, and Antioch,
and they spoke the word to no one except Jews.
^{20}But among them were some men of Cyprus and Cyrene who,
on coming to Antioch, spoke to the Hellenists also,
proclaiming the Lord Jesus.
^{21}The hand of the Lord was with them,
and a great number became believers and turned to the Lord.
^{22}News of this came to the ears of the church in Jerusalem,
and they sent Barnabas to Antioch.

^{23}When he came and saw the grace of God, he rejoiced,
and he exhorted them all to remain faithful to the Lord with steadfast devotion;
^{24}for he was a good man, full of the Holy Spirit and of faith.
And a great many people were brought to the Lord.
^{25}Then Barnabas went to Tarsus to look for Saul,
^{26}and when he had found him, he brought him to Antioch.
So it was that for an entire year
they met with the church and taught a great many people,
and it was in Antioch that the disciples were first called "Christians."

^{27}At that time prophets came down from Jerusalem to Antioch.
^{28}One of them named Agabus stood up and predicted by the Spirit
that there would be a severe famine over all the world;
and this took place during the reign of Claudius.
^{29}The disciples determined that according to their ability,
each would send relief to the believers living in Judea;
^{30}this they did, sending it to the elders by Barnabas and Saul.

$^{13:1}$Now in the church at Antioch there were prophets and teachers:
Barnabas, Simeon who was called Niger,
Lucius of Cyrene, Manaen a member of the court of Herod the ruler, and Saul.
^{2}While they were worshiping the Lord and fasting,
the Holy Spirit said,
"Set apart for me Barnabas and Saul for the work to which I have called them."
^{3}Then after fasting and praying
they laid their hands on them and sent them off.

The word of the Lord.

GOSPEL: MATTHEW 10:7–16

The Holy Gospel according to Matthew, the tenth chapter.

Jesus said to the twelve:
[7]"As you go, proclaim the good news,
'The kingdom of heaven has come near.'
[8]Cure the sick, raise the dead, cleanse the lepers, cast out demons.
You received without payment; give without payment.
[9]Take no gold, or silver, or copper in your belts,
[10]no bag for your journey, or two tunics, or sandals, or a staff;
for laborers deserve their food.

[11]"Whatever town or village you enter, find out who in it is worthy,
and stay there until you leave.
[12]As you enter the house, greet it.
[13]If the house is worthy, let your peace come upon it;
but if it is not worthy, let your peace return to you.
[14]If anyone will not welcome you or listen to your words,
shake off the dust from your feet as you leave that house or town.
[15]Truly I tell you,
it will be more tolerable for the land of Sodom and Gomorrah
        on the day of judgment
than for that town.

[16]"See, I am sending you out like sheep into the midst of wolves;
so be wise as serpents and innocent as doves."

The Gospel of the Lord.

The Nativity of
St. John the Baptist

JUNE 24

FIRST READING: Malachi 3:1–4

A reading from Malachi:

¹See, I am sending my messenger to prepare the way before me,
and the Lord whom you seek will suddenly come to his temple.
The messenger of the covenant in whom you delight—
indeed, he is coming, says the Lord of hosts.
²But who can endure the day of his coming,
and who can stand when he appears?

For he is like a refiner's fire and like fullers' soap;
³he will sit as a refiner and purifier of silver,
and he will purify the descendants of Levi
and refine them like gold and silver,
until they present offerings to the Lord in righteousness.
⁴Then the offering of Judah and Jerusalem will be pleasing to the Lord
as in the days of old and as in former years.

The word of the Lord.

PSALMODY: Psalm 141

SECOND READING: Acts 13:13–26

A reading from Acts:

¹³Paul and his companions set sail from Paphos
and came to Perga in Pamphylia.
John, however, left them and returned to Jerusalem;
¹⁴but they went on from Perga and came to Antioch in Pisidia.
And on the sabbath day they went into the synagogue and sat down.
¹⁵After the reading of the law and the prophets,
the officials of the synagogue sent them a message, saying,
"Brothers, if you have any word of exhortation for the people, give it."

¹⁶So Paul stood up and with a gesture began to speak:
"You Israelites, and others who fear God, listen.

17The God of this people Israel chose our ancestors
and made the people great during their stay in the land of Egypt,
and with uplifted arm he led them out of it.
18For about forty years he put up with them in the wilderness.
19After he had destroyed seven nations in the land of Canaan,
he gave them their land as an inheritance
20for about four hundred fifty years.
After that he gave them judges until the time of the prophet Samuel.
21Then they asked for a king;
and God gave them Saul son of Kish, a man of the tribe of Benjamin,
who reigned for forty years.
22When he had removed him, he made David their king.
In his testimony about him he said,
'I have found David, son of Jesse, to be a man after my heart,
who will carry out all my wishes.'
23Of this man's posterity God has brought to Israel a Savior,
Jesus, as he promised;
24before his coming John had already proclaimed a baptism of repentance
to all the people of Israel.
25And as John was finishing his work, he said,
'What do you suppose that I am? I am not he.
No, but one is coming after me;
I am not worthy to untie the thong of the sandals on his feet.'

26"My brothers, you descendants of Abraham's family,
and others who fear God,
to us the message of this salvation has been sent."

The word of the Lord.

GOSPEL: LUKE 1:57–67 [68–80]

The Holy Gospel according to Luke, the first chapter.

57Now the time came for Elizabeth to give birth, and she bore a son.
58Her neighbors and relatives heard that the Lord had shown his great mercy
        to her,
and they rejoiced with her.

59On the eighth day they came to circumcise the child,
and they were going to name him Zechariah after his father.
60But his mother said, "No; he is to be called John."
61They said to her, "None of your relatives has this name."
62Then they began motioning to his father
to find out what name he wanted to give him.
63He asked for a writing tablet and wrote,
"His name is John."
And all of them were amazed.

⁶⁴Immediately his mouth was opened and his tongue freed,
and he began to speak, praising God.
⁶⁵Fear came over all their neighbors,
and all these things were talked about
throughout the entire hill country of Judea.
⁶⁶All who heard them pondered them and said,
"What then will this child become?"
For, indeed, the hand of the Lord was with him.

⁶⁷Then his father Zechariah was filled with the Holy Spirit
and spoke this prophecy:
    [⁶⁸"Blessed be the Lord God of Israel,
        for he has looked favorably on his people and redeemed them.
    ⁶⁹He has raised up a mighty savior for us
        in the house of his servant David,
    ⁷⁰as he spoke through the mouth of his holy prophets from of old,
        ⁷¹that we would be saved from our enemies and from the hand of all
            who hate us.
    ⁷²Thus he has shown the mercy promised to our ancestors,
        and has remembered his holy covenant,
    ⁷³the oath that he swore to our ancestor Abraham,
        to grant us ⁷⁴that we, being rescued from the hands of our enemies,
    might serve him without fear, ⁷⁵in holiness and righteousness
        before him all our days.

    ⁷⁶"And you, child, will be called the prophet of the Most High;
        for you will go before the Lord to prepare his ways,
    ⁷⁷to give knowledge of salvation to his people
        by the forgiveness of their sins.
    ⁷⁸By the tender mercy of our God,
        the dawn from on high will break upon us,
    ⁷⁹to give light to those who sit in darkness and in the shadow of death,
        to guide our feet into the way of peace."

⁸⁰The child grew and became strong in spirit,
and he was in the wilderness until the day he appeared publicly to Israel.]

The Gospel of the Lord.

St. Peter and St. Paul, Apostles

JUNE 29

FIRST READING: Ezekiel 34:11–16

A reading from Ezekiel:

[11]Thus says the Lord GOD:
I myself will search for my sheep, and will seek them out.
[12]As shepherds seek out their flocks
when they are among their scattered sheep,
so I will seek out my sheep.
I will rescue them from all the places to which they have been scattered
on a day of clouds and thick darkness.
[13]I will bring them out from the peoples and gather them from the countries,
and will bring them into their own land;
and I will feed them on the mountains of Israel,
by the watercourses, and in all the inhabited parts of the land.
[14]I will feed them with good pasture,
and the mountain heights of Israel shall be their pasture;
there they shall lie down in good grazing land,
and they shall feed on rich pasture on the mountains of Israel.
[15]I myself will be the shepherd of my sheep,
and I will make them lie down, says the Lord GOD.
[16]I will seek the lost, and I will bring back the strayed,
and I will bind up the injured, and I will strengthen the weak,
but the fat and the strong I will destroy.
I will feed them with justice.

The word of the Lord.

PSALMODY: Psalm 87:1–3, 5–7   *Psalm 87:1–2, 4–6* LBW/BCP

SECOND READING: 1 CORINTHIANS 3:16–23

A reading from First Corinthians:

[16]Do you not know that you are God's temple
and that God's Spirit dwells in you?
[17]If anyone destroys God's temple, God will destroy that person.
For God's temple is holy, and you are that temple.

[18]Do not deceive yourselves.
If you think that you are wise in this age,
you should become fools so that you may become wise.
[19]For the wisdom of this world is foolishness with God.
For it is written,
    "He catches the wise in their craftiness,"
[20]and again,
    "The Lord knows the thoughts of the wise,
        that they are futile."
[21]So let no one boast about human leaders.
For all things are yours,
[22]whether Paul or Apollos or Cephas
or the world or life or death or the present or the future—
all belong to you,
[23]and you belong to Christ,
and Christ belongs to God.

The word of the Lord.

The Holy Gospel according to Mark, the eighth chapter.

[27]Jesus went on with his disciples to the villages of Caesarea Philippi;
and on the way he asked his disciples,
"Who do people say that I am?"
[28]And they answered him,
"John the Baptist; and others, Elijah;
and still others, one of the prophets."
[29]He asked them, "But who do you say that I am?"
Peter answered him, "You are the Messiah."
[30]And he sternly ordered them not to tell anyone about him.

[31]Then he began to teach them
that the Son of Man must undergo great suffering,
and be rejected by the elders, the chief priests, and the scribes,
and be killed, and after three days rise again.
[32]He said all this quite openly.
And Peter took him aside and began to rebuke him.
[33]But turning and looking at his disciples, he rebuked Peter and said,
"Get behind me, Satan!
For you are setting your mind not on divine things but on human things."

[34]He called the crowd with his disciples, and said to them,
"If any want to become my followers,
let them deny themselves and take up their cross and follow me.
[35]For those who want to save their life will lose it,
and those who lose their life for my sake, and for the sake of the gospel,
will save it."

The Gospel of the Lord.

ST. MARY MAGDALENE

JULY 22

FIRST READING: RUTH 1:6–18
Or Exodus 2:1–10, following

A reading from Ruth:

⁶Naomi started to return with her daughters-in-law Orpah and Ruth
　　from the country of Moab,
for she had heard in the country of Moab
that the LORD had considered his people
and given them food.
⁷So she set out from the place where she had been living,
she and her two daughters-in-law,
and they went on their way to go back to the land of Judah.
⁸But Naomi said to her two daughters-in-law,
"Go back each of you to your mother's house.
May the LORD deal kindly with you,
as you have dealt with the dead and with me.
⁹The LORD grant that you may find security,
each of you in the house of your husband."
Then she kissed them, and they wept aloud.

¹⁰They said to her, "No, we will return with you to your people."
¹¹But Naomi said,
"Turn back, my daughters, why will you go with me?
Do I still have sons in my womb that they may become your husbands?
¹²Turn back, my daughters, go your way,
for I am too old to have a husband.
Even if I thought there was hope for me,
even if I should have a husband tonight and bear sons,
¹³would you then wait until they were grown?
Would you then refrain from marrying?
No, my daughters, it has been far more bitter for me than for you,
because the hand of the LORD has turned against me."

¹⁴Then they wept aloud again.
Orpah kissed her mother-in-law, but Ruth clung to her.

¹⁵So she said,
"See, your sister-in-law has gone back to her people and to her gods;
return after your sister-in-law."
¹⁶But Ruth said,
    "Do not press me to leave you
        or to turn back from following you!
    Where you go, I will go;
        where you lodge, I will lodge;
    your people shall be my people,
        and your God my God.
    ¹⁷Where you die, I will die—
        there will I be buried.
    May the LORD do thus and so to me,
        and more as well,
    if even death parts me from you!"
¹⁸When Naomi saw that she was determined to go with her,
she said no more to her.

The word of the Lord.

OR: EXODUS 2:1–10

A reading from Exodus:

¹Now a man from the house of Levi went and married a Levite woman.
²The woman conceived and bore a son;
and when she saw that he was a fine baby, she hid him three months.
³When she could hide him no longer she got a papyrus basket for him,
and plastered it with bitumen and pitch;
she put the child in it and placed it among the reeds on the bank of the river.
⁴His sister stood at a distance, to see what would happen to him.

⁵The daughter of Pharaoh came down to bathe at the river,
while her attendants walked beside the river.
She saw the basket among the reeds and sent her maid to bring it.
⁶When she opened it, she saw the child.
He was crying, and she took pity on him.
"This must be one of the Hebrews' children," she said.
⁷Then his sister said to Pharaoh's daughter,
"Shall I go and get you a nurse from the Hebrew women
to nurse the child for you?"
⁸Pharaoh's daughter said to her, "Yes."
So the girl went and called the child's mother.
⁹Pharaoh's daughter said to her,
"Take this child and nurse it for me, and I will give you your wages."
So the woman took the child and nursed it.

[10]When the child grew up, she brought him to Pharaoh's daughter,
and she took him as her son.
She named him Moses, "because," she said,
"I drew him out of the water."

The word of the Lord.

PSALMODY: PSALM 73:23–28

Psalm 73:23–29 LBW/BCP

SECOND READING: ACTS 13:26–33a

A reading from Acts:

[26]"My brothers, you descendants of Abraham's family,
and others who fear God,
to us the message of this salvation has been sent.
[27]Because the residents of Jerusalem and their leaders did not recognize him
or understand the words of the prophets that are read every sabbath,
they fulfilled those words by condemning him.
[28]Even though they found no cause for a sentence of death,
they asked Pilate to have him killed.
[29]When they had carried out everything that was written about him,
they took him down from the tree and laid him in a tomb.

[30]"But God raised him from the dead;
[31]and for many days he appeared to those who came up with him
from Galilee to Jerusalem,
and they are now his witnesses to the people.
[32]And we bring you the good news that what God promised to our ancestors
[33]he has fulfilled for us, their children, by raising Jesus."

The word of the Lord.

GOSPEL: JOHN 20:1–2, 11–18

The Holy Gospel according to John, the 20th chapter.

¹Early on the first day of the week, while it was still dark,
Mary Magdalene came to the tomb
and saw that the stone had been removed from the tomb.
²So she ran and went to Simon Peter and the other disciple,
the one whom Jesus loved, and said to them,
"They have taken the Lord out of the tomb,
and we do not know where they have laid him."

¹¹Mary stood weeping outside the tomb.
As she wept, she bent over to look into the tomb;
¹²and she saw two angels in white,
sitting where the body of Jesus had been lying,
one at the head and the other at the feet.
¹³They said to her, "Woman, why are you weeping?"
She said to them,
"They have taken away my Lord, and I do not know where they have laid him."
¹⁴When she had said this, she turned around and saw Jesus standing there,
but she did not know that it was Jesus.
¹⁵Jesus said to her,
"Woman, why are you weeping? Whom are you looking for?"
Supposing him to be the gardener, she said to him,
"Sir, if you have carried him away, tell me where you have laid him,
and I will take him away."

¹⁶Jesus said to her, "Mary!"
She turned and said to him in Hebrew,
"Rabbouni!" (which means Teacher).
¹⁷Jesus said to her,
"Do not hold on to me, because I have not yet ascended to the Father.
But go to my brothers and say to them,
'I am ascending to my Father and your Father, to my God and your God.' "
¹⁸Mary Magdalene went and announced to the disciples,
"I have seen the Lord";
and she told them that he had said these things to her.

The Gospel of the Lord.

ST. JAMES THE ELDER, APOSTLE

JULY 25

FIRST READING: 1 KINGS 19:9–18

A reading from First Kings:

⁹At Horeb, the mount of God,
Elijah came to a cave, and spent the night there.
Then the word of the LORD came to him, saying,
"What are you doing here, Elijah?"
¹⁰He answered, "I have been very zealous for the LORD, the God of hosts;
for the Israelites have forsaken your covenant, thrown down your altars,
and killed your prophets with the sword.
I alone am left, and they are seeking my life, to take it away."
¹¹He said, "Go out and stand on the mountain before the LORD,
for the LORD is about to pass by."

Now there was a great wind, so strong that it was splitting mountains
and breaking rocks in pieces before the LORD,
but the LORD was not in the wind;
and after the wind an earthquake,
but the LORD was not in the earthquake;
¹²and after the earthquake a fire,
but the LORD was not in the fire;
and after the fire a sound of sheer silence.
¹³When Elijah heard it, he wrapped his face in his mantle
and went out and stood at the entrance of the cave.

Then there came a voice to him that said,
"What are you doing here, Elijah?"
¹⁴He answered,
"I have been very zealous for the LORD, the God of hosts;
for the Israelites have forsaken your covenant, thrown down your altars,
and killed your prophets with the sword.
I alone am left, and they are seeking my life, to take it away."
¹⁵Then the LORD said to him,
"Go, return on your way to the wilderness of Damascus;
when you arrive, you shall anoint Hazael as king over Aram.
¹⁶Also you shall anoint Jehu son of Nimshi as king over Israel;
and you shall anoint Elisha son of Shaphat of Abel-meholah
as prophet in your place.

¹⁷Whoever escapes from the sword of Hazael, Jehu shall kill;
and whoever escapes from the sword of Jehu, Elisha shall kill.
¹⁸Yet I will leave seven thousand in Israel,
all the knees that have not bowed to Baal,
and every mouth that has not kissed him."

The word of the Lord.

PSALMODY: PSALM 7:1–10   *Psalm 7:1–11* LBW/BCP

SECOND READING: ACTS 11:27—12:3a

A reading from Acts:

²⁷At that time when Barnabas and Saul were in Antioch,
prophets came down from Jerusalem to Antioch.
²⁸One of them named Agabus stood up and predicted by the Spirit
that there would be a severe famine over all the world;
and this took place during the reign of Claudius.
²⁹The disciples determined that according to their ability,
each would send relief to the believers living in Judea;
this they did, sending it to the elders by Barnabas and Saul.

¹²:¹About that time
King Herod laid violent hands upon some who belonged to the church.
²He had James, the brother of John, killed with the sword.
³After he saw that it pleased the Jews, he proceeded to arrest Peter also.

The word of the Lord.

The Holy Gospel according to Mark, the tenth chapter.

[35]James and John, the sons of Zebedee, came forward to Jesus and said to him,
  "Teacher, we want you to do for us whatever we ask of you."
[36]And he said to them, "What is it you want me to do for you?"
[37]And they said to him,
"Grant us to sit, one at your right hand and one at your left, in your glory."
[38]But Jesus said to them,
"You do not know what you are asking.
Are you able to drink the cup that I drink,
or be baptized with the baptism that I am baptized with?"
[39]They replied, "We are able."
Then Jesus said to them,
"The cup that I drink you will drink;
and with the baptism with which I am baptized, you will be baptized;
[40]but to sit at my right hand or at my left is not mine to grant,
but it is for those for whom it has been prepared."

[41]When the ten heard this, they began to be angry with James and John.
[42]So Jesus called them and said to them,
"You know that among the Gentiles
those whom they recognize as their rulers lord it over them,
and their great ones are tyrants over them.
[43]But it is not so among you;
but whoever wishes to become great among you must be your servant,
[44]and whoever wishes to be first among you must be slave of all.
[45]For the Son of Man came not to be served but to serve,
and to give his life a ransom for many."

The Gospel of the Lord.

MARY, MOTHER OF OUR LORD

AUGUST 15

FIRST READING: Isaiah 61:7–11

A reading from Isaiah:

7Because their shame was double,
　　and dishonor was proclaimed as their lot,
therefore they shall possess a double portion;
　　everlasting joy shall be theirs.

8For I the Lord love justice,
　　I hate robbery and wrongdoing;
I will faithfully give them their recompense,
　　and I will make an everlasting covenant with them.
9Their descendants shall be known among the nations,
　　and their offspring among the peoples;
all who see them shall acknowledge
　　that they are a people whom the Lord has blessed.
10I will greatly rejoice in the Lord,
　　my whole being shall exult in my God;
for he has clothed me with the garments of salvation,
　　he has covered me with the robe of righteousness,
as a bridegroom decks himself with a garland,
　　and as a bride adorns herself with her jewels.
11For as the earth brings forth its shoots,
　　and as a garden causes what is sown in it to spring up,
so the Lord God will cause righteousness and praise
　　to spring up before all the nations.

The word of the Lord.

PSALMODY: Psalm 45:10–15　　　　　　　　　　　*Psalm 45:11–16* LBW/BCP

SECOND READING: Galatians 4:4–7

A reading from Galatians:

4When the fullness of time had come,
God sent his Son, born of a woman, born under the law,
5in order to redeem those who were under the law,

so that we might receive adoption as children. [6]And because you are children,
God has sent the Spirit of his Son into our hearts,
crying, "Abba! Father!"
[7]So you are no longer a slave but a child,
and if a child then also an heir, through God.

The word of the Lord.

GOSPEL: LUKE 1:46–55

The Holy Gospel according to Luke, the first chapter.

[46]Mary said,
"My soul magnifies the Lord,
    [47]and my spirit rejoices in God my Savior,
[48]for he has looked with favor on the lowliness of his servant.
    Surely, from now on all generations will call me blessed;
[49]for the Mighty One has done great things for me,
    and holy is his name.
[50]His mercy is for those who fear him
    from generation to generation.
[51]He has shown strength with his arm;
    he has scattered the proud in the thoughts of their hearts.
[52]He has brought down the powerful from their thrones,
    and lifted up the lowly;
[53]he has filled the hungry with good things,
    and sent the rich away empty.
[54]He has helped his servant Israel,
    in remembrance of his mercy,
[55]according to the promise he made to our ancestors,
    to Abraham and to his descendants forever."

The Gospel of the Lord.

St. Bartholomew, Apostle

AUGUST 24

FIRST READING: Exodus 19:1–6

A reading from Exodus:

¹On the third new moon after the Israelites had gone out of the land of Egypt,
on that very day, they came into the wilderness of Sinai.
²They had journeyed from Rephidim, entered the wilderness of Sinai,
and camped in the wilderness;
Israel camped there in front of the mountain.
³Then Moses went up to God;
the Lord called to him from the mountain, saying,
"Thus you shall say to the house of Jacob, and tell the Israelites:
⁴You have seen what I did to the Egyptians,
and how I bore you on eagles' wings and brought you to myself.
⁵Now therefore, if you obey my voice and keep my covenant,
you shall be my treasured possession out of all the peoples.
Indeed, the whole earth is mine,
⁶but you shall be for me a priestly kingdom and a holy nation.
These are the words that you shall speak to the Israelites."

The word of the Lord.

PSALMODY: Psalm 12

SECOND READING: 1 Corinthians 12:27–31a

A reading from First Corinthians:

²⁷Now you are the body of Christ and individually members of it.
²⁸And God has appointed in the church first apostles,
second prophets, third teachers;
then deeds of power, then gifts of healing,
forms of assistance, forms of leadership, various kinds of tongues.
²⁹Are all apostles? Are all prophets? Are all teachers?
Do all work miracles? Do all possess gifts of healing?
³⁰Do all speak in tongues? Do all interpret?
³¹But strive for the greater gifts.

The word of the Lord.

The Holy Gospel according to John, the first chapter.

[43]The next day Jesus decided to go to Galilee.
He found Philip and said to him, "Follow me."
[44]Now Philip was from Bethsaida, the city of Andrew and Peter.
[45]Philip found Nathanael and said to him,
"We have found him about whom Moses in the law and also the prophets
          wrote,
Jesus son of Joseph from Nazareth."
[46]Nathanael said to him, "Can anything good come out of Nazareth?"
Philip said to him, "Come and see."

[47]When Jesus saw Nathanael coming toward him, he said of him,
"Here is truly an Israelite in whom there is no deceit!"
[48]Nathanael asked him, "Where did you get to know me?"
Jesus answered, "I saw you under the fig tree before Philip called you."
[49]Nathanael replied,
"Rabbi, you are the Son of God! You are the King of Israel!"
[50]Jesus answered,
"Do you believe because I told you that I saw you under the fig tree?
You will see greater things than these."
[51]And he said to him,
"Very truly, I tell you, you will see heaven opened
and the angels of God ascending and descending upon the Son of Man."

The Gospel of the Lord.

HOLY CROSS DAY

SEPTEMBER 14

FIRST READING: NUMBERS 21:4b–9

A reading from Numbers:

From Mount Hor the Israelites set out,
⁴ᵇbut the people became impatient on the way.
⁵The people spoke against God and against Moses,
"Why have you brought us up out of Egypt to die in the wilderness?
For there is no food and no water, and we detest this miserable food."
⁶Then the LORD sent poisonous serpents among the people,
and they bit the people, so that many Israelites died.

⁷The people came to Moses and said,
"We have sinned by speaking against the LORD and against you;
pray to the LORD to take away the serpents from us."
So Moses prayed for the people.
⁸And the LORD said to Moses,
"Make a poisonous serpent, and set it on a pole;
and everyone who is bitten shall look at it and live."
⁹So Moses made a serpent of bronze, and put it upon a pole;
and whenever a serpent bit someone,
that person would look at the serpent of bronze and live.

The word of the Lord.

PSALMODY: PSALM 98:1–4* or PSALM 78:1–2, 34–38   **Psalm 98:1–5* LBW/BCP

SECOND READING: 1 CORINTHIANS 1:18–24

A reading from First Corinthians:

¹⁸The message about the cross is foolishness to those who are perishing,
but to us who are being saved it is the power of God.
¹⁹For it is written,
    "I will destroy the wisdom of the wise,
        and the discernment of the discerning I will thwart."
²⁰Where is the one who is wise?
Where is the scribe?

Where is the debater of this age?
Has not God made foolish the wisdom of the world?

[21]For since, in the wisdom of God,
the world did not know God through wisdom,
God decided, through the foolishness of our proclamation,
to save those who believe.
[22]For Jews demand signs and Greeks desire wisdom,
[23]but we proclaim Christ crucified,
a stumbling block to Jews and foolishness to Gentiles,
[24]but to those who are the called, both Jews and Greeks,
Christ the power of God and the wisdom of God.

The word of the Lord.

GOSPEL: JOHN 3:13–17

The Holy Gospel according to John, the third chapter.

Jesus said:
[13]"No one has ascended into heaven
except the one who descended from heaven,
the Son of Man.
[14]And just as Moses lifted up the serpent in the wilderness,
so must the Son of Man be lifted up,
[15]that whoever believes in him may have eternal life.

[16]"For God so loved the world that he gave his only Son,
so that everyone who believes in him may not perish
but may have eternal life.
[17]Indeed, God did not send the Son into the world to condemn the world,
but in order that the world might be saved through him."

The Gospel of the Lord.

St. Matthew, Apostle and Evangelist

SEPTEMBER 21

FIRST READING: Ezekiel 2:8—3:11

A reading from Ezekiel:

⁸You, mortal, hear what I say to you;
do not be rebellious like that rebellious house;
open your mouth and eat what I give you.
⁹I looked, and a hand was stretched out to me,
and a written scroll was in it.
¹⁰He spread it before me;
it had writing on the front and on the back,
and written on it were words of lamentation and mourning and woe.

³:¹He said to me, O mortal, eat what is offered to you;
eat this scroll, and go, speak to the house of Israel.
²So I opened my mouth, and he gave me the scroll to eat.
³He said to me, Mortal, eat this scroll that I give you
and fill your stomach with it.
Then I ate it; and in my mouth it was as sweet as honey.

⁴He said to me: Mortal, go to the house of Israel
and speak my very words to them.
⁵For you are not sent to a people of obscure speech and difficult language,
but to the house of Israel—
⁶not to many peoples of obscure speech and difficult language,
whose words you cannot understand.
Surely, if I sent you to them, they would listen to you.
⁷But the house of Israel will not listen to you,
for they are not willing to listen to me;
because all the house of Israel have a hard forehead and a stubborn heart.
⁸See, I have made your face hard against their faces,
and your forehead hard against their foreheads.
⁹Like the hardest stone, harder than flint, I have made your forehead;
do not fear them or be dismayed at their looks,
for they are a rebellious house.
¹⁰He said to me: Mortal, all my words that I shall speak to you
receive in your heart and hear with your ears;
¹¹then go to the exiles, to your people, and speak to them.

Say to them, "Thus says the Lord GOD";
whether they hear or refuse to hear.

The word of the Lord.

PSALMODY: Psalm 119:33–40

SECOND READING: Ephesians 2:4–10

A reading from Ephesians:

[4]God, who is rich in mercy,
out of the great love with which he loved us
[5]even when we were dead through our trespasses,
made us alive together with Christ—by grace you have been saved—
[6]and raised us up with him
and seated us with him in the heavenly places in Christ Jesus,
[7]so that in the ages to come
he might show the immeasurable riches of his grace
in kindness toward us in Christ Jesus.
[8]For by grace you have been saved through faith,
and this is not your own doing;
it is the gift of God—
[9]not the result of works, so that no one may boast.
[10]For we are what he has made us,
created in Christ Jesus for good works,
which God prepared beforehand to be our way of life.

The word of the Lord.

The Holy Gospel according to Matthew, the ninth chapter.

[9]As Jesus was walking along,
he saw a man called Matthew sitting at the tax booth;
and he said to him, "Follow me."
And he got up and followed him.

[10]And as he sat at dinner in the house,
many tax collectors and sinners came
and were sitting with him and his disciples.
[11]When the Pharisees saw this, they said to his disciples,
"Why does your teacher eat with tax collectors and sinners?"
[12]But when he heard this, he said,
"Those who are well have no need of a physician,
but those who are sick.
[13]Go and learn what this means,
'I desire mercy, not sacrifice.'
For I have come to call not the righteous but sinners."

The Gospel of the Lord.

ST. MICHAEL AND ALL ANGELS

SEPTEMBER 29

FIRST READING: DANIEL 10:10–14; 12:1–3

A reading from Daniel:

¹⁰A hand touched me and roused me to my hands and knees.
¹¹He said to me, "Daniel, greatly beloved,
pay attention to the words that I am going to speak to you.
Stand on your feet, for I have now been sent to you."
So while he was speaking this word to me, I stood up trembling.
¹²He said to me, "Do not fear, Daniel,
for from the first day that you set your mind to gain understanding
and to humble yourself before your God,
your words have been heard, and I have come because of your words.
¹³But the prince of the kingdom of Persia opposed me twenty-one days.
So Michael, one of the chief princes, came to help me,
and I left him there with the prince of the kingdom of Persia,
¹⁴and have come to help you understand what is to happen to your people
at the end of days.
For there is a further vision for those days.

¹²:¹"At that time Michael, the great prince,
the protector of your people, shall arise.
There shall be a time of anguish,
such as has never occurred since nations first came into existence.
But at that time your people shall be delivered,
everyone who is found written in the book.
²Many of those who sleep in the dust of the earth shall awake,
some to everlasting life, and some to shame and everlasting contempt.
³Those who are wise shall shine like the brightness of the sky,
and those who lead many to righteousness,
like the stars forever and ever."

The word of the Lord.

PSALMODY: PSALM 103:1–5, 20–22

SECOND READING: REVELATION 12:7–12

A reading from Revelation:

[7]War broke out in heaven;
Michael and his angels fought against the dragon.
The dragon and his angels fought back,
[8]but they were defeated, and there was no longer any place for them in heaven.
[9]The great dragon was thrown down,
that ancient serpent, who is called the Devil and Satan,
the deceiver of the whole world—
he was thrown down to the earth, and his angels were thrown down with him.

[10]Then I heard a loud voice in heaven, proclaiming,
    "Now have come the salvation and the power
        and the kingdom of our God
        and the authority of his Messiah,
    for the accuser of our comrades has been thrown down,
        who accuses them day and night before our God.
[11]But they have conquered him by the blood of the Lamb
        and by the word of their testimony,
    for they did not cling to life even in the face of death.
[12]Rejoice then, you heavens
        and those who dwell in them!
    But woe to the earth and the sea,
        for the devil has come down to you
    with great wrath,
        because he knows that his time is short!"

The word of the Lord.

GOSPEL: LUKE 10:17–20

The Holy Gospel according to Luke, the tenth chapter.

[17]The seventy returned with joy, saying,
"Lord, in your name even the demons submit to us!"
[18]He said to them,
"I watched Satan fall from heaven like a flash of lightning.
[19]See, I have given you authority to tread on snakes and scorpions,
and over all the power of the enemy;
and nothing will hurt you.
[20]Nevertheless, do not rejoice at this,
that the spirits submit to you,
but rejoice that your names are written in heaven."

The Gospel of the Lord.

St. Luke, Evangelist

OCTOBER 18

FIRST READING: Isaiah 43:8–13

Or Isaiah 35:5–8, following

A reading from Isaiah:

⁸Bring forth the people who are blind, yet have eyes,
    who are deaf, yet have ears!
⁹Let all the nations gather together,
    and let the peoples assemble.
Who among them declared this,
    and foretold to us the former things?
Let them bring their witnesses to justify them,
    and let them hear and say, "It is true."
¹⁰You are my witnesses, says the Lord,
    and my servant whom I have chosen,
so that you may know and believe me
    and understand that I am he.
Before me no god was formed,
    nor shall there be any after me.
¹¹I, I am the Lord,
    and besides me there is no savior.
¹²I declared and saved and proclaimed,
    when there was no strange god among you;
    and you are my witnesses, says the Lord.
¹³I am God, and also henceforth I am He;
    there is no one who can deliver from my hand;
    I work and who can hinder it?

The word of the Lord.

OR: Isaiah 35:5–8

A reading from Isaiah:

⁵Then the eyes of the blind shall be opened,
    and the ears of the deaf unstopped;
⁶then the lame shall leap like a deer,
    and the tongue of the speechless sing for joy.

For waters shall break forth in the wilderness,
    and streams in the desert;
[7]the burning sand shall become a pool,
    and the thirsty ground springs of water;
the haunt of jackals shall become a swamp,
    the grass shall become reeds and rushes.

[8]A highway shall be there,
    and it shall be called the Holy Way;
the unclean shall not travel on it,
    but it shall be for God's people;
    no traveler, not even fools, shall go astray.

The word of the Lord.

PSALMODY: PSALM 124

SECOND READING: 2 TIMOTHY 4:5–11

A reading from Second Timothy:

[5]As for you, always be sober, endure suffering,
do the work of an evangelist, carry out your ministry fully.

[6]As for me, I am already being poured out as a libation,
and the time of my departure has come.
[7]I have fought the good fight,
I have finished the race,
I have kept the faith.
[8]From now on there is reserved for me the crown of righteousness,
which the Lord, the righteous judge, will give me on that day,
and not only to me but also to all who have longed for his appearing.

[9]Do your best to come to me soon,
[10]for Demas, in love with this present world,
has deserted me and gone to Thessalonica;
Crescens has gone to Galatia, Titus to Dalmatia.
[11]Only Luke is with me.
Get Mark and bring him with you, for he is useful in my ministry.

The word of the Lord.

The Holy Gospel according to Luke, the first and twenty-fourth chapters.

Luke writes:
¹Since many have undertaken to set down an orderly account
of the events that have been fulfilled among us,
²just as they were handed on to us
by those who from the beginning were eyewitnesses and servants of the word,
³I too decided, after investigating everything carefully from the very first,
to write an orderly account for you, most excellent Theophilus,
⁴so that you may know the truth concerning the things
about which you have been instructed.

²⁴:⁴⁴Before he ascended, Jesus said to the disciples and their companions:
"These are my words that I spoke to you while I was still with you—
that everything written about me in the law of Moses,
the prophets, and the psalms must be fulfilled."
⁴⁵Then he opened their minds to understand the scriptures,
⁴⁶and he said to them, "Thus it is written,
that the Messiah is to suffer and to rise from the dead on the third day,
⁴⁷and that repentance and forgiveness of sins is to be proclaimed in his name
to all nations, beginning from Jerusalem.
⁴⁸You are witnesses of these things.
⁴⁹And see, I am sending upon you what my Father promised;
so stay here in the city until you have been clothed with power from on high."

⁵⁰Then he led them out as far as Bethany,
and, lifting up his hands, he blessed them.
⁵¹While he was blessing them,
he withdrew from them and was carried up into heaven.
⁵²And they worshiped him, and returned to Jerusalem with great joy;
⁵³and they were continually in the temple blessing God.

The Gospel of the Lord.

ST. SIMON AND ST. JUDE, APOSTLES

OCTOBER 28

FIRST READING: JEREMIAH 26:[1–6] 7–16

A reading from Jeremiah:

[¹At the beginning of the reign of King Jehoiakim son of Josiah of Judah,
this word came from the LORD:
²Thus says the LORD:
Stand in the court of the LORD's house,
and speak to all the cities of Judah that come to worship in the house
        of the LORD;
speak to them all the words that I command you;
do not hold back a word.
³It may be that they will listen, all of them,
and will turn from their evil way,
that I may change my mind about the disaster
that I intend to bring on them because of their evil doings.
⁴You shall say to them:
Thus says the LORD: If you will not listen to me,
to walk in my law that I have set before you,
⁵and to heed the words of my servants the prophets
whom I send to you urgently—
though you have not heeded—
⁶then I will make this house like Shiloh,
and I will make this city a curse for all the nations of the earth.]

⁷The priests and the prophets and all the people
heard Jeremiah speaking these words in the house of the LORD.
⁸And when Jeremiah had finished speaking
all that the LORD had commanded him to speak to all the people,
then the priests and the prophets and all the people laid hold of him,
saying, "You shall die!
⁹Why have you prophesied in the name of the LORD, saying,
'This house shall be like Shiloh,
and this city shall be desolate, without inhabitant'?"
And all the people gathered around Jeremiah in the house of the LORD.

¹⁰When the officials of Judah heard these things,
they came up from the king's house to the house of the LORD
and took their seat in the entry of the New Gate of the house of the LORD.

¹¹Then the priests and the prophets said to the officials and to all the people,
"This man deserves the sentence of death
because he has prophesied against this city,
as you have heard with your own ears."

¹²Then Jeremiah spoke to all the officials and all the people, saying,
"It is the LORD who sent me to prophesy
against this house and this city all the words you have heard.
¹³Now therefore amend your ways and your doings,
and obey the voice of the LORD your God,
and the LORD will change his mind about the disaster
that he has pronounced against you.
¹⁴But as for me, here I am in your hands.
Do with me as seems good and right to you.
¹⁵Only know for certain that if you put me to death,
you will be bringing innocent blood upon yourselves
and upon this city and its inhabitants,
for in truth the LORD sent me to you to speak all these words in your ears."

¹⁶Then the officials and all the people said to the priests and the prophets,
"This man does not deserve the sentence of death,
for he has spoken to us in the name of the LORD our God."

The word of the Lord.

PSALMODY: PSALM 11

SECOND READING: 1 JOHN 4:1–6

A reading from First John:

¹Beloved, do not believe every spirit,
but test the spirits to see whether they are from God;
for many false prophets have gone out into the world.
²By this you know the Spirit of God:
every spirit that confesses that Jesus Christ has come in the flesh is from God,
³and every spirit that does not confess Jesus is not from God.
And this is the spirit of the antichrist,
of which you have heard that it is coming;
and now it is already in the world.

⁴Little children, you are from God, and have conquered them;
for the one who is in you is greater than the one who is in the world.
⁵They are from the world;
therefore what they say is from the world, and the world listens to them.

[6]We are from God.
Whoever knows God listens to us,
and whoever is not from God does not listen to us.
From this we know the spirit of truth and the spirit of error.

The word of the Lord.

GOSPEL: JOHN 14:21–27

The Holy Gospel according to John, the 14th chapter.

Jesus said to the disciples:
[21]"They who have my commandments and keep them are those who love me;
and those who love me will be loved by my Father,
and I will love them and reveal myself to them."
[22]Judas (not Iscariot) said to him,
"Lord, how is it that you will reveal yourself to us, and not to the world?"
[23]Jesus answered him,
"Those who love me will keep my word, and my Father will love them,
and we will come to them and make our home with them.
[24]Whoever does not love me does not keep my words;
and the word that you hear is not mine, but is from the Father who sent me.

[25]"I have said these things to you while I am still with you.
[26]But the Advocate, the Holy Spirit, whom the Father will send in my name,
will teach you everything,
and remind you of all that I have said to you.
[27]Peace I leave with you; my peace I give to you.
I do not give to you as the world gives.
Do not let your hearts be troubled, and do not let them be afraid."

The Gospel of the Lord.

REFORMATION DAY

OCTOBER 31

REFORMATION SUNDAY: OCTOBER 26, 1997   OCTOBER 29, 2000   OCTOBER 26, 2003

FIRST READING: JEREMIAH 31:31–34

A reading from Jeremiah:

³¹The days are surely coming, says the LORD,
when I will make a new covenant with the house of Israel
        and the house of Judah.
³²It will not be like the covenant that I made with their ancestors
when I took them by the hand to bring them out of the land of Egypt—
a covenant that they broke, though I was their husband, says the LORD.

³³But this is the covenant that I will make with the house of Israel
after those days, says the LORD:
I will put my law within them,
and I will write it on their hearts;
and I will be their God, and they shall be my people.
³⁴No longer shall they teach one another,
or say to each other, "Know the LORD,"
for they shall all know me,
from the least of them to the greatest, says the LORD;
for I will forgive their iniquity, and remember their sin no more.

The word of the Lord.

PSALMODY: PSALM 46

SECOND READING: ROMANS 3:19–28

A reading from Romans:

¹⁹Now we know that whatever the law says,
it speaks to those who are under the law,
so that every mouth may be silenced,
and the whole world may be held accountable to God.
²⁰For "no human being will be justified in his sight"
by deeds prescribed by the law,
for through the law comes the knowledge of sin.

21But now, apart from law, the righteousness of God has been disclosed,
and is attested by the law and the prophets,
22the righteousness of God through faith in Jesus Christ for all who believe.
For there is no distinction,
23since all have sinned and fall short of the glory of God;
24they are now justified by his grace as a gift,
through the redemption that is in Christ Jesus,
25whom God put forward as a sacrifice of atonement by his blood,
effective through faith.
He did this to show his righteousness,
because in his divine forbearance
he had passed over the sins previously committed;
26it was to prove at the present time that he himself is righteous
and that he justifies the one who has faith in Jesus.

27Then what becomes of boasting?
It is excluded.
By what law? By that of works?
No, but by the law of faith.
28For we hold that a person is justified by faith apart from works
        prescribed by the law.

The word of the Lord.

GOSPEL: JOHN 8:31–36

The Holy Gospel according to John, the eighth chapter.

31Jesus said to the Jews who had believed in him,
"If you continue in my word, you are truly my disciples;
32and you will know the truth,
and the truth will make you free."
33They answered him,
"We are descendants of Abraham and have never been slaves to anyone.
What do you mean by saying, 'You will be made free'?"

34Jesus answered them,
"Very truly, I tell you, everyone who commits sin is a slave to sin.
35The slave does not have a permanent place in the household;
the son has a place there forever.

36"So if the Son makes you free, you will be free indeed."

The Gospel of the Lord.

ALL SAINTS DAY

NOVEMBER 1

ALL SAINTS SUNDAY: NOVEMBER 2, 1997   NOVEMBER 5, 2000   NOVEMBER 2, 2003

FIRST READING: ISAIAH 25:6–9   *Alternate Reading: Wisdom of Solomon 3:1–9 (p. 409)*

A reading from Isaiah:

⁶On this mountain the LORD of hosts will make for all peoples
a feast of rich food, a feast of well-aged wines,
of rich food filled with marrow, of well-aged wines strained clear.
⁷And he will destroy on this mountain
the shroud that is cast over all peoples,
the sheet that is spread over all nations;
he will swallow up death forever.
⁸Then the Lord GOD will wipe away the tears from all faces,
and the disgrace of his people he will take away from all the earth,
for the LORD has spoken.
⁹It will be said on that day,
Lo, this is our God; we have waited for him, so that he might save us.
This is the LORD for whom we have waited;
let us be glad and rejoice in his salvation.

The word of the Lord.

PSALMODY: PSALM 24

SECOND READING: REVELATION 21:1–6a

A reading from Revelation:

¹I saw a new heaven and a new earth;
for the first heaven and the first earth had passed away,
and the sea was no more.
²And I saw the holy city, the new Jerusalem,
coming down out of heaven from God,
prepared as a bride adorned for her husband.
³And I heard a loud voice from the throne saying,
    "See, the home of God is among mortals.
    He will dwell with them as their God;
    they will be his peoples,
    and God himself will be with them;
    ⁴he will wipe every tear from their eyes.
    Death will be no more;
    mourning and crying and pain will be no more,
    for the first things have passed away."

⁵And the one who was seated on the throne said,
"See, I am making all things new."
Also he said, "Write this, for these words are trustworthy and true."
⁶Then he said to me, "It is done!
I am the Alpha and the Omega,
the beginning and the end."

The word of the Lord.

The Holy Gospel according to John, the eleventh chapter.

[32]When Mary came where Jesus was and saw him,
she knelt at his feet and said to him,
"Lord, if you had been here, my brother would not have died."
[33]When Jesus saw her weeping,
and the Jews who came with her also weeping,
he was greatly disturbed in spirit and deeply moved.
[34]He said, "Where have you laid him?"
They said to him, "Lord, come and see."
[35]Jesus began to weep.
[36]So the Jews said, "See how he loved him!"
[37]But some of them said,
"Could not he who opened the eyes of the blind man
have kept this man from dying?"

[38]Then Jesus, again greatly disturbed, came to the tomb.
It was a cave, and a stone was lying against it.
[39]Jesus said, "Take away the stone."
Martha, the sister of the dead man, said to him,
"Lord, already there is a stench because he has been dead four days."
[40]Jesus said to her,
"Did I not tell you that if you believed, you would see the glory of God?"

[41]So they took away the stone.
And Jesus looked upward and said,
"Father, I thank you for having heard me.
[42]I knew that you always hear me,
but I have said this for the sake of the crowd standing here,
so that they may believe that you sent me."
[43]When he had said this, he cried with a loud voice,
"Lazarus, come out!"
[44]The dead man came out,
his hands and feet bound with strips of cloth,
and his face wrapped in a cloth.
Jesus said to them, "Unbind him, and let him go."

The Gospel of the Lord.

NEW YEAR'S EVE
DECEMBER 31

FIRST READING: ECCLESIASTES 3:1–13

A reading from Ecclesiastes:

¹For everything there is a season, and a time for every matter under heaven:
    ²a time to be born, and a time to die;
    a time to plant, and a time to pluck up what is planted;
    ³a time to kill, and a time to heal;
    a time to break down, and a time to build up;
    ⁴a time to weep, and a time to laugh;
    a time to mourn, and a time to dance;
    ⁵a time to throw away stones, and a time to gather stones together;
    a time to embrace, and a time to refrain from embracing;
    ⁶a time to seek, and a time to lose;
    a time to keep, and a time to throw away;
    ⁷a time to tear, and a time to sew;
    a time to keep silence, and a time to speak;
    ⁸a time to love, and a time to hate;
    a time for war, and a time for peace.

⁹What gain have the workers from their toil?
¹⁰I have seen the business that God has given to everyone to be busy with.
¹¹He has made everything suitable for its time;
moreover he has put a sense of past and future into their minds,
yet they cannot find out what God has done from the beginning to the end.
¹²I know that there is nothing better for them than to be happy
and enjoy themselves as long as they live;
¹³moreover, it is God's gift
that all should eat and drink and take pleasure in all their toil.

The word of the Lord.

PSALMODY: PSALM 8

SECOND READING: Revelation 21:1–6a

A reading from Revelation:

¹I saw a new heaven and a new earth;
for the first heaven and the first earth had passed away,
and the sea was no more.
²And I saw the holy city, the new Jerusalem,
coming down out of heaven from God,
prepared as a bride adorned for her husband.
³And I heard a loud voice from the throne saying,
    "See, the home of God is among mortals.
    He will dwell with them as their God;
    they will be his peoples,
    and God himself will be with them;
    ⁴he will wipe every tear from their eyes.
    Death will be no more;
    mourning and crying and pain will be no more,
    for the first things have passed away."

⁵And the one who was seated on the throne said,
"See, I am making all things new."
Also he said,
"Write this, for these words are trustworthy and true."
⁶ᵃThen he said to me,
"It is done! I am the Alpha and the Omega, the beginning and the end."

The word of the Lord.

GOSPEL: Matthew 25:31–46

The Holy Gospel according to Matthew, the 25th chapter.

Jesus said to the disciples:
³¹"When the Son of Man comes in his glory, and all the angels with him,
then he will sit on the throne of his glory.
³²All the nations will be gathered before him,
and he will separate people one from another
as a shepherd separates the sheep from the goats,
³³and he will put the sheep at his right hand and the goats at the left.

³⁴"Then the king will say to those at his right hand,
'Come, you that are blessed by my Father,
inherit the kingdom prepared for you from the foundation of the world;
³⁵for I was hungry and you gave me food,
I was thirsty and you gave me something to drink,
I was a stranger and you welcomed me,
³⁶I was naked and you gave me clothing,
I was sick and you took care of me,

I was in prison and you visited me.'
^{37}Then the righteous will answer him,
'Lord, when was it that we saw you hungry and gave you food,
or thirsty and gave you something to drink?
^{38}And when was it that we saw you a stranger and welcomed you,
or naked and gave you clothing?
^{39}And when was it that we saw you sick or in prison and visited you?'
^{40}And the king will answer them,
'Truly I tell you,
just as you did it to one of the least of these who are members of my family,
you did it to me.'

^{41}"Then he will say to those at his left hand,
'You that are accursed,
depart from me into the eternal fire prepared for the devil and his angels;
^{42}for I was hungry and you gave me no food,
I was thirsty and you gave me nothing to drink,
^{43}I was a stranger and you did not welcome me,
naked and you did not give me clothing,
sick and in prison and you did not visit me.'
^{44}Then they also will answer,
'Lord, when was it that we saw you hungry or thirsty
or a stranger or naked or sick or in prison,
and did not take care of you?'
^{45}Then he will answer them,
'Truly I tell you,
just as you did not do it to one of the least of these,
you did not do it to me.'
^{46}And these will go away into eternal punishment,
but the righteous into eternal life."

The Gospel of the Lord.

Day of Thanksgiving

CANADA: OCTOBER 13, 1997 OCTOBER 9, 2000 OCTOBER 13, 2003

U.S.A.: NOVEMBER 27, 1997 NOVEMBER 23, 2000 NOVEMBER 27, 2003

FIRST READING: JOEL 2:21–27

A reading from Joel:

²¹Do not fear, O soil;
    be glad and rejoice,
    for the LORD has done great things!
²²Do not fear, you animals of the field,
    for the pastures of the wilderness are green;
the tree bears its fruit,
    the fig tree and vine give their full yield.

²³O children of Zion, be glad
    and rejoice in the LORD your God;
for he has given the early rain for your vindication,
    he has poured down for you abundant rain,
    the early and the later rain, as before.
²⁴The threshing floors shall be full of grain,
    the vats shall overflow with wine and oil.

²⁵I will repay you for the years
    that the swarming locust has eaten,
the hopper, the destroyer, and the cutter,
    my great army, which I sent against you.

²⁶You shall eat in plenty and be satisfied,
    and praise the name of the LORD your God,
    who has dealt wondrously with you.
And my people shall never again be put to shame.
²⁷You shall know that I am in the midst of Israel,
    and that I, the LORD, am your God and there is no other.
And my people shall never again
    be put to shame.

The word of the Lord.

PSALMODY: PSALM 126

SECOND READING: 1 Timothy 2:1–7

A reading from First Timothy:

¹First of all, then,
I urge that supplications, prayers, intercessions, and thanksgivings
be made for everyone,
²for kings and all who are in high positions,
so that we may lead a quiet and peaceable life in all godliness and dignity.
³This is right and is acceptable in the sight of God our Savior,
⁴who desires everyone to be saved and to come to the knowledge of the truth.
⁵For
    there is one God;
        there is also one mediator between God and humankind,
    Christ Jesus, himself human,
        ⁶who gave himself a ransom for all
—this was attested at the right time.
⁷For this I was appointed a herald and an apostle
(I am telling the truth, I am not lying),
a teacher of the Gentiles in faith and truth.

The word of the Lord.

The Holy Gospel according to Matthew, the sixth chapter.

Jesus said,
[25]"I tell you,
do not worry about your life,
what you will eat or what you will drink,
or about your body, what you will wear.
Is not life more than food, and the body more than clothing?
[26]Look at the birds of the air;
they neither sow nor reap nor gather into barns,
and yet your heavenly Father feeds them.
Are you not of more value than they?
[27]And can any of you by worrying
add a single hour to your span of life?
[28]And why do you worry about clothing?
Consider the lilies of the field, how they grow;
they neither toil nor spin,
[29]yet I tell you, even Solomon in all his glory
was not clothed like one of these.
[30]But if God so clothes the grass of the field,
which is alive today and tomorrow is thrown into the oven,
will he not much more clothe you—you of little faith?

[31]"Therefore do not worry, saying,
'What will we eat?' or 'What will we drink?' or 'What will we wear?'
[32]For it is the Gentiles who strive for all these things;
and indeed your heavenly Father knows that you need all these things.
[33]But strive first for the kingdom of God and his righteousness,
and all these things will be given to you as well."

The Gospel of the Lord.

APPENDIX A

SEMI-CONTINUOUS FIRST READINGS AND PSALMODY

S UNDAY BETWEEN
M AY 29 AND J UNE 4 INCLUSIVE
(if after Trinity Sunday)

PROPER 4

JUNE 1, 1997

FIRST READING: 1 S AMUEL 3:1–10 [11–20]

A reading from First Samuel:

¹Now the boy Samuel was ministering to the L ORD under Eli.
The word of the L ORD was rare in those days;
visions were not widespread.
²At that time Eli,
whose eyesight had begun to grow dim so that he could not see,
was lying down in his room;
³the lamp of God had not yet gone out,
and Samuel was lying down in the temple of the L ORD,
where the ark of God was.
⁴Then the L ORD called, "Samuel! Samuel!"
and he said, "Here I am!"
⁵and ran to Eli, and said, "Here I am, for you called me."
But he said, "I did not call; lie down again."
So he went and lay down.

⁶The L ORD called again, "Samuel!"
Samuel got up and went to Eli, and said,
"Here I am, for you called me."
But he said, "I did not call, my son; lie down again."
⁷Now Samuel did not yet know the L ORD,
and the word of the L ORD had not yet been revealed to him.

⁸The L ORD called Samuel again, a third time.
And he got up and went to Eli, and said, "Here I am, for you called me."
Then Eli perceived that the L ORD was calling the boy.
⁹Therefore Eli said to Samuel,
"Go, lie down; and if he calls you, you shall say,
'Speak, L ORD, for your servant is listening.' "
So Samuel went and lay down in his place.

¹⁰Now the L ORD came and stood there,
calling as before, "Samuel! Samuel!"
And Samuel said, "Speak, for your servant is listening."

[11Then the LORD said to Samuel,
"See, I am about to do something in Israel
that will make both ears of anyone who hears of it tingle.
12On that day I will fulfill against Eli all that I have spoken concerning his
        house,
from beginning to end.
13For I have told him that I am about to punish his house forever,
for the iniquity that he knew,
because his sons were blaspheming God, and he did not restrain them.
14Therefore I swear to the house of Eli
that the iniquity of Eli's house shall not be expiated by sacrifice or offering
        forever."

15Samuel lay there until morning;
then he opened the doors of the house of the LORD.
Samuel was afraid to tell the vision to Eli.
16But Eli called Samuel and said, "Samuel, my son."
He said, "Here I am."
17Eli said, "What was it that he told you? Do not hide it from me.
May God do so to you and more also,
if you hide anything from me of all that he told you."
18So Samuel told him everything and hid nothing from him.
Then he said, "It is the LORD; let him do what seems good to him."

19As Samuel grew up,
the LORD was with him and let none of his words fall to the ground.
20And all Israel from Dan to Beer-sheba
knew that Samuel was a trustworthy prophet of the LORD.]

The word of the Lord.

PSALMODY: PSALM 139:1–6, 13–18

Readings continue on p. 194

Sunday Between
June 5 and 11 inclusive
(if after Trinity Sunday)
PROPER 5
JUNE 8, 1997

FIRST READING: 1 SAMUEL 8:4–11 [12–15] 16–20; [11:14–15]

A reading from First Samuel:

⁴All the elders of Israel gathered together and came to Samuel at Ramah,
⁵and said to him, "You are old and your sons do not follow in your ways;
appoint for us, then, a king to govern us, like other nations."
⁶But the thing displeased Samuel when they said,
"Give us a king to govern us."
Samuel prayed to the LORD, ⁷and the LORD said to Samuel,
"Listen to the voice of the people in all that they say to you;
for they have not rejected you,
but they have rejected me from being king over them.
⁸Just as they have done to me,
from the day I brought them up out of Egypt to this day,
forsaking me and serving other gods,
so also they are doing to you.
⁹Now then, listen to their voice;
only—you shall solemnly warn them,
and show them the ways of the king who shall reign over them."

¹⁰So Samuel reported all the words of the LORD to the people
who were asking him for a king.
¹¹He said,
"These will be the ways of the king who will reign over you:
he will take your sons and appoint them to his chariots and to be his
        horsemen,
and to run before his chariots;
[¹²and he will appoint for himself commanders of thousands and commanders
        of fifties,
and some to plow his ground and to reap his harvest,
and to make his implements of war and the equipment of his chariots.
¹³He will take your daughters to be perfumers and cooks and bakers.
¹⁴He will take the best of your fields and vineyards and olive orchards
and give them to his courtiers.
¹⁵He will take one-tenth of your grain and of your vineyards
and give it to his officers and his courtiers.]

¹⁶He will take your male and female slaves,
and the best of your cattle and donkeys,
and put them to his work.
¹⁷He will take one-tenth of your flocks,
and you shall be his slaves.
¹⁸And in that day you will cry out because of your king,
whom you have chosen for yourselves;
but the LORD will not answer you in that day."

¹⁹But the people refused to listen to the voice of Samuel;
they said, "No! but we are determined to have a king over us,
²⁰so that we also may be like other nations,
and that our king may govern us and go out before us and fight our battles."

[¹¹:¹⁴Samuel said to the people,
"Come, let us go to Gilgal and there renew the kingship."
¹⁵So all the people went to Gilgal,
and there they made Saul king before the LORD in Gilgal.
There they sacrificed offerings of well-being before the LORD,
and there Saul and all the Israelites rejoiced greatly.]

The word of the Lord.

PSALMODY: PSALM 138

Readings continue on p. 197

SUNDAY BETWEEN
JUNE 12 AND 18 INCLUSIVE
(if after Trinity Sunday)
PROPER 6
JUNE 15, 1997

FIRST READING: 1 SAMUEL 15:34—16:13

A reading from First Samuel:

34Samuel went to Ramah;
and Saul went up to his house in Gibeah of Saul.
35Samuel did not see Saul again until the day of his death,
but Samuel grieved over Saul.
And the LORD was sorry that he had made Saul king over Israel.

16:1The LORD said to Samuel,
"How long will you grieve over Saul?
I have rejected him from being king over Israel.
Fill your horn with oil and set out;
I will send you to Jesse the Bethlehemite,
for I have provided for myself a king among his sons."
2Samuel said, "How can I go?
If Saul hears of it, he will kill me."
And the LORD said, "Take a heifer with you, and say,
'I have come to sacrifice to the LORD.'
3Invite Jesse to the sacrifice,
and I will show you what you shall do;
and you shall anoint for me the one whom I name to you."
4Samuel did what the LORD commanded, and came to Bethlehem.
The elders of the city came to meet him trembling, and said,
"Do you come peaceably?"
5He said, "Peaceably; I have come to sacrifice to the LORD;
sanctify yourselves and come with me to the sacrifice."
And he sanctified Jesse and his sons and invited them to the sacrifice.

6When they came, he looked on Eliab and thought,
"Surely the LORD's anointed is now before the LORD."
7But the LORD said to Samuel,
"Do not look on his appearance or on the height of his stature,
because I have rejected him;
for the LORD does not see as mortals see;
they look on the outward appearance,

but the LORD looks on the heart."

⁸Then Jesse called Abinadab, and made him pass before Samuel.
He said, "Neither has the LORD chosen this one."
⁹Then Jesse made Shammah pass by.
And he said, "Neither has the LORD chosen this one."
¹⁰Jesse made seven of his sons pass before Samuel,
and Samuel said to Jesse, "The LORD has not chosen any of these."
¹¹Samuel said to Jesse, "Are all your sons here?"
And he said,
"There remains yet the youngest, but he is keeping the sheep."
And Samuel said to Jesse,
"Send and bring him; for we will not sit down until he comes here."
¹²He sent and brought him in.
Now he was ruddy, and had beautiful eyes, and was handsome.
The LORD said, "Rise and anoint him; for this is the one."
¹³Then Samuel took the horn of oil,
and anointed him in the presence of his brothers;
and the spirit of the LORD came mightily upon David from that day forward.
Samuel then set out and went to Ramah.

The word of the Lord.

PSALMODY: PSALM 20

Readings continue on p. 200

S U N D A Y   B E T W E E N
J U N E 19 A N D 25 I N C L U S I V E
(if after Trinity Sunday)

PROPER 7

JUNE 22, 1997   JUNE 25, 2000   JUNE 22, 2003

FIRST READING: 1 Samuel 17:[1a, 4–11, 19–23] 32–49
Or 1 Samuel 17:57—18:5, 10–16, following

A reading from First Samuel:

[¹Now the Philistines gathered their armies for battle;
⁴And there came out from the camp of the Philistines
a champion named Goliath, of Gath,
whose height was six cubits and a span.
⁵He had a helmet of bronze on his head,
and he was armed with a coat of mail;
the weight of the coat was five thousand shekels of bronze.
⁶He had greaves of bronze on his legs
and a javelin of bronze slung between his shoulders.
⁷The shaft of his spear was like a weaver's beam,
and his spear's head weighed six hundred shekels of iron;
and his shield-bearer went before him.
⁸He stood and shouted to the ranks of Israel,
"Why have you come out to draw up for battle?
Am I not a Philistine, and are you not servants of Saul?
Choose a man for yourselves, and let him come down to me.
⁹If he is able to fight with me and kill me,
then we will be your servants;
but if I prevail against him and kill him,
then you shall be our servants and serve us."
¹⁰And the Philistine said, "Today I defy the ranks of Israel!
Give me a man, that we may fight together."
¹¹When Saul and all Israel heard these words of the Philistine,
they were dismayed and greatly afraid.

¹⁹Now Saul, and they, and all the men of Israel, were in the valley of Elah,
fighting with the Philistines.
²⁰David rose early in the morning, left the sheep with a keeper,
took the provisions, and went as Jesse had commanded him.
He came to the encampment as the army was going forth to the battle line,
shouting the war cry.
²¹Israel and the Philistines drew up for battle, army against army.

^{22}David left the things in charge of the keeper of the baggage,
ran to the ranks, and went and greeted his brothers.
^{23}As he talked with them, the champion, the Philistine of Gath,
	Goliath by name,
came up out of the ranks of the Philistines,
and spoke the same words as before.
And David heard him.]

^{32}David said to Saul, "Let no one's heart fail because of him;
your servant will go and fight with this Philistine."
^{33}Saul said to David,
"You are not able to go against this Philistine to fight with him;
for you are just a boy, and he has been a warrior from his youth."
^{34}But David said to Saul,
"Your servant used to keep sheep for his father;
and whenever a lion or a bear came, and took a lamb from the flock,
^{35}I went after it and struck it down, rescuing the lamb from its mouth;
and if it turned against me, I would catch it by the jaw,
strike it down, and kill it.
^{36}Your servant has killed both lions and bears;
and this uncircumcised Philistine shall be like one of them,
since he has defied the armies of the living God."
^{37}David said,
"The LORD, who saved me from the paw of the lion and from the paw of the
	bear,
will save me from the hand of this Philistine."
So Saul said to David, "Go, and may the LORD be with you!"

^{38}Saul clothed David with his armor;
he put a bronze helmet on his head and clothed him with a coat of mail.
^{39}David strapped Saul's sword over the armor,
and he tried in vain to walk, for he was not used to them.
Then David said to Saul,
"I cannot walk with these; for I am not used to them."
So David removed them.
^{40}Then he took his staff in his hand, and chose five smooth stones
	from the wadi,
and put them in his shepherd's bag, in the pouch;
his sling was in his hand, and he drew near to the Philistine.

^{41}The Philistine came on and drew near to David,
with his shield-bearer in front of him.
^{42}When the Philistine looked and saw David, he disdained him,
for he was only a youth, ruddy and handsome in appearance.
^{43}The Philistine said to David,
"Am I a dog, that you come to me with sticks?"
And the Philistine cursed David by his gods.

⁴⁴The Philistine said to David,
"Come to me, and I will give your flesh to the birds of the air
and to the wild animals of the field."
⁴⁵But David said to the Philistine,
"You come to me with sword and spear and javelin;
but I come to you in the name of the LORD of hosts,
the God of the armies of Israel, whom you have defied.
⁴⁶This very day the LORD will deliver you into my hand,
and I will strike you down and cut off your head;
and I will give the dead bodies of the Philistine army
this very day to the birds of the air and to the wild animals of the earth,
so that all the earth may know that there is a God in Israel,
⁴⁷and that all this assembly may know
that the LORD does not save by sword and spear;
for the battle is the LORD's and he will give you into our hand."

⁴⁸When the Philistine drew nearer to meet David,
David ran quickly toward the battle line to meet the Philistine.
⁴⁹David put his hand in his bag, took out a stone, slung it,
and struck the Philistine on his forehead;
the stone sank into his forehead,
and he fell face down on the ground.

The word of the Lord.

Readings continue on p. 203

OR: 1 SAMUEL 17:57—18:5, 10–16

A reading from First Samuel:

⁵⁷On David's return from killing the Philistine,
Abner took him and brought him before Saul,
with the head of the Philistine in his hand.
⁵⁸Saul said to him, "Whose son are you, young man?"
And David answered,
"I am the son of your servant Jesse the Bethlehemite."

18:1When David had finished speaking to Saul,
the soul of Jonathan was bound to the soul of David,
and Jonathan loved him as his own soul.
²Saul took him that day and would not let him return to his father's house.
³Then Jonathan made a covenant with David,
because he loved him as his own soul.
⁴Jonathan stripped himself of the robe that he was wearing,
and gave it to David,
and his armor, and even his sword and his bow and his belt.

[5]David went out and was successful wherever Saul sent him;
as a result, Saul set him over the army.
And all the people, even the servants of Saul, approved.

[10]The next day an evil spirit from God rushed upon Saul,
and he raved within his house,
while David was playing the lyre, as he did day by day.
Saul had his spear in his hand; [11]and Saul threw the spear,
for he thought, "I will pin David to the wall."
But David eluded him twice.

[12]Saul was afraid of David,
because the LORD was with him but had departed from Saul.
[13]So Saul removed him from his presence,
and made him a commander of a thousand;
and David marched out and came in, leading the army.
[14]David had success in all his undertakings;
for the LORD was with him.
[15]When Saul saw that he had great success, he stood in awe of him.
[16]But all Israel and Judah loved David;
for it was he who marched out and came in leading them.

The word of the Lord.

PSALMODY: PSALM 9:9–20 or PSALM 133

Readings continue on p. 203

FIRST READING: 2 SAMUEL 1:1, 17–27

A reading from Second Samuel:

[1]After the death of Saul,
when David had returned from defeating the Amalekites,
David remained two days in Ziklag.

[17]David intoned this lamentation over Saul and his son Jonathan.
[18](He ordered that The Song of the Bow be taught to the people of Judah;
it is written in the Book of Jashar.)
He said:
   [19]Your glory, O Israel, lies slain upon your high places!
      How the mighty have fallen!
   [20]Tell it not in Gath,
      proclaim it not in the streets of Ashkelon;
   or the daughters of the Philistines will rejoice,
      the daughters of the uncircumcised will exult.

   [21]You mountains of Gilboa,
      let there be no dew or rain upon you,
      nor bounteous fields!
   For there the shield of the mighty was defiled,
      the shield of Saul, anointed with oil no more.

   [22]From the blood of the slain,
      from the fat of the mighty,
   the bow of Jonathan did not turn back,
      nor the sword of Saul return empty.

   [23]Saul and Jonathan, beloved and lovely!
      In life and in death they were not divided;
   they were swifter than eagles,
      they were stronger than lions.

²⁴O daughters of Israel, weep over Saul,
    who clothed you with crimson, in luxury,
    who put ornaments of gold on your apparel.

²⁵How the mighty have fallen
    in the midst of the battle!

Jonathan lies slain upon your high places.
    ²⁶I am distressed for you, my brother Jonathan;
greatly beloved were you to me;
    your love to me was wonderful,
    passing the love of women.

²⁷How the mighty have fallen,
    and the weapons of war perished!

The word of the Lord.

PSALMODY: PSALM 130

Readings continue on p. 206

FIRST READING: 2 SAMUEL 5:1–5, 9–10

A reading from Second Samuel:

¹All the tribes of Israel came to David at Hebron, and said,
"Look, we are your bone and flesh.
²For some time, while Saul was king over us,
it was you who led out Israel and brought it in.
The LORD said to you:
It is you who shall be shepherd of my people Israel,
you who shall be ruler over Israel."
³So all the elders of Israel came to the king at Hebron;
and King David made a covenant with them at Hebron before the LORD,
and they anointed David king over Israel.

⁴David was thirty years old when he began to reign,
and he reigned forty years.
⁵At Hebron he reigned over Judah seven years and six months;
and at Jerusalem he reigned over all Israel and Judah thirty-three years.

⁹David occupied the stronghold, and named it the city of David.
David built the city all around from the Millo inward.
¹⁰And David became greater and greater,
for the LORD, the God of hosts, was with him.

The word of the Lord.

PSALMODY: PSALM 48

Readings continue on p. 210

Sunday between
July 10 and 16 inclusive

PROPER 10

JULY 13, 1997   JULY 16, 2000   JULY 13, 2003

FIRST READING: 2 SAMUEL 6:1–5, 12b–19

A reading from Second Samuel:

¹David again gathered all the chosen men of Israel, thirty thousand.
²David and all the people with him set out and went from Baale-judah,
to bring up from there the ark of God,
which is called by the name of the LORD of hosts who is enthroned on the
          cherubim.
³They carried the ark of God on a new cart,
and brought it out of the house of Abinadab, which was on the hill.
Uzzah and Ahio, the sons of Abinadab,
were driving the new cart ⁴with the ark of God;
and Ahio went in front of the ark.
⁵David and all the house of Israel were dancing before the LORD with all their
          might,
with songs and lyres and harps and tambourines and castanets and cymbals.

¹²ᵇSo David went and brought up the ark of God
from the house of Obed-edom to the city of David with rejoicing;
¹³and when those who bore the ark of the LORD had gone six paces,
he sacrificed an ox and a fatling.
¹⁴David danced before the LORD with all his might;
David was girded with a linen ephod.
¹⁵So David and all the house of Israel brought up the ark of the LORD
          with shouting,
and with the sound of the trumpet.

¹⁶As the ark of the LORD came into the city of David,
Michal daughter of Saul looked out of the window,
and saw King David leaping and dancing before the LORD;
and she despised him in her heart.

¹⁷They brought in the ark of the LORD,
and set it in its place, inside the tent that David had pitched for it;
and David offered burnt offerings and offerings of well-being before the LORD.
¹⁸When David had finished offering the burnt offerings

and the offerings of well-being,
he blessed the people in the name of the L<small>ORD</small> of hosts,
¹⁹and distributed food among all the people,
the whole multitude of Israel, both men and women,
to each a cake of bread, a portion of meat, and a cake of raisins.
Then all the people went back to their homes.

The word of the Lord.

PSALMODY: PSALM** 24**

Readings continue on p. 214

SUNDAY BETWEEN
JULY 17 AND 23 INCLUSIVE

PROPER 11

JULY 20, 1997   *JULY 23, 2000*   *JULY 20, 2003*

FIRST READING: 2 SAMUEL 7:1–14a

A reading from Second Samuel:

¹Now when David the king was settled in his house,
and the LORD had given him rest from all his enemies around him,
²the king said to the prophet Nathan,
"See now, I am living in a house of cedar,
but the ark of God stays in a tent."
³Nathan said to the king,
"Go, do all that you have in mind; for the LORD is with you."

⁴But that same night the word of the LORD came to Nathan:
⁵Go and tell my servant David:
Thus says the LORD: Are you the one to build me a house to live in?
⁶I have not lived in a house
since the day I brought up the people of Israel from Egypt to this day,
but I have been moving about in a tent and a tabernacle.
⁷Wherever I have moved about among all the people of Israel,
did I ever speak a word with any of the tribal leaders of Israel,
whom I commanded to shepherd my people Israel, saying,
"Why have you not built me a house of cedar?"

⁸Now therefore thus you shall say to my servant David:
Thus says the LORD of hosts: I took you from the pasture,
from following the sheep to be prince over my people Israel;
⁹and I have been with you wherever you went,
and have cut off all your enemies from before you;
and I will make for you a great name,
like the name of the great ones of the earth.
¹⁰And I will appoint a place for my people Israel and will plant them,
so that they may live in their own place, and be disturbed no more;
and evildoers shall afflict them no more, as formerly,
¹¹from the time that I appointed judges over my people Israel;
and I will give you rest from all your enemies.
Moreover the LORD declares to you that the LORD will make you a house.
¹²When your days are fulfilled and you lie down with your ancestors,

I will raise up your offspring after you,
who shall come forth from your body,
and I will establish his kingdom.
[13]He shall build a house for my name,
and I will establish the throne of his kingdom forever.
[14]I will be a father to him,
and he shall be a son to me.

The word of the Lord.

PSALMODY: PSALM 89:20–37

Readings continue on p. 217

☩

S U N D A Y   B E T W E E N
J U L Y   2 4   A N D   3 0   I N C L U S I V E

PROPER 12

JULY 27, 1997   *JULY 30, 2000*   *JULY 27, 2003*

FIRST READING: 2 SAMUEL 11:1–15

A reading from Second Samuel:

[1]In the spring of the year, the time when kings go out to battle,
David sent Joab with his officers and all Israel with him;
they ravaged the Ammonites, and besieged Rabbah.
But David remained at Jerusalem.

[2]It happened, late one afternoon,
when David rose from his couch
and was walking about on the roof of the king's house,
that he saw from the roof a woman bathing;
the woman was very beautiful.
[3]David sent someone to inquire about the woman.
It was reported, "This is Bathsheba daughter of Eliam,
the wife of Uriah the Hittite."
[4]So David sent messengers to get her,
and she came to him, and he lay with her.
(Now she was purifying herself after her period.)
Then she returned to her house.
[5]The woman conceived;
and she sent and told David, "I am pregnant."

[6]So David sent word to Joab,
"Send me Uriah the Hittite."
And Joab sent Uriah to David.
[7]When Uriah came to him,
David asked how Joab and the people fared,
and how the war was going.
[8]Then David said to Uriah,
"Go down to your house, and wash your feet."
Uriah went out of the king's house,
and there followed him a present from the king.
[9]But Uriah slept at the entrance of the king's house with all the servants
        of his lord,
and did not go down to his house.

¹⁰When they told David, "Uriah did not go down to his house,"
David said to Uriah, "You have just come from a journey.
Why did you not go down to your house?"
¹¹Uriah said to David,
"The ark and Israel and Judah remain in booths;
and my lord Joab and the servants of my lord are camping in the open field;
shall I then go to my house, to eat and to drink,
and to lie with my wife?
As you live, and as your soul lives, I will not do such a thing."
¹²Then David said to Uriah,
"Remain here today also, and tomorrow I will send you back."
So Uriah remained in Jerusalem that day.
On the next day, ¹³David invited him to eat and drink in his presence
and made him drunk;
and in the evening he went out to lie on his couch with the servants
        of his lord,
but he did not go down to his house.

¹⁴In the morning David wrote a letter to Joab,
and sent it by the hand of Uriah.
¹⁵In the letter he wrote,
"Set Uriah in the forefront of the hardest fighting,
and then draw back from him,
so that he may be struck down and die."

The word of the Lord.

PSALMODY: PSALM 14

Readings continue on p. 220

PROPER 13

AUGUST 3, 1997   AUGUST 6, 2000   AUGUST 3, 2003

FIRST READING: 2 SAMUEL 11:26—12:13a

A reading from Second Samuel:

²⁶When the wife of Uriah heard that her husband was dead,
she made lamentation for him.
²⁷When the mourning was over,
David sent and brought her to his house, and she became his wife,
and bore him a son.

But the thing that David had done displeased the LORD,
¹²:¹and the LORD sent Nathan to David.
He came to him, and said to him,
"There were two men in a certain city,
the one rich and the other poor.
²The rich man had very many flocks and herds;
³but the poor man had nothing but one little ewe lamb,
which he had bought.
He brought it up,
and it grew up with him and with his children;
it used to eat of his meager fare, and drink from his cup,
and lie in his bosom,
and it was like a daughter to him.
⁴Now there came a traveler to the rich man,
and he was loath to take one of his own flock or herd
to prepare for the wayfarer who had come to him,
but he took the poor man's lamb,
and prepared that for the guest who had come to him."

⁵Then David's anger was greatly kindled against the man.
He said to Nathan,
"As the LORD lives, the man who has done this deserves to die;
⁶he shall restore the lamb fourfold,
because he did this thing, and because he had no pity."

⁷Nathan said to David, "You are the man!
Thus says the LORD, the God of Israel:

I anointed you king over Israel,
and I rescued you from the hand of Saul;
⁸I gave you your master's house,
and your master's wives into your bosom,
and gave you the house of Israel and of Judah;
and if that had been too little, I would have added as much more.
⁹Why have you despised the word of the LORD,
to do what is evil in his sight?
You have struck down Uriah the Hittite with the sword,
and have taken his wife to be your wife,
and have killed him with the sword of the Ammonites.
¹⁰Now therefore the sword shall never depart from your house,
for you have despised me,
and have taken the wife of Uriah the Hittite to be your wife.
¹¹Thus says the LORD:
I will raise up trouble against you from within your own house;
and I will take your wives before your eyes,
and give them to your neighbor,
and he shall lie with your wives in the sight of this very sun.
¹²For you did it secretly;
but I will do this thing before all Israel, and before the sun."
¹³David said to Nathan,
"I have sinned against the LORD."

The word of the Lord.

PSALMODY: PSALM 51:1–12

Readings continue on p. 224

S U N D A Y B E T W E E N
A U G U S T 7 A N D 13 I N C L U S I V E

PROPER 14

AUGUST 10, 1997   *AUGUST 13, 2000*   *AUGUST 10, 2003*

FIRST READING: 2 SAMUEL 18:5–9, 15, 31–33

A reading from Second Samuel:

⁵King David ordered Joab and Abishai and Ittai, saying,
"Deal gently for my sake with the young man Absalom."
And all the people heard
when the king gave orders to all the commanders concerning Absalom.

⁶So the army went out into the field against Israel;
and the battle was fought in the forest of Ephraim.
⁷The men of Israel were defeated there by the servants of David,
and the slaughter there was great on that day, twenty thousand men.
⁸The battle spread over the face of all the country;
and the forest claimed more victims that day than the sword.

⁹Absalom happened to meet the servants of David.
Absalom was riding on his mule,
and the mule went under the thick branches of a great oak.
His head caught fast in the oak,
and he was left hanging between heaven and earth,
while the mule that was under him went on.
¹⁵And ten young men, Joab's armor-bearers,
surrounded Absalom and struck him, and killed him.

³¹Then the Cushite came; and the Cushite said,
"Good tidings for my lord the king!
For the LORD has vindicated you this day,
delivering you from the power of all who rose up against you."
³²The king said to the Cushite,
"Is it well with the young man Absalom?"
The Cushite answered,
"May the enemies of my lord the king,
and all who rise up to do you harm, be like that young man."

³³The king was deeply moved,
and went up to the chamber over the gate, and wept;

and as he went, he said,
"O my son Absalom, my son, my son Absalom!
Would I had died instead of you,
O Absalom, my son, my son!"

The word of the Lord.

PSALMODY: PSALM 130

Readings continue on p. 227

S U N D A Y   B E T W E E N
A U G U S T   14   A N D   20   I N C L U S I V E

PROPER 15

AUGUST 17, 1997   *AUGUST 20, 2000*   *AUGUST 17, 2003*

FIRST READING: 1 KINGS 2:10–12; 3:3–14

A reading from First Kings:

10David slept with his ancestors,
and was buried in the city of David.
11The time that David reigned over Israel was forty years;
he reigned seven years in Hebron,
and thirty-three years in Jerusalem.
12So Solomon sat on the throne of his father David;
and his kingdom was firmly established.

3:3Solomon loved the LORD,
walking in the statutes of his father David;
only, he sacrificed and offered incense at the high places.
4The king went to Gibeon to sacrifice there,
for that was the principal high place;
Solomon used to offer a thousand burnt offerings on that altar.

5At Gibeon the LORD appeared to Solomon in a dream by night;
and God said, "Ask what I should give you."
6And Solomon said,
"You have shown great and steadfast love to your servant my father David,
because he walked before you in faithfulness, in righteousness,
and in uprightness of heart toward you;
and you have kept for him this great and steadfast love,
and have given him a son to sit on his throne today.
7And now, O LORD my God,
you have made your servant king in place of my father David,
although I am only a little child;
I do not know how to go out or come in.
8And your servant is in the midst of the people whom you have chosen,
a great people, so numerous they cannot be numbered or counted.
9Give your servant therefore an understanding mind to govern your people,
able to discern between good and evil;
for who can govern this your great people?"

[^10]It pleased the Lord that Solomon had asked this. [^11]God said to him,
"Because you have asked this,
and have not asked for yourself long life or riches,
or for the life of your enemies,
but have asked for yourself understanding to discern what is right,
[^12]I now do according to your word.
Indeed I give you a wise and discerning mind;
no one like you has been before you
and no one like you shall arise after you.
[^13]I give you also what you have not asked,
both riches and honor all your life;
no other king shall compare with you.
[^14]If you will walk in my ways,
keeping my statutes and my commandments,
as your father David walked,
then I will lengthen your life."

The word of the Lord.

PSALMODY: PSALM 111

Readings continue on p. 230

S U N D A Y   B E T W E E N
A U G U S T   21   A N D   27   I N C L U S I V E

PROPER 16

AUGUST 24, 1997   *AUGUST 27, 2000*   *AUGUST 24, 2003*

FIRST READING: 1 KINGS 8:[1, 6, 10–11] 22–30, 41–43

A reading from First Kings:

[¹Solomon assembled the elders of Israel and all the heads of the tribes,
the leaders of the ancestral houses of the Israelites,
before King Solomon in Jerusalem,
to bring up the ark of the covenant of the LORD out of the city of David,
which is Zion.
⁶Then the priests brought the ark of the covenant of the LORD to its place,
in the inner sanctuary of the house, in the most holy place,
underneath the wings of the cherubim.
¹⁰And when the priests came out of the holy place,
a cloud filled the house of the LORD,
¹¹so that the priests could not stand to minister because of the cloud;
for the glory of the LORD filled the house of the LORD.]

²²Then Solomon stood before the altar of the LORD
in the presence of all the assembly of Israel,
and spread out his hands to heaven.
²³He said, "O LORD, God of Israel,
there is no God like you in heaven above or on earth beneath,
keeping covenant and steadfast love for your servants
who walk before you with all their heart,
²⁴the covenant that you kept for your servant my father David
as you declared to him;
you promised with your mouth
and have this day fulfilled with your hand.
²⁵Therefore, O LORD, God of Israel,
keep for your servant my father David that which you promised him, saying,
'There shall never fail you a successor before me to sit on the throne of Israel,
if only your children look to their way,
to walk before me as you have walked before me.'
²⁶Therefore, O God of Israel, let your word be confirmed,
which you promised to your servant my father David.

²⁷"But will God indeed dwell on the earth?
Even heaven and the highest heaven cannot contain you,

much less this house that I have built!
²⁸Regard your servant's prayer and his plea, O Lᴏʀᴅ my God,
heeding the cry and the prayer that your servant prays to you today;
²⁹that your eyes may be open night and day toward this house,
the place of which you said, 'My name shall be there,'
that you may heed the prayer that your servant prays toward this place.
³⁰Hear the plea of your servant and of your people Israel
when they pray toward this place;
O hear in heaven your dwelling place;
heed and forgive.

⁴¹"Likewise when a foreigner, who is not of your people Israel,
comes from a distant land because of your name
⁴²—for they shall hear of your great name,
your mighty hand, and your outstretched arm—
when a foreigner comes and prays toward this house,
⁴³then hear in heaven your dwelling place,
and do according to all that the foreigner calls to you,
so that all the peoples of the earth may know your name and fear you,
as do your people Israel,
and so that they may know
that your name has been invoked on this house that I have built."

The word of the Lord.

PSALMODY: Psᴀʟᴍ 84

Readings continue on p. 233

FIRST READING: SONG OF SOLOMON 2:8–13

A reading from Song of Solomon:

⁸The voice of my beloved!
    Look, he comes,
leaping upon the mountains,
    bounding over the hills.
⁹My beloved is like a gazelle
    or a young stag.
Look, there he stands
    behind our wall,
gazing in at the windows,
    looking through the lattice.

¹⁰My beloved speaks and says to me:
"Arise, my love, my fair one,
    and come away;
¹¹for now the winter is past,
    the rain is over and gone.
¹²The flowers appear on the earth;
    the time of singing has come,
and the voice of the turtledove
    is heard in our land.
¹³The fig tree puts forth its figs,
    and the vines are in blossom;
    they give forth fragrance.
Arise, my love, my fair one,
    and come away."

The word of the Lord.

PSALMODY: PSALM 45:1–2, 6–9

Readings continue on p. 236

SUNDAY BETWEEN
SEPTEMBER 4 AND 10 INCLUSIVE
PROPER 18

SEPTEMBER 7, 1997   SEPTEMBER 10, 2000   SEPTEMBER 7, 2003

FIRST READING: PROVERBS 22:1–2, 8–9, 22–23

A reading from Proverbs:

¹A good name is to be chosen rather than great riches,
    and favor is better than silver or gold.
²The rich and the poor have this in common:
    the LORD is the maker of them all.

⁸Whoever sows injustice will reap calamity,
    and the rod of anger will fail.
⁹Those who are generous are blessed,
    for they share their bread with the poor.
²²Do not rob the poor because they are poor,
    or crush the afflicted at the gate;
²³for the LORD pleads their cause
    and despoils of life those who despoil them.

The word of the Lord.

PSALMODY: PSALM 125

Readings continue on p. 239

SUNDAY BETWEEN
SEPTEMBER 11 AND 17 INCLUSIVE

PROPER 19

SEPTEMBER 14, 1997   *SEPTEMBER 17, 2000*   *SEPTEMBER 14, 2003*

FIRST READING: PROVERBS 1:20–33

A reading from Proverbs:

²⁰Wisdom cries out in the street;
    in the squares she raises her voice.
²¹At the busiest corner she cries out;
    at the entrance of the city gates she speaks:
²²"How long, O simple ones, will you love being simple?
How long will scoffers delight in their scoffing
    and fools hate knowledge?
²³Give heed to my reproof;
I will pour out my thoughts to you;
    I will make my words known to you.
²⁴Because I have called and you refused,
    have stretched out my hand and no one heeded,
²⁵and because you have ignored all my counsel
    and would have none of my reproof,
²⁶I also will laugh at your calamity;
    I will mock when panic strikes you,
²⁷when panic strikes you like a storm,
    and your calamity comes like a whirlwind,
    when distress and anguish come upon you.

²⁸"Then they will call upon me, but I will not answer;
    they will seek me diligently, but will not find me.
²⁹Because they hated knowledge
    and did not choose the fear of the LORD,
³⁰would have none of my counsel,
    and despised all my reproof,
³¹therefore they shall eat the fruit of their way
    and be sated with their own devices.
³²For waywardness kills the simple,
    and the complacency of fools destroys them;
³³but those who listen to me will be secure
    and will live at ease, without dread of disaster."

The word of the Lord.

PSALMODY: PSALM 19 or WISDOM OF SOLOMON 7:26—8:1

Readings continue on p. 242

FIRST READING: Proverbs 31:10–31

A reading from Proverbs:

¹⁰A capable wife who can find?
　She is far more precious than jewels.
¹¹The heart of her husband trusts in her,
　and he will have no lack of gain.
¹²She does him good, and not harm,
　all the days of her life.
¹³She seeks wool and flax,
　and works with willing hands.
¹⁴She is like the ships of the merchant,
　she brings her food from far away.
¹⁵She rises while it is still night
　and provides food for her household
　and tasks for her servant girls.
¹⁶She considers a field and buys it;
　with the fruit of her hands she plants a vineyard.
¹⁷She girds herself with strength,
　and makes her arms strong.
¹⁸She perceives that her merchandise is profitable.
　Her lamp does not go out at night.
¹⁹She puts her hands to the distaff,
　and her hands hold the spindle.
²⁰She opens her hand to the poor,
　and reaches out her hands to the needy.
²¹She is not afraid for her household when it snows,
　for all her household are clothed in crimson.
²²She makes herself coverings;
　her clothing is fine linen and purple.

²³Her husband is known in the city gates,
　taking his seat among the elders of the land.
²⁴She makes linen garments and sells them;
　she supplies the merchant with sashes.
²⁵Strength and dignity are her clothing,
　and she laughs at the time to come.

²⁶She opens her mouth with wisdom,
   and the teaching of kindness is on her tongue.
²⁷She looks well to the ways of her household,
   and does not eat the bread of idleness.
²⁸Her children rise up and call her happy;
   her husband too, and he praises her:
²⁹"Many women have done excellently,
   but you surpass them all."
³⁰Charm is deceitful, and beauty is vain,
   but a woman who fears the LORD is to be praised.
³¹Give her a share in the fruit of her hands,
   and let her works praise her in the city gates.

The word of the Lord.

PSALMODY: PSALM 1

Readings continue on p. 245

FIRST READING: Esther 7:1–6, 9–10; 9:20–22

A reading from Esther:

¹King Ahasuerus and Haman went in to feast with Queen Esther.
²On the second day, as they were drinking wine,
the king again said to Esther,
"What is your petition, Queen Esther?
It shall be granted you.
And what is your request?
Even to the half of my kingdom, it shall be fulfilled."
³Then Queen Esther answered,
"If I have won your favor, O king, and if it pleases the king,
let my life be given me—that is my petition—
and the lives of my people—that is my request.
⁴For we have been sold, I and my people,
to be destroyed, to be killed, and to be annihilated.
If we had been sold merely as slaves, men and women,
I would have held my peace;
but no enemy can compensate for this damage to the king."

⁵Then King Ahasuerus said to Queen Esther,
"Who is he, and where is he, who has presumed to do this?"
⁶Esther said, "A foe and enemy, this wicked Haman!"
Then Haman was terrified before the king and the queen.
⁹Then Harbona, one of the eunuchs in attendance on the king, said,
"Look, the very gallows that Haman has prepared for Mordecai,
whose word saved the king,
stands at Haman's house, fifty cubits high."
And the king said, "Hang him on that."
¹⁰So they hanged Haman on the gallows that he had prepared for Mordecai.
Then the anger of the king abated.

9:20Mordecai recorded these things,
and sent letters to all the Jews who were in all the provinces
     of King Ahasuerus,
both near and far,

²¹enjoining them that they should keep the fourteenth day of the month Adar
and also the fifteenth day of the same month, year by year,
²²as the days on which the Jews gained relief from their enemies,
and as the month that had been turned for them from sorrow into gladness
and from mourning into a holiday;
that they should make them days of feasting and gladness,
days for sending gifts of food to one another and presents to the poor.

The word of the Lord.

PSALMODY: PSALM 124

Readings continue on p. 249

S U N D A Y   B E T W E E N
O C T O B E R   2   A N D   8   I N C L U S I V E

PROPER 22

OCTOBER 5, 1997 · OCTOBER 8, 2000 · OCTOBER 5, 2003

FIRST READING: JOB 1:1; 2:1–10

A reading from Job:

¹There was once a man in the land of Uz whose name was Job.
That man was blameless and upright,
one who feared God and turned away from evil.

²:¹One day the heavenly beings came to present themselves before the LORD,
and Satan also came among them to present himself before the LORD.
²The LORD said to Satan, "Where have you come from?"
Satan answered the LORD,
"From going to and fro on the earth,
and from walking up and down on it."
³The LORD said to Satan,
"Have you considered my servant Job?
There is no one like him on the earth,
a blameless and upright man who fears God and turns away from evil.
He still persists in his integrity,
although you incited me against him, to destroy him for no reason."
⁴Then Satan answered the LORD, "Skin for skin!
All that people have they will give to save their lives.
⁵But stretch out your hand now and touch his bone and his flesh,
and he will curse you to your face."
⁶The LORD said to Satan,
"Very well, he is in your power; only spare his life."

⁷So Satan went out from the presence of the LORD,
and inflicted loathsome sores on Job
from the sole of his foot to the crown of his head.
⁸Job took a potsherd with which to scrape himself,
and sat among the ashes.
⁹Then his wife said to him,
"Do you still persist in your integrity?
Curse God, and die."

APPENDIX A: SUNDAY BETWEEN OCTOBER 2 AND 8

APPENDIX A: SUNDAY BETWEEN OCTOBER 2 AND 8 · 389

[10]But he said to her,
"You speak as any foolish woman would speak.
Shall we receive the good at the hand of God, and not receive the bad?"
In all this Job did not sin with his lips.

The word of the Lord.

PSALMODY: PSALM 26

Readings continue on p. 252

SUNDAY BETWEEN OCTOBER 9 AND 15 INCLUSIVE

PROPER 23

OCTOBER 12, 1997 *OCTOBER 15, 2000* *OCTOBER 12, 2003*

FIRST READING: JOB 23:1–9, 16–17

A reading from Job:

1Job answered:
2"Today also my complaint is bitter;
his hand is heavy despite my groaning.
3Oh, that I knew where I might find him,
that I might come even to his dwelling!
4I would lay my case before him,
and fill my mouth with arguments.
5I would learn what he would answer me,
and understand what he would say to me.
6Would he contend with me in the greatness of his power?
No; but he would give heed to me.
7There an upright person could reason with him,
and I should be acquitted forever by my judge.

8"If I go forward, he is not there;
or backward, I cannot perceive him;
9on the left he hides, and I cannot behold him;
I turn to the right, but I cannot see him.
16God has made my heart faint;
the Almighty has terrified me;
17If only I could vanish in darkness,
and thick darkness would cover my face!"

The word of the Lord.

PSALMODY: PSALM 22:1–15

Readings continue on p. 255

✠

SUNDAY BETWEEN
OCTOBER 16 AND 22 INCLUSIVE

PROPER 24

OCTOBER 19, 1997   OCTOBER 22, 2000   OCTOBER 19, 2003

FIRST READING: JOB 38:1–7 [34–41]

A reading from Job:

¹The LORD answered Job out of the whirlwind:
²"Who is this that darkens counsel by words without knowledge?
³Gird up your loins like a man,
    I will question you, and you shall declare to me.

⁴"Where were you when I laid the foundation of the earth?
    Tell me, if you have understanding.
⁵Who determined its measurements—surely you know!
    Or who stretched the line upon it?
⁶On what were its bases sunk,
    or who laid its cornerstone
⁷when the morning stars sang together
    and all the heavenly beings shouted for joy?

[³⁴"Can you lift up your voice to the clouds,
    so that a flood of waters may cover you?
³⁵Can you send forth lightnings, so that they may go
    and say to you, 'Here we are'?
³⁶Who has put wisdom in the inward parts,
    or given understanding to the mind?
³⁷Who has the wisdom to number the clouds?
    Or who can tilt the waterskins of the heavens,
³⁸when the dust runs into a mass
    and the clods cling together?
³⁹Can you hunt the prey for the lion,
    or satisfy the appetite of the young lions,
⁴⁰when they crouch in their dens,
    or lie in wait in their covert?
⁴¹Who provides for the raven its prey,
    when its young ones cry to God,
    and wander about for lack of food?"]

The word of the Lord.

PSALMODY: PSALM 104:1–9, 24, 35c

Readings continue on p. 259

S U N D A Y   B E T W E E N
O C T O B E R   **23**   A N D   **29**   I N C L U S I V E

PROPER 25

OCTOBER 26, 1997   *OCTOBER 29, 2000*   *OCTOBER 26, 2003*

FIRST READING: JOB 42:1–6, 10–17

A reading from Job:

¹Job answered the LORD:
²"I know that you can do all things,
    and that no purpose of yours can be thwarted.
³'Who is this that hides counsel without knowledge?'
Therefore I have uttered what I did not understand,
    things too wonderful for me, which I did not know.
⁴'Hear, and I will speak;
    I will question you, and you declare to me.'
⁵I had heard of you by the hearing of the ear,
    but now my eye sees you;
⁶therefore I despise myself,
    and repent in dust and ashes."

¹⁰And the LORD restored the fortunes of Job when he had prayed for his friends;
and the LORD gave Job twice as much as he had before.
¹¹Then there came to him all his brothers and sisters
and all who had known him before,
and they ate bread with him in his house;
they showed him sympathy
and comforted him for all the evil that the LORD had brought upon him;
and each of them gave him a piece of money and a gold ring.

¹²The LORD blessed the latter days of Job more than his beginning;
and he had fourteen thousand sheep, six thousand camels,
a thousand yoke of oxen, and a thousand donkeys.
¹³He also had seven sons and three daughters.
¹⁴He named the first Jemimah, the second Keziah, and the third
        Keren–happuch.
¹⁵In all the land there were no women so beautiful as Job's daughters;
and their father gave them an inheritance along with their brothers.
¹⁶After this Job lived one hundred and forty years,

and saw his children, and his children's children, four generations. [17]And Job died, old and full of days.

The word of the Lord.

PSALMODY: PSALM 34:1–8 [19–22]

Readings continue on p. 262

PROPER 26

NOVEMBER 2, 1997   *NOVEMBER 5, 2000*   *NOVEMBER 2, 2003*

FIRST READING: RUTH 1:1–18

A reading from Ruth:

¹In the days when the judges ruled, there was a famine in the land,
and a certain man of Bethlehem in Judah went to live in the country of Moab,
he and his wife and two sons.
²The name of the man was Elimelech and the name of his wife Naomi,
and the names of his two sons were Mahlon and Chilion;
they were Ephrathites from Bethlehem in Judah.
They went into the country of Moab and remained there.
³But Elimelech, the husband of Naomi, died,
and she was left with her two sons.
⁴These took Moabite wives;
the name of the one was Orpah and the name of the other Ruth.
When they had lived there about ten years,
⁵both Mahlon and Chilion also died,
so that the woman was left without her two sons and her husband.

⁶Then she started to return with her daughters-in-law from the country
        of Moab,
for she had heard in the country of Moab
that the Lord had considered his people and given them food.
⁷So she set out from the place where she had been living,
she and her two daughters-in-law,
and they went on their way to go back to the land of Judah.
⁸But Naomi said to her two daughters-in-law,
"Go back each of you to your mother's house.
May the Lord deal kindly with you,
as you have dealt with the dead and with me.
⁹The Lord grant that you may find security,
each of you in the house of your husband."
Then she kissed them, and they wept aloud.
¹⁰They said to her,
"No, we will return with you to your people."
¹¹But Naomi said, "Turn back, my daughters, why will you go with me?
Do I still have sons in my womb that they may become your husbands?

¹²Turn back, my daughters, go your way,
for I am too old to have a husband.
Even if I thought there was hope for me,
even if I should have a husband tonight and bear sons,
¹³would you then wait until they were grown?
Would you then refrain from marrying?
No, my daughters, it has been far more bitter for me than for you,
because the hand of the Lord has turned against me."
¹⁴Then they wept aloud again.
Orpah kissed her mother-in-law, but Ruth clung to her.

¹⁵So she said,
"See, your sister-in-law has gone back to her people and to her gods;
return after your sister-in-law."
¹⁶But Ruth said,
    "Do not press me to leave you
        or to turn back from following you!
    Where you go, I will go;
        where you lodge, I will lodge;
    your people shall be my people,
        and your God my God.
    ¹⁷Where you die, I will die—
        there will I be buried.
    May the Lord do thus and so to me,
        and more as well,
        if even death parts me from you!"
¹⁸When Naomi saw that she was determined to go with her,
she said no more to her.

The word of the Lord.

PSALMODY: Psalm 146

Readings continue on p. 264

FIRST READING: RUTH 3:1–5; 4:13–17

A reading from Ruth:

¹Naomi said to Ruth,
"My daughter, I need to seek some security for you,
so that it may be well with you.
²Now here is our kinsman Boaz,
with whose young women you have been working.
See, he is winnowing barley tonight at the threshing floor.
³Now wash and anoint yourself,
and put on your best clothes and go down to the threshing floor;
but do not make yourself known to the man
until he has finished eating and drinking.
⁴When he lies down, observe the place where he lies;
then, go and uncover his feet and lie down;
and he will tell you what to do."
⁵She said to her, "All that you tell me I will do."

⁴:¹³So Boaz took Ruth and she became his wife.
When they came together, the LORD made her conceive, and she bore a son.
¹⁴Then the women said to Naomi,
"Blessed be the LORD, who has not left you this day without next-of-kin;
and may his name be renowned in Israel!
¹⁵He shall be to you a restorer of life and a nourisher of your old age;
for your daughter-in-law who loves you,
who is more to you than seven sons, has borne him."
¹⁶Then Naomi took the child and laid him in her bosom,
and became his nurse.
¹⁷The women of the neighborhood gave him a name, saying,
"A son has been born to Naomi."
They named him Obed; he became the father of Jesse, the father of David.

The word of the Lord.

PSALMODY: PSALM 127

Readings continue on p. 266

FIRST READING: 1 SAMUEL 1:4–20

A reading from First Samuel:

⁴On the day when Elkanah sacrificed,
he would give portions to his wife Peninnah and to all her sons and daughters;
⁵but to Hannah he gave a double portion, because he loved her,
though the LORD had closed her womb.
⁶Her rival used to provoke her severely,
to irritate her, because the LORD had closed her womb.
⁷So it went on year by year;
as often as she went up to the house of the LORD, she used to provoke her.
Therefore Hannah wept and would not eat.
⁸Her husband Elkanah said to her,
"Hannah, why do you weep? Why do you not eat?
Why is your heart sad? Am I not more to you than ten sons?"

⁹After they had eaten and drunk at Shiloh,
Hannah rose and presented herself before the LORD.
Now Eli the priest was sitting on the seat beside the doorpost of the temple
       of the LORD.
¹⁰She was deeply distressed and prayed to the LORD, and wept bitterly.
¹¹She made this vow: "O LORD of hosts,
if only you will look on the misery of your servant,
and remember me, and not forget your servant,
but will give to your servant a male child,
then I will set him before you as a nazirite until the day of his death.
He shall drink neither wine nor intoxicants,
and no razor shall touch his head."

¹²As she continued praying before the LORD,
Eli observed her mouth.
¹³Hannah was praying silently; only her lips moved,
but her voice was not heard;
therefore Eli thought she was drunk.
¹⁴So Eli said to her,
"How long will you make a drunken spectacle of yourself?

Put away your wine."
¹⁵But Hannah answered,
"No, my lord, I am a woman deeply troubled;
I have drunk neither wine nor strong drink,
but I have been pouring out my soul before the LORD.
¹⁶Do not regard your servant as a worthless woman,
for I have been speaking out of my great anxiety and vexation all this time."
¹⁷Then Eli answered, "Go in peace;
the God of Israel grant the petition you have made to him."
¹⁸And she said, "Let your servant find favor in your sight."
Then the woman went to her quarters, ate and drank with her husband,
and her countenance was sad no longer.

¹⁹They rose early in the morning and worshiped before the LORD;
then they went back to their house at Ramah.
Elkanah knew his wife Hannah, and the LORD remembered her.
²⁰In due time Hannah conceived and bore a son.
She named him Samuel,
for she said, "I have asked him of the LORD."

The word of the Lord.

PSALMODY: 1 SAMUEL 2:1–10

Readings continue on p. 269

CHRIST THE KING
Last Sunday after Pentecost[†]
PROPER 29

NOVEMBER 23, 1997   NOVEMBER 26, 2000   NOVEMBER 23, 2003

FIRST READING: 2 SAMUEL 23:1–7

A reading from Second Samuel:

1Now these are the last words of David:
 The oracle of David, son of Jesse,
 the oracle of the man whom God exalted,
the anointed of the God of Jacob,
 the favorite of the Strong One of Israel:

2The spirit of the LORD speaks through me,
 his word is upon my tongue.
3The God of Israel has spoken,
 the Rock of Israel has said to me:
One who rules over people justly,
 ruling in the fear of God,
4is like the light of morning,
 like the sun rising on a cloudless morning,
 gleaming from the rain on the grassy land.
5Is not my house like this with God?
 For he has made with me an everlasting covenant,
 ordered in all things and secure.
Will he not cause to prosper
 all my help and my desire?
6But the godless are all like thorns that are thrown away;
 for they cannot be picked up with the hand;
7to touch them one uses an iron bar
 or the shaft of a spear.
 And they are entirely consumed in fire on the spot.

The word of the Lord.

PSALMODY: PSALM 132:1–12 [13–18]

Readings continue on p. 272

[†]*Sunday between November 20 and 26 inclusive*

APPENDIX B

READINGS FROM THE APOCRYPHAL BOOKS

Second Sunday after Christmas

JANUARY 5, 1997　　JANUARY 2, 2000　　JANUARY 5, 2003

FIRST READING: Sɪʀᴀᴄʜ 24:1–12

A reading from Sirach:

[1]Wisdom praises herself,
  and tells of her glory in the midst of her people.
[2]In the assembly of the Most High she opens her mouth,
  and in the presence of his hosts she tells of her glory:

[3]"I came forth from the mouth of the most High,
  and covered the earth like a mist.
[4]I dwelt in the highest heavens,
  and my throne was in a pillar of cloud.
[5]Alone I compassed the vault of heaven
  and traversed the depths of the abyss.
[6]Over waves of the sea, over all the earth,
  and over every people and nation I have held sway."
[7]Among all these I sought a resting place;
  in whose territory should I abide?

[8]"Then the Creator of all things gave me a command,
  and my Creator chose the place for my tent.
He said, 'Make your dwelling in Jacob,
  and in Israel receive your inheritance.'
[9]Before the ages, in the beginning, he created me,
  and for all the ages I shall not cease to be.
[10]In the holy tent I ministered before him,
  and so I was established in Zion.

[11]"Thus in the beloved city he gave me a resting place,
  and in Jerusalem was my domain.
[12]I took root in an honored people,
  in the portion of the Lord, his heritage."

The word of the Lord.

PSALMODY: Wɪsᴅᴏᴍ ᴏꜰ Sᴏʟᴏᴍᴏɴ 10:15–21

Readings continue on p. 30

The Resurrection of Our Lord
Vigil of Easter

MARCH 29, 1997   APRIL 22, 2000   APRIL 19, 2003

SIXTH READING: BARUCH 3:9–15, 32—4:4

A reading from Baruch:

9Hear the commandments of life, O Israel;
    give ear, and learn wisdom!
10Why is it, O Israel, why is it that you are in the land of your enemies,
    that you are growing old in a foreign country,
that you are defiled with the dead,
    11that you are counted among those in Hades?
12You have forsaken the fountain of wisdom.
13If you had walked in the way of God,
    you would be living in peace forever.
14Learn where there is wisdom,
    where there is strength,
    where there is understanding,
so that you may at the same time discern
    where there is length of days, and life,
    where there is light for the eyes, and peace.

15Who has found her place?
    And who has entered her storehouses?

32But the one who knows all things knows her,
    he found her by his understanding.
The one who prepared the earth for all time
    filled it with four-footed creatures;
33the one who sends forth the light, and it goes;
    he called it, and it obeyed him, trembling;
34the stars shone in their watches, and were glad;
    he called them, and they said, "Here we are!"
    They shone with gladness for him who made them.
35This is our God;
    no other can be compared to him.
36He found the whole way to knowledge,
    and gave her to his servant Jacob
    and to Israel, whom he loved.
37Afterward she appeared on earth
    and lived with humankind.

4:1She is the book of the commandments of God,
 the law that endures forever.
All who hold her fast will live,
 and those who forsake her will die.
2Turn, O Jacob, and take her;
 walk toward the shining of her light.
3Do not give your glory to another,
 or your advantages to an alien people.
4Happy are we, O Israel,
 for we know what is pleasing to God.

The word of the Lord.

RESPONSE: PSALM 19

Readings continue on p. 137

Readings continue on p. 137

SUNDAY BETWEEN
JUNE 26 AND JULY 2 INCLUSIVE

PROPER 8

JUNE 29, 1997   JULY 2, 2000   JUNE 29, 2003

FIRST READING: WISDOM OF SOLOMON 1:13–15; 2:23–24

A reading from the Wisdom of Solomon:

[13]God did not make death,
and he does not delight in the death of the living.
[14]For he created all things so that they might exist;
the generative forces of the world are wholesome,
and there is no destructive poison in them,
and the dominion of Hades is not on earth.
[15]For righteousness is immortal.

[2:23]For God created us for incorruption,
and made us in the image of his own eternity,
[24]but through the devil's envy death entered the world,
and those who belong to his company experience it.

The word of the Lord.

PSALMODY: PSALM 30

Readings continue on p. 206

SUNDAY BETWEEN SEPTEMBER 18 AND 24 INCLUSIVE

PROPER 20

SEPTEMBER 21, 1997　　　*SEPTEMBER 24, 2000*　　　*SEPTEMBER 21, 2003*

FIRST READING: WISDOM OF SOLOMON 1:16—2:1, 12–22

A reading from the Wisdom of Solomon:

¹⁶The ungodly by their words and deeds summoned death;
considering him a friend, they pined away
and made a covenant with him,
because they are fit to belong to his company.
²:¹For they reasoned unsoundly, saying to themselves,
"Short and sorrowful is our life,
and there is no rememdy when a life comes to its end,
and no one has been known to return from Hades.

¹²"Let us lie in wait for the righteous man,
because he is inconvenient to us and opposes our actions;
he reproaches us for sins against the law,
and accuses us of sins against our training.
¹³He professes to have knowledge of God,
and calls himself a child of the Lord.
¹⁴He became to us a reproof of our thoughts;
¹⁵the very sight of him is a burden to us,
because his manner of life is unlike that of others,
and his ways are strange.
¹⁶We are considered by him as something base,
and he avoids our ways as unclean;
he calls the last end of the righteous happy,
and boasts that God is his father.
¹⁷Let us see if his words are true,
and let us test what will happen at the end of his life;
¹⁸for if the righteous man is God's child, he will help him,
and will deliver him from the hand of his adversaries.
¹⁹Let us test him with insult and torture,
so that we may find out how gentle he is,
and make trial of his forbearance.
²⁰Let us condemn him to a shameful death,
for, according to what he says, he will be protected."

[21]Thus they reasoned, but they were led astray,
for their wickedness blinded them,
[22]and they did not know the secret purposes of God,
nor hoped for the wages of holiness,
nor discerned the prize for blameless souls.

The word of the Lord.

PSALMODY: PSALM 54

Readings continue on p. 245

ALL SAINTS DAY

NOVEMBER 1

ALL SAINTS SUNDAY: NOVEMBER 2, 1997 NOVEMBER 5, 2000 NOVEMBER 2, 2003

FIRST READING: WISDOM OF SOLOMON 3:1–9

A reading from the Wisdom of Solomon:

¹The souls of the righteous are in the hand of God,
and no torment will ever touch them.
²In the eyes of the foolish they seemed to have died,
and their departure was thought to be a disaster,
³and their going from us to be their destruction;
but they are at peace.

⁴For though in the sight of others they were punished,
their hope is full of immortality.
⁵Having been disciplined a little, they will receive great good,
because God tested them and found them worthy of himself;
⁶like gold in the furnace he tried them,
and like a sacrificial burnt offering he accepted them.

⁷In the time of their visitation they will shine forth,
and will run like sparks through the stubble.
⁸They will govern nations and rule over peoples,
and the Lord will reign over them forever.
⁹Those who trust in him will understand truth,
and the faithful will abide with him in love,
because grace and mercy are upon his holy ones,
and he watches over his elect.

The word of the Lord.

PSALMODY: PSALM 24

Readings continue on p. 344

INDEX

Semi-continuous set of readings, found in Appendix A